Elastic Language

Elastic language carries non-specific and stretchable meaning, as in 'He loves her, kind of'. It is used like a slingshot, targeting various strategic goals. Consolidating current research and charting new directions, this book develops a refreshing theory of elasticity, empirically attested by natural language data from tension-prone encounters between Australian Customs officers and passengers. The theory proposes three principles (fluidity, stretchability and strategy) and offers a systematic look at how elastic language, as a sliding scale, works to balance strengthening and weakening speech tones, to firm and soften a speaker's stance, and to reveal and evade the truth. The comparative analysis of forms, functions and context confirms that elastic language is fluid, stretchable and strategic. It serves both cooperative and competitive functions, and social and speech factors impact on its use. This book will appeal to students and researchers working in pragmatics, applied linguistics, sociolinguistics, discourse analysis, and communication.

- Proposes a new conceptual framework for vague language and hedging.
- Uses stimulating data from interesting situations to support arguments.
- Presents mixed methods research for data analysis, which will appeal to both quantitative and qualitative researchers.

DR GRACE Q. ZHANG is an Associate Professor at Curtin University, Australia. She was awarded a PhD in linguistics by the University of Edinburgh in 1996, and has published extensively on elastic/vague language.

Elastic Language
How and Why We Stretch Our Words

Grace Q. Zhang
Curtin University

CAMBRIDGE
UNIVERSITY PRESS

CAMBRIDGE
UNIVERSITY PRESS

University Printing House, Cambridge CB2 8BS, United Kingdom

One Liberty Plaza, 20th Floor, New York, NY 10006, USA

477 Williamstown Road, Port Melbourne, VIC 3207, Australia

314-321, 3rd Floor, Plot 3, Splendor Forum, Jasola District Centre, New Delhi - 110025, India

79 Anson Road, #06-04/06, Singapore 079906

Cambridge University Press is part of the University of Cambridge.

It furthers the University's mission by disseminating knowledge in the pursuit of education, learning and research at the highest international levels of excellence.

www.cambridge.org
Information on this title: www.cambridge.org/9781108718912

© Grace Q. Zhang 2015

This publication is in copyright. Subject to statutory exception and to the provisions of relevant collective licensing agreements, no reproduction of any part may take place without the written permission of Cambridge University Press.

First published 2015
First paperback edition 2019

A catalogue record for this publication is available from the British Library

Library of Congress Cataloging in Publication data
Zhang, Grace Qiao, author.
Elastic language: how and why we stretch our words / Grace Zhang.
    pages   cm
Includes bibliographical references and index.
ISBN 978-1-107-02844-9 (Hardback)
1. Pragmatics–Social aspects.   2. Semantics   3. Plays on words.   4. Vagueness (Philosophy)   5. Speech acts (Linguistics)   6. Sociolinguistics–Research.
7. Language and languages–Philosophy.   I. Title.
P99.4.P72Z53 2015
401'.45–dc23   2015016635

ISBN 978-1-107-02844-9 Hardback
ISBN 978-1-108-71891-2 Paperback

Cambridge University Press has no responsibility for the persistence or accuracy of URLs for external or third-party internet websites referred to in this publication, and does not guarantee that any content on such websites is, or will remain, accurate or appropriate.

This book is dedicated to my parents
Shimin and Lanyin Zhang

Contents

List of figures   *page* ix
List of tables   x
Preface   xiii
Acknowledgements   xv
Conventional notations   xvi

1 Introduction   1
    1.1 A pragmatics-oriented approach   2
    1.2 Definitions   4
    1.3 The purposes of this study   6
    1.4 Organisation of the book   8
    1.5 Summary   8

2 Theoretical foundations   10
    2.1 Vagueness and vague language   10
    2.2 Vague language, hedging and others   20
    2.3 Linguistic categories   25
    2.4 Pragmatic functions   37
    2.5 Vague language and institutional discourses   45
    2.6 Summary   47

3 Elasticity theory   49
    3.1 Cooperative Principle and Relevance Theory   49
    3.2 Zhang's seminal work on elasticity of vague language   55
    3.3 Elasticity theory   57
    3.4 Summary   64

4 Methodology   66
    4.1 A mixed methods research   66
    4.2 Data and rationales   67
    4.3 Data analysis   72
    4.4 Limitation of research   74
    4.5 Summary   76

5 Linguistic realisation of elastic language   78
    5.1 Overall lexical pattern   78
    5.2 Approximate stretchers   81

viii   Contents

5.3	General stretchers	88
5.4	Scalar stretchers	97
5.5	Epistemic stretchers	104
5.6	Padding expressions	113
5.7	Linguistic patterns of elastic language as a manifestation of elasticity	121
5.8	Summary	123

6 Strategies of elastic language   126

6.1	Just-right elastic	127
6.2	Rapport elastic	130
6.3	Mitigating elastic	135
6.4	Intensifying elastic	140
6.5	Self-protection elastic	143
6.6	Evasive elastic	146
6.7	Strategic functions of elastic language as a manifestation of elasticity	151
6.8	Summary	154

7 Elastic language, power and gender   157

7.1	Power	158
7.2	Gender	172
7.3	Summary	181

8 Elastic language and speech factors   184

8.1	Speech event: drug vs non-drug cases	184
8.2	Speech genre: monologue vs dialogue	191
8.3	Language competence: L1 vs L2	198
8.4	Summary	207

9 General discussion   209

9.1	Stretchers, pragmatic functions and maxims	209
9.2	Co-constructed and negotiated elastic language	210
9.3	Cooperative and competitive elastic language	212
9.4	Universal and specific elastic language	215
9.5	Communicative hero or villain?	216
9.6	Summary	218

10 Conclusions and implications   220

10.1	How is elastic language distributed?	221
10.2	What are the pragmatic functions of elastic language?	221
10.3	How does elastic language interact with social and speech factors?	222
10.4	Implications	224
10.5	Future research	225

References   227
Index   241

Figures

1.1	Stretching operation	*page* 5
3.1	Stretching in multi-directions	62
7.1	Frequency of stretchers used by officers and passengers	160
7.2	Frequency of stretchers used by male and female speakers	174
8.1	Frequency of stretchers used in drug and non-drug cases	186
8.2	Frequency of stretchers used in monologue and dialogue	193
8.3	Frequency of stretchers used by L1 and L2 English speakers	200

Tables

2.1	Comparison of semantic and pragmatic meanings	*page* 16
2.2	Differences between vagueness and VL	19
2.3	Differences between VL and related concepts	25
2.4	Taxonomy of VL	27
2.5	Approximators	28
2.6	Vague quantifiers	29
2.7	Vague category indicators with *and/or*	31
2.8	Three types of stance marker	34
2.9	Four lexical categories of EL	36
2.10	Pragmatic functions of VL	38
2.11	Categories of EL pragmatic function in this study	44
3.1	Membership of *about 20*	60
3.2	Four maxims	63
5.1	Twenty most frequent stretchers	79
5.2	Twenty most frequent stretchers by category	80
5.3	Eight stretchers to be analysed	80
5.4	Frequency of *about* clusters	81
5.5	Frequency of *some* clusters	86
5.6	Frequency of *anything* clusters	89
5.7	Frequency of *something* clusters	93
5.8	Scalar stretchers	98
5.9	Frequency of top 10 *very* clusters	100
5.10	Comparison of top 10 *very* clusters in Zhang and Cheng (per 10,000 words)	100
5.11	Frequency of two major *quite* clusters	102
5.12	Epistemic stance markers in three varieties of English (per 10,000 words)	106
5.13	Frequency of *probably* clusters	107
5.14	Three frequent *sort of* clusters	110
6.1	Stretchers and strategies of EL	152
6.2	Realisation of EL strategies	153

List of tables

7.1	Frequency of stretchers used by officers and passengers	160
7.2	Different interactional styles between men and women	172
7.3	Frequency of stretchers used by male and female speakers	174
7.4	Differences between men and women statistically verified	181
8.1	Frequency of stretchers used in drug and non-drug cases	185
8.2	Frequency of stretchers used in monologue and dialogue	191
8.3	Frequency of stretchers used by L1 and L2 English speakers	199
8.4	Statistically verified differences attributed to the three speech factors	207
9.1	Statistically verified differences relating to the influences of five factors	215

Preface

More than three decades ago, when I began my Masters study in China, I little knew that I was embarking on a research journey that would last for thirty years and more. During the search for my Masters topic, I happened to read an article written by the late Professor Wu Tieping, the founder of fuzzy linguistics in China. The article introduced into linguistic study the fuzzy set theory developed by Lotfi A. Zadeh in 1965. The refreshing ideas inspired me to start researching vague language, and my thesis discussed vague meanings in Mandarin Chinese. The topic was so fascinating that my PhD also focused on the semantics of vague quantifiers. Since then my interest has not waned: vague language is full of uncharted territories, and my extensive publications offer a map for the first ventures into this field.

The study of vague language as an area of enquiry is non-conventional and somewhat peripheral to traditional linguistic studies. There exists negativity towards the concept of vague language. John Sinclair mentioned in his Forward to Joanna Channell's 1994 book *Vague Language* that the title worried the series editors initially, as they were unsure if the intended readership would accept it (p. xviii). Sinclair explained that vagueness has negative connotations and teachers would normally not endorse vagueness as part of the repertoire of communication. However, they decided to use the title because, as Sinclair says, there is nothing shameful in mentioning vagueness, and our language allows us to avoid precision and committal: without vagueness our communication would be severely inadequate. In the introduction to her 2007 work on vague language, Joan Cutting mentioned that her colleagues used vague language to humour her, for example ending an email to her with 'see you whenever it is, if not before'. There is still some way to go before we fully appreciate the nature of vague language.

My long but fruitful 'vague' journey has been challenging and fascinating, and thoroughly enjoyable. I work hard to justify the legitimacy of my work by convincing people that vague language is an integral part of our language. The ability to use vague language is as important as, if not more important than, the ability to use other types of language (e.g. precise language). To put vague language on the linguistic map, and ensure it is understood and valued as it deserves, I continue to work, and to refine the topic. For instance, in this book the negative 'vague language' has been replaced with 'elastic language' to emphasise the real nature of this type of language and to resite it as a positive form. I hope this book is a small step towards staking a claim for the status of elastic language in linguistic studies.

Why and how do we stretch our words? This book attempts to answer the question by developing an elasticity theory to explain how stretching works, something lacking in the existing literature. Grounded in naturally occurring data in institutional (Australian Customs) settings, the book provides an account of the nature and function of elastic language. Participants in the data stretch language to negotiate and construct meanings, balance strengthening and weakening speech tones, firm and soften their stance, and adopt socially mandated roles in responding to a type of situation and their expected function in that situation. As a valuable resource, this book will be useful to students and researchers engaged in pragmatics, applied linguistics, sociolinguistics, discourse analysis, and communication.

Acknowledgements

I am immensely indebted to the anonymous reviewers and the final clearance reader for the insightful feedback that has been incorporated into this book. I am also extremely grateful for Cambridge University Press editor Helen Barton's encouragement and support; she was always ready to help, an absolute pleasure to work with. The invaluable help provided by Glennis Starling, Bethany Gaunt, Gaia Poggiogalli, Sherleena Sandou, and other staff members of Cambridge University Press in the copy-editing process and production is also greatly appreciated. A big thank you also goes to Margaret Johnson, Xiaodan Zhang, Anne Guan, Peyman Sabet, Samantha Hornsby, Karen Wittcomb, Peter Robinson, and the transcribers of Way With Words, for their magnificent assistance in various stages of this project.

Writing this book needed time; I cannot thank enough for the wonderful and much needed support from Lina Pelliccione, my Head of School at Curtin University. I also appreciate the help given by my colleagues.

Without the kind permission of the Australian Customs and Border Protection Service in Sydney, this project would not have been possible, and I am very grateful for their generosity. I would also like to acknowledge, with gratitude, research grants awarded by Curtin University (AAPI and Humanities) that facilitated the production of the manuscript for this book. Thanks are due to Kristopher J. Preacher for his generous help with statistical calculations and his convenient online tool *Calculation for the chi-square test* (2010–2015), and to Mike Scott for his analysis software *WordSmith* (version 6.0, 2008). To any whom I may have failed to mention, I extend my gratitude.

Finally, I thank my loving parents Shimin Zhang and Lanyin Zhang, who have my eternal gratitude, and my husband Zhigang Guan and daughter Anne Guan, for bearing with me while I wrote this book. Without their unconditional love and unwavering support, this project would not have been completed, and I am grateful to them from the bottom of my heart.

Conventional notations

...	unfinished sentence
all capital letters	stressed prosodically, emphasising the words
(pause)	a pause of more than two seconds
=	latching between utterances, which indicates speech or vocal noise concurrent with the previous one
underline	noted by the author for emphasis
italics	indicating a word or phrase that will be discussed
( )	situational comments, noticeable non-verbal activities
wo:::rd	prolongation of a sound, stretching the preceding sound: more colons indicate more stretch
1:2:3	episode 1, extract 2, speaking turn 3

1 Introduction

If we accept that science is all about probabilities and in the eye of science nothing is certain, then it should not be difficult to accept that our language may express all kinds of uncertainty and fluidity.

The title of this book is 'elastic language' (EL, exemplified by *probably* and *maybe*), instead of 'vague language' (VL). Misconceptions about VL's nature and function have resulted in some negative attitudes (Overstreet and Yule 1997b). The conventional term 'vague' has a somewhat negative connotation; replacing it with 'elastic' offers instead a positive representation of what this type of language really is. For the convenience and continuity of discussion, in this book sometimes EL and VL are, where appropriate, used interchangeably, especially when referencing VL-related literature.

Words are slingshots with a rubber band, and speakers 'stretch' their words to serve communicative purposes (Zhang 2011). We stretch them in both clear and unclear ways. As Sperber and Wilson (1985/86: 161) state, 'the linguistic meaning is generally ambiguous, it may be elliptical or vague'. Language is inherently vague (e.g. Channell 1994; Peirce 1902; Rowland 2007), but this is not a deficiency. It occurs even in so-called 'precise' contexts such as mathematical language (Rowland 2007) and legal language (Cotterill 2007; Crystal and Davy 1969). Strategic use of language is essential in successful communication, and being vague is one of many strategies.

VL is not ad hoc; it is a pervasive phenomenon and an indispensable part of our language (Russell 1923). Channell (1994: 196), one of the earlier VL researchers, states that VL is a considerable part of language use and that 'we cannot, in any theory of language, treat it as the exception rather than the rule'. VL is unavoidable; for example 'talking and thinking by means of "about", "nearly" is a necessity' (Guilbaud 1977: 126). Similarly, Stubbs states,

> When we speak or write, we are rarely very clear, precise, or explicit about what we mean – and perhaps could not be – but are, on the contrary, vague, indirect, and unclear about just what we are committed to. This often appears superficially to be an inadequacy of human language: but only for those who hold a rather crude view of what is maximally efficient in communication. Being vague and indirect can have many uses. (Stubbs 1986a: 1)

Stubbs suggests that using VL is actually our normal way of communication. It is not inadequate; on the contrary, it has multiple functions. This view is supported by Jucker, Smith and Lüdge (2003), whose findings based on conversational English data among university students are that vague expressions are more informative than exact numbers. For example, 'many friends came to his birthday party' carries more information than 'twenty friends came to his birthday party'. *Many* implies 'he is popular'; this implicature is not present with the use of *twenty*.

It is commonly considered counterproductive to talk about VL. Ruzaitė (2007: 1) observes that traditionally researchers clearly prioritised precision, and people 'fetishise' precision and treat VL as an excessive and unwanted feature. VL can be a source of 'fascination for all of us who love languages and language learning', but can also be a source of 'frustration for those who would prefer meanings, like bars of soap, to hold still long enough for us to capture them' (Hatch and Brown 1995: 60). Bolinger (1975: 205) says that 'meanings are as elusive as a piece of wet soap in a bathtub'. VL is one of the 'wet soaps', and how well one can control it is a manifestation of one's pragmatic competence (Fraser 2010). VL 'plays a huge role in human communication' (van Deemter 2010: 93), and without it no flexible and adequate communication could be achieved (Daitz 1956; Ullmann 1962). VL maintains versatile communication; for example, it can smooth over an embarrassing situation or evade certain sensitive questions.

For decades, linguistic studies have considered accurate language to be desirable, paying little attention to VL. The issue of vagueness is controversial and neglected (Ruzaitė 2007: 1) because it poses challenges to theories in linguistics. While some works on VL are insightful, they mostly focus on the nature and function of VL. An overarching theoretical framework to explain how and why VL works is lacking – especially a well-developed pragmatic account that captures the behaviours of VL adequately. In my other work (Zhang 2011), I provide a theoretical explanation of VL through the notion of elasticity, in that fluid utterances are stretched for various pragmatic purposes. A complete theory of language 'must have vagueness as an integral component' (Channell 1994: 5). Drawn on naturally occurring data, this book intends to develop a fully fledged elasticity theory to fill the gap in current VL studies.

1.1 A pragmatics-oriented approach

There is no categorical and fully agreed boundary between semantics and pragmatics, and this study does not attempt to find one. While there is an *interaction* between semantics and pragmatics (Levinson 1983: 372), the two fields have different focuses and priorities. Semantic and pragmatic meanings are different in that semantic meaning is 'what is encoded in the language itself, independent of any particular speaker or context of utterance', and pragmatic meaning is 'conveyed, or intended to be conveyed' by the use of a particular utterance in a particular context, which includes 'what is inferred as well as subtleties that do not affect truth and falsity, that is, the appropriateness of the mapping between utterances and states of affairs' (Birner 2013: 294). In this study, context is defined in the sense of Cruse, in that it is 'an essential factor in the interpretation of utterances and expressions' (2006: 35), consisting of 'previous utterances (discourse context), participants in the speech event, their interrelations, knowledge, and goals, and the social and physical setting of the speech event' (2006: 136). Context is used in a broad sense, including interactional context, situational context, and extra-situational context (Janney 2002: 458). The definition of pragmatics this study adopts is that of Kecskes:

Pragmatics is about meaning; it is about language use and the users. It is about how the language system is employed in social encounters by human beings. In this process, which is one of the most creative human enterprises, communicators (who are speaker-producers and hearer-interpreters at the same time) manipulate language to shape and infer meaning in a socio-cultural context. (Kecskes 2014: 21)

This definition stresses the interaction of meaning with language use, users, and social encounters, which is the position of this study.

The two research questions in pragmatics, according to Kecskes, are: (1) why do we choose to say what we say? (production), and (2) why do we understand things the way we do? (comprehension). Cruse states, 'a very rough working distinction is that semantics is concerned with the stable meaning resources of language-as-a-system and pragmatics with the use of that system for communicating, on particular occasions and in particular contexts' (2006: 2). In simplified terms, semantics focuses on language system and pragmatics on language use. Semantics deals with sentences and grammaticality, and pragmatics looks at utterances and acceptability (Chapman 2011). For example, as Chapman observes, semanticists and logicians explain vagueness in terms of logic and truth conditionality, while pragmatists introduce ideas of implicit and explicit messages and the gap between literal and intended meaning.

The modern use of the term 'pragmatics' can be traced to Charles Morris, who defines it as the study of 'the relations of signs to the objects to which the signs are applicable', and pragmatics as the study of 'the relation of signs to interpreters' (1938: 6). While the central topics of linguistic pragmatics are 'those aspects of meaning which are dependent on context' Cruse (2006: 3), pragmatics is 'the study of how contextual factors interact with linguistic meaning in the interpretation of utterances' (Wilson and Sperber 2012: 1). Pragmatics does not involve truth-conditional meaning; it typically studies issues such as politeness phenomena, reference and deixis, implicatures, and speech acts, a breadth of focus that has led to its commonly being regarded as a 'waste bucket'. Ariel (2000) calls it a 'big tent' to describe its heterogeneous characteristics.

There is a view that semantics and pragmatics cannot be separated (e.g. Ruzaitė 2007), and that the two are 'inextricably tied together' (Lakoff 1973: 474). However, this study sides with Channell's argument that semantic constructs are 'fleshless skeletons', only coming alive when put into language use; hence 'pragmatic rules are probabilistic, and semantic rules are categorical' (1994: 29–30). Given that pragmatics looks at how contextual factors interact with the interpretation of utterances (Wilson and Sperber 2012: 1) and VL is essentially a pragmatic matter (e.g. Channell 1994; Sadock 1977), this study adopts a pragmatic approach in that the focus is on the intended meaning of VL contextualised in a particular discourse. Discourse in this study refers to language use relative to pragmatic and social situations, and to the language determining how people interact with each other. In particular, it includes previous and following utterances, where meaning is implied in relation to running texts, ongoing interactions, situations, communicative purposes and interactants.

This study is pragmatic in nature, primarily investigating pragmatic vagueness, as the truth-conditional meaning is less relevant in real-life communication. Particularly it looks at the interactional meaning between speaker and hearer, how a speaker conveys an intended meaning using VL, and ways in which this intended meaning serves moment-to-moment communicative goals.

1.2 Definitions

Two definitions are discussed at the outset: EL and elasticity (an in-depth discussion can be found in Chapter 3). It is difficult to reach a consensus, but the working definitions align this research with previous studies, and inform the following analyses.

1.2.1 Elastic language

What is EL? EL is fluid and stretchable. 'Stretch' is used here as a metaphor, referring to ways in which we adjust, modify, and manipulate our words to accommodate particular discursive needs. Its operation can be described as follows:

In Figure 1.1, A is an utterance. When stretched, it becomes utterance B. For example:

JOHN: What do you think about our new colleague?
MARY: Well, sometimes he is extremely charming, but other times he is a little bit odd.

1.2 Definitions

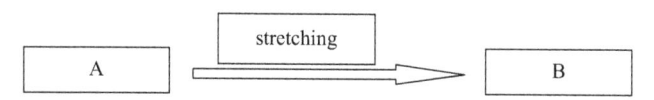

Figure 1.1 Stretching operation

When Mary describes her impression, she stretches to strengthen a favourable comment by using *extremely* and hedge an unfavourable comment by using *a little bit*. What enables Mary to do this is that our language is fluid and stretchable: that is, EL is an important part of communication.

The working definition of EL refers to language that inherently and strategically conveys fluidity and stretchability. EL carries non-specific and stretchable meaning, in that the speaker either cannot be more specific or (more often) strategically makes it less specific.

The definition of EL is developed from that of VL, which has been in use for decades; see Section 2.1.2 for details. Based on my previous work (Zhang 2011), the definition of EL in this study highlights the overlapping nature of language. While EL and VL are similar linguistic phenomena, the differences are twofold. First, they carry different connotations, with the term 'EL' seeming more positive and VL more negative. Second, they have different focuses: VL gives prominence to the uncertainty and under-specification of language, EL to its fluid and elastic nature.

1.2.2 Elasticity

Elasticity has a metaphorical origin and is related to the word elastic. The literal meaning of 'elastic' refers to something (e.g. a piece of string) able to stretch and resume its original shape. The metaphorical meaning of elastic adopted in this study is its general sense: the springy nature of language that makes it able to adjust readily to different contexts and communicative goals, rather than a specific process of stretching out and bouncing back. The term 'elasticity' aims to accentuate the positive and effective profile of EL.

Glinert (2010: 57–8) uses 'elasticity' in his study of political apologising, where it is described as stretching words like a rubber band. In my 2011 work, I propose that the concept of elasticity may be applied to VL as a strategic feature of VL. I define elasticity as VL that 'can be stretched and negotiated to suit the moment-to-moment communicative needs' (Zhang 2011: 573); elasticity is a manifestation of VL's non-specificity, dependent upon context and communicative purpose, enabling language to stretch in multiple directions, upward, downward, and horizontally.

The use of elasticity aims to mitigate the negative connotation of the word vague, as vague words are often viewed as similar to 'weasel words' (e.g. Dobson 2010: 28), indicating a degree of disapproval: weasel words are commonly perceived to communicate a vague or ambiguous meaning. The term 'elastic' reflects the dynamic nature of linguistic expressions, and is free of the negative connotation associated with vague. Elasticity in this study refers to the tendency of utterances to be fluid, stretchable and strategic. 'Fluidity' is manifested as unspecific and overlapping, context-dependent and socially variable; 'stretch' refers to extending or modifying the scope or meaning of an expression, and is a technical term with no negative connotation. Stretchability is manifested as rubber-band-like and with multiple trajectories. Strategicness refers to an elaborate and systematic linguistic behaviour aimed to achieve communicative goals. In this study, elasticity is manifested particularly by the frequency, form and functions of the language, which will vary between different groups of speakers, among other variables.

This study introduces a new term, 'stretch work', referring to the way we treat the elasticity of language as a rubber band, capable of adapting to change or a variety of situations. The working of strategic elasticity is based on the elastic nature of language and communication. There are also other two coined terms: 'elasticise' and 'elasticisation'. Elasticise refers to the act of realising elasticity to suit communicative goals, and elasticisation refers to the realisation of elasticity. For example, on the continuum between *red* and *not red*, in 'his face is extremely red' *extremely* stretches the degree of redness to the higher end. In 'his face is kind of red' *kind of* stretches the degree of redness to the lower end. *Extremely* and *kind of* elasticise the degree of redness; the elasticisation stretches in different directions on the continuum of redness.

In my other work (Zhang 2011: 579) I use the metaphor of a slingshot to describe elastic communication. It has three stages: stretch, aim/adjust, and release/hit. The ways in which the slingshot is stretched depend upon the communicative target. Language tends to be adjusted constantly in practice, and it is possible that the clarity of the target influences the clarity of the language: the clearer the target, the more accurate the language. This study adds that a correlation between target and accuracy of language may not always be the case: it is equally possible that the target is clear, but the language may be kept vague for strategic reasons.

1.3 The purposes of this study

For decades there has been a bias against VL. Channell (1994: 1) states that it is a commonly held view that '"good" usage involves (among other things) clarity and precision. Hence, it is believed that vagueness, ambiguity, imprecision, and general woolliness are to be avoided.' As a result, linguistic studies tend to consider accurate language desirable, and pay less attention to VL. Research on VL tends to be somewhat non-mainstream, although the field has been drawing increasingly more attention in recent years.

1.3 The purposes of this study

Systematic and theoretical research on VL is still somewhat lacking. Existing work on VL from pragmatic perspectives include that of Channel (1994), Cutting (2007), Ruzaitė (2007), and others. Channell's monograph is seminal and has been widely cited. As she puts it, the purpose of her book is more descriptive than theoretical (1994: 31). Cutting's work is a collection of essays covering topics such as vagueness and genre, the psychology of vagueness, and cross-cultural vagueness. Ruzaitė concentrates on approximators and quantifiers in British and American English in educational settings. These major works on VL focus on important areas, but there is still a need to conceptualise the VL phenomenon and the working of VL, to provide an underlying theoretical account integrating empirical evidence that will elevate its study to a new level.

The purpose of this book is to establish such a framework as a small step towards developing a broad and multi-layered account to explicate the use of EL. The theory is tested against empirical evidence, drawing on naturally occurring data from encounters between Australian Customs officers and passengers. This study is one of few attempts to look at the strategic manipulation of EL in tension-prone institutional discourse. It expands and refines Zhang's (2011) concept of elasticity by investigating how elasticity theory is confirmed by the empirical evidence. There are three specific research questions.

1 How is EL distributed?
2 What are the pragmatic functions of EL?
3 How does EL interact with social and speech factors?

To address these questions, three steps are taken. The first is to examine the linguistic manifestation of elasticity in terms of EL form and distribution to show what EL is used and how it is used; the second is to analyse the pragmatic manifestation of elasticity to show why EL is employed; and the third is to investigate the impacts of social (power and gender) and speech-related (speech events, speech genre and language competence) factors on the behaviour of EL. This should produce a rich and rigorous study of EL. The analyses occur at lexical, phrasal, discursive, and social levels. The quantitative analysis provides a general and macro picture of participants' preferences in using EL, offering a strong foundation for other discussion. As quantitative analysis alone may not reveal specific stretching strategies used, there is need for a qualitative analysis that will provide a detailed micro picture of how EL is stretched. As the frequency, form, and function of EL may vary across social groups, the theoretical framework of this study is verified by investigating the interactional mechanisms emerging from the data: for example, is it valid to claim that men are more confrontational than women? Will passengers use more evasive strategies than officers?

This study uncovers what, how and why speakers employ EL and how hearers respond. It examines how inferred meanings are co-constructed in conflict-filled negotiations, and reveals stretch work in the linguistic realisation of EL and power plays in the process of resolving a situation. It investigates how communication games are played using EL: what elasticisation is, how it is produced, and, more importantly, what it does for each participant. The findings shed light on the pragmatics of EL. In particular, the tension-prone institutional corpus provides new resources, and the intercultural aspect of this study adds to its overall importance.

1.4 Organisation of the book

This book consists of ten chapters. This introductory chapter has set the tone, providing working definitions and research questions. Chapter 2 is a critical overview of existing literature on VL, including the two essential concepts of vagueness and VL. There are also conceptual comparisons between VL and other related phenomena such as hedging, implicitness, and indirectness. Chapter 2, informed by previous studies, provides linguistic realisations of EL and categories of EL function that are used in analysis in the following chapters. Chapter 3 is dedicated to a discussion of elasticity theory, including its principles, properties, structure, processes and mechanisms. Before presenting the theory, the chapter reviews Grice's (1975) maxims and the concept of 'loose talk' proposed in Sperber and Wilson's (1985/86; 1995 [1986]) work. Chapter 4 covers the mixed methods approach of this study, both quantitative and qualitative. It describes the data set and data analysis. Chapter 5 is an analysis of EL frequency and clustering, and Chapter 6 considers the pragmatic functions of EL. Chapter 7 looks at the impact of two social factors, power and gender, on EL. Chapter 8 discusses the relationship between speech-related factors and EL, including the differences between monologue and dialogue, drug and non-drug cases (level of severity), and L1 (first language speaker) and L2 (second language speaker). Chapter 9 is a general discussion of the findings of previous chapters. The book ends in Chapter 10 with conclusions and implications.

1.5 Summary

EL is indispensable in our communication, yet it does not get the attention it deserves. Two decades ago, Channell published her seminal book on VL, noting that 'there is as yet no major study of linguistic vagueness; and no generally agreed approach to it' (1994: 20). Two decades later, there has been increasing interest in the field, and a few major studies have emerged such as those of Cutting (2007) and Ruzaitė (2007). However, a theoretical framework is still not established. This study is a small step towards the goal of developing a theoretical framework of EL, and its use of the word 'elastic' is a deliberate ploy to reposition VL as a positive feature of language. It takes a pragmatic perspective on EL, viewing it through the lens of elasticity theory. EL inherently, deliberately and strategically conveys fluidity and stretchability. The concept of elasticity refers to the tendency of springy utterances that are fluid, stretchable and strategic. The purpose of this book is to explore the ways in which EL is stretched in terms of frequency of EL, its pragmatic functions, and the interaction between EL and social and speech-related factors.

2 Theoretical foundations

This chapter is an overview of the existing literature on VL to align this study with previous works and inform conceptual continuity, and to provide a source of the coding system for the linguistic realisation of EL and categories of pragmatic function adapted in the data analysis.

2.1 Vagueness and vague language

There are different focuses on the concepts of vagueness and VL. Drave (2002: 26) argues that it is necessary to make a distinction between the two concepts to represent different research traditions: VL is a natural-language concept and a concern of linguists, but vagueness is a logical concept and a concern of philosophers. This study adds that vagueness may also be a concern of semanticists, who study meaning using a formal semantic approach. The distinction is relevant when vagueness and VL are used as technical terms; the distinction may blur when the two concepts are used in a general sense.

Research traditions differ in their positions on issues relating to vagueness and VL. For example, there are two opinions about whether language is all vague. Based on a traditional and logic-based view, semantic vagueness refers to expressions whose meaning involves reference to a category with a fuzzy boundary (Crystal 2008: 23). Applying this definition, all language, particularly all category names, could be treated as inherently vague. This type of vagueness has an extremely broad scope, potentially including all categorisation except proper names. Zadeh (cited in Tong, Nguyen, Yager and Ovchinnikov 1987) proposes a *very* test to decide between fuzzy and not fuzzy: any word which can be modified by *very* is fuzzy. Ruzaitė (2007: 35) points out that the *very* test is only applicable to adjectives. One of my previous works, Zhang (1998), proposes other tests to distinguish four concepts: fuzziness, vagueness, generality and ambiguity.

Any reference that does not give a precise referent can be treated as vague. This also applies to cognitive-oriented approaches: for example, Sperber and Wilson (1995 [1986]) claim that indeterminacy is an inherent aspect of language and that no proposition can be entirely determined as to meaning.

Ruzaitė (2007) provides a useful review of vagueness in areas such as philosophy, cognitive linguistics and corpus linguistics.

2.1.1 Vagueness

Early research on vagueness is mostly from the perspective of philosophy and formal linguistics, where vagueness is defined in terms of truth conditions. Russell states that 'vagueness and precision are considered as features which either belong or don't belong to a representation, of which language is an example' (1923: 85), and 'a representation is *vague* when the relation of the representing system to the represented system is not one–one, but one–many' (1923: 89). Russell argues that vagueness only associates with representation, not with actual things in the world. For example, the category 'product of Australia' (written on a rice sack) is vague because the category boundary is fluid. That is, it is unclear what exactly can be considered a member of the category of 'product of Australia'. However, the rice in the sack is not vague, because vagueness refers to concepts, not the actual things concepts represent.

Fuzziness, like vagueness, is dealt with in fuzzy set theory[1] (Zadeh 1965) through a graded membership. This theory enables researchers to look at language with the notion that not everything is black and white: there are grey areas in language communication. This idea guides the study of VL in a fundamental way. Works applying Zadeh's fuzzy set theory to language studies include Lakoff's (1973) seminal work, McCawley (1981), Wu (1999), and Chen and Wu (2002). In Lakoff's view, a certain degree of fuzziness exists around the componential boundaries of fuzzy categories. Sassoon (2013: 3) considers that vagueness conveys 'partial information about the interpretation of predicates like *tall* and *heap*, namely, the impossibility of drawing a clear boundary between members and non-members of their extensions'. That is, interpretation varies from individual to individual, from situation to situation. My PhD project examines fuzzy quantifiers and confirms that they are compositional, in that fuzzy quantifiers of the same type function in the same way to generate a constant semantic pattern which is systematic and predictable (Zhang 1996).

---

[1] A standard set theory considers categories in an all-or-none manner: an individual is either in the set or outside the set. However, there are categories which are not well defined. For example, the category of young people has a fuzzy boundary, so it is not clear whether or not a 35 year-old belongs to the category of young people. This is because there is gradation of youngness. To compensate for the limitation of the standard set theory, Zadeh (1965) devised fuzzy set theory to examine categories with fuzzy boundaries. They can be represented through a degree of membership between 0 and 1. For example, a 35 year-old can belong to *young people* to some degree, say 60%. Zadeh's theory is 'a natural and ingenious extension of the classical theory of sets' (Lakoff 1987: 22).

An expression is fuzzy 'if it has a characteristic of referential opacity' (Zhang 1998: 15) and no clear-cut meaning boundary (Zhang 2004). Fuzzy is a technical term, excluding the notions of misused, mistaken, not well defined, and the like. For example, in a supermarket, if 'product of Australia' is written on a rice sack: what exactly does it mean? Does it mean that the rice in the sack grew AND was packaged in Australia, or only grew in Australia, or was only packaged in Australia? Similarly, with something being 'made in Australia', does it mean this thing was wholly or partially made in Australia, or that the materials were imported and only packaged in Australia? Fuzziness occurs in the application of certain criteria to establish a category.

Crystal (2008: 204) states that the term 'fuzzy' originated from fuzzy mathematics; according to some linguists, fuzziness refers to indeterminacy in the linguistic analysis of a unit or pattern, exemplified by *cup*, *glass*, *sort of*, *rather*, and *quite*. They represent a semantic category which has an invariant core but a variable or fuzzy boundary, permitting a flexible application of a wide range of entities, given an appropriate context. The view that fuzziness is a form of indeterminacy is supported in Zhang (1998: 20), who says that 'one distinct characteristic of fuzziness is that it has no clear-cut referential applicability. Take *tallness* as an example: its general or definitional meaning may be defined as 'a greater height than a norm or an average'; thus, it is not fuzzy. Fuzziness emerges when we try to work out the concept's reference. Using a cognitive approach, Chen and Wu (2002) argue that the internal structure made up of 'centre' and 'boundary' is the reflection of a fuzzy semantic category. The boundary of the prototype category is always fuzzy and cannot be clearly defined. They state that fuzziness is one of the essential characteristics of semantic categorisation, which refers to concepts having fuzzy edges: grey areas where the application of one lexeme over another is fluid.

There is also the notorious sorites paradox of vague concepts. For example, if someone is not bald, then if he loses one hair he should still not be bald. Repeating this $n - 1$ enough times, even when no hair is left he will still not be bald: so when does he become bald enough to be a bald man? To solve this paradox, Raffman proposes a new theory of multiple range vagueness. Using a non-contextualist approach, she (2014: xii) argues that 'vagueness is a form of multiple references, and the competent use of a vague word is characterised by arbitrary divergences among competent speakers' applications of it'. She calls vague words 'unruly', lacking clear boundaries of application: for example, no clear line divides 'product of Australia' from 'non-product of Australia'. Drawing on a psychological study (observing how people use vague words), Raffman finds that people interpret vague words in multiple ways, arbitrarily different but equally competent. For example, the interpretation of 'product of Australia' is based on a range of goods that is arbitrarily

2.1 Vagueness and vague language

different but equally satisfying the criteria of the category; no one is preferred over another, and the paradox can be solved.

Relevance Theory is a cognitive account of pragmatics, claiming 'approximately true' is not the case for VL because usually a literal truth-conditional meaning exists in a vague proposition: 'The truth-conditional relation between propositions and the state of affairs they represent remains unaltered: what varies is how closely the proposition expressed is taken to represent the speaker's thought' (Sperber and Wilson 1991: 546). By introducing the concept of 'loose use', Sperber and Wilson provide a solution to the baldness paradox: they treat *bald* as an all-or-none classic set: no hair at all, so that technically, anyone who has one hair is not bald. However, as a loose use it is perfectly appropriate to say that someone with one hair or very little hair is bald. There is leeway in terms of where a line can be drawn, depending upon context. According to Sperber and Wilson, it is equally false to claim that a man with one hair or a man with a full head of hair is bald: 'what distinguishes them is not the fact that one is true and the other false, but the fact that one is an acceptable loose use because many of its logical and contextual implications are true, whereas the other is unacceptable since a hearer would be able to derive from it virtually no true descriptive information about the state of affairs it purports to represent' (1986: 165). Further discussion of loose use appears in Section 3.1.

Vague expressions do not have a specific meaning (Carter and McCarthy 2006). Powell (1985: 48) states that 'a vaguely denoting expression is one for which a speaker does not possess an unequivocal core of meaning', so that uncertainty focuses on peripheral members, not the core meaning of a vague word. For example, the core meaning of *many* is 'a significant number', which is abstract and rather agreeable (Moxey and Sanford 1993). When it comes to the application of this core meaning, vagueness occurs: 10 people may be *many* in a bedroom, but not in a lecture theatre.

Vagueness and fuzziness are interchangeable in principle, but different research traditions have different preferences for their use. Fuzziness tends to be used in works following fuzzy logic traditions (e.g. Crystal 2008; Lakoff 1973; McCawley 1981; Zadeh 1965; Zhang 1998); otherwise vagueness tends to be used. Fuzziness mainly refers to membership of a category, and 'many everyday conceptual categories are not well defined': for example, *middle-aged* covers what ages (Cruse 2006: 69)? The fuzziness of category boundaries is caused by a lack of clear diagnostic criteria for membership, a speaker's uncertainty about whether certain items belong to the category or not, different judgements in different contexts, and disagreement between speakers regarding membership. As this study concentrates on the use of EL rather than the semantic application of a vague expression, it uses the term 'vagueness' rather than 'fuzziness', because the focus is pragmatic vagueness and non-fuzzy-logic tradition.

2.1.2 Vague language

VL conveys intrinsic uncertainty by rendering the same proposition with more than one expression and, more importantly, is 'purposely and unabashedly vague' (Sadock 1977, cited in Channell 1994: 20). There is little agreement about VL (Channell 1994: 18; Cotterill 2007: 98). Adolphs, Atkins and Harvey (2007: 62) say that 'defining VL is a problematic endeavour, and VL is itself, arguably, a vague concept'. Most things around us are vaguely defined, and to mistake them as crisply defined 'is perhaps best seen as a useful fiction' (van Deemter 2010: 69).

While it is neither the intention, nor feasible, to provide a universally acceptable definition of VL here, this study presents a position that underpins its development. More than 100 years ago, Peirce (1902: 748) defined vagueness from a semantic perspective: 'a proposition is vague when there are possible states of things concerning which it is intrinsically uncertain whether, had they been contemplated by the speaker, he would have regarded them as excluded or allowed by the proposition'. By 'intrinsically', Peirce means that vagueness comes from the indeterminacy of our habits of language, and that language does not force us to come up with a clear-cut decision on whether or not certain elements fit in a category. In a similar vein, Russell (1923: 90) states that vagueness is 'a matter of degree, depending upon the extent of the possible differences between different systems represented by the same representation. Accuracy, on the contrary, is an ideal limit.' Burnett (2012: 2–3) states that 'those advocating a semantic view propose that the puzzling properties of vague language arise from aspects of the semantic denotation of scalar constituents'. The semantic approach identifies vagueness primarily on the referential boundary of an expression. For example, I define a vague expression as a linguistic unit (word, phrase, or sentence) with opaque referential application (Zhang 1998). Take *middle-aged* as an example: 40 years old may seem to be a clear-cut example of middle age, but a grey area exists when the number moves away from 40. It is debatable if a 50-year-old is *middle-aged*, and opinions may vary from individual to individual, from context to context. Thus, *middle-aged* is an expression with undetermined referents. Crystal (2008: 23) confirms that semantic vagueness usually refers to expressions whose meaning involves reference to a category with fuzzy boundaries. Burnett summarises a semantic definition of vagueness through three related properties:

borderline cases (objects for which it is difficult or even impossible to tell whether they satisfy the predicate), *fuzzy boundaries* (the observation that there appear to be no sharp boundaries between cases of a vague predicate and its negation), and *susceptibility to the sorites paradox* (a paradox for systems based on classical first order logic that follows from the fuzzy boundaries property). (Burnett 2012: 2)

2.1 Vagueness and vague language

As Burnett states, the semantic-oriented definitions of vagueness emphasise the unspecified referential boundary of an expression in the form of borderline cases, fuzzy boundaries and the sorites paradox. They highlight overlapping and grey areas, where the application of one particular lexeme over another is debatable. Consequently, classical semantic theories are ill equipped to analyse vague predicates and non-classical approaches are called for, such as applying fuzzy logic (Zadeh 1965) to vagueness (Lakoff 1973). Zadeh's fuzzy logic considers fuzziness[2] a matter of degree: that is, an element belongs to a category to a certain extent rather than having a straight yes-or-no membership.

Different from the semantic orientation, a pragmatic explanation of vagueness focuses on the strategic features of VL in use. VL is inherently or purposively vague (Powell 1985: 31), used to deliberately refer to people and things in an imprecise way exemplified by phrases such as *kind of*, *reasonably*, and *less than* (Carter and McCarthy 2006: 928). Cheng (2007: 162) makes it clear that vague expressions 'can be interpreted based on the particular context in which they occur, and that VL signals to the hearer that the utterance, or part of it, is not to be interpreted precisely'. Cheng's definition has two elements: VL is not an open set, a concept that is useful to distinguish VL from other phenomena such as implicitness and implicature (see Section 2.2 for details); and VL is both context-dependable and context-irresolvable. Ruzaitė states that 'vague language is a natural, usually purposeful and multifunctional linguistic phenomenon that involves imprecision and is employed for certain communicative strategies' (2007: 28). She particularly emphasises the strategic aspect of VL.

There have been attempts to distinguish semantic vagueness and pragmatic vagueness. For example, Wilson and Sperber (2012: 19–20) consider *old* and *ovoid* to be vague linguistic senses, and therefore semantically vague. In their view, pragmatic vagueness refers to an expression with precise semantic meaning where vagueness emerges when it is pragmatically interpreted in context. For example, *at five o'clock* in 'the lecture starts at five o'clock' is not strictly true, because lecturers rarely start at exactly the appointed time. So it is an approximation, and such an approximation is a pragmatic vagueness. Technically speaking, Wilson and Sperber are right to distinguish the two different categories; however, while *old* and *ovoid* are semantically vague, they can also be pragmatically vague, because their interpretations may vary from context to context. Vagueness and the standards of precision vary from context to context (Lewis 1979). Some expressions (such as *old* and *ovoid*) can

---

[2] Used as technical terms, fuzziness and vagueness are similar in nature, but are preferred by different disciplines. Fuzziness originated from fuzzy set theory and fuzzy logic (Zadeh 1965), and so is primarily adopted by mathematics and the like. Vagueness tends to be used by linguistics and the like.

16 Theoretical foundations

Table 2.1 *Comparison of semantic and pragmatic meanings*

Semantic meaning (literal or dictionary)	Pragmatic meaning (interpretation in context)	Example
1 Vague	vague	Many students attended class.
2 Precise	precise	1 + 1 = 2
3 Precise	vague	I'll be back at 8 p.m. today.
4 Ambiguous	precise	He is looking for glasses, because he cannot see clearly.

be both semantically and pragmatically vague, while others (such as *at five o'clock*) are pragmatically vague only.

Semantic vagueness closely involves literal meanings. 'An utterance may be said to have a literal meaning which is capable of being either true or false when the result of combining its linguistic sense with its reference is a proposition' (Wilson and Sperber 2012: 49–50). They argue that people don't care about the literal meaning; for example, in 'the lecture starts at 10 o'clock', they do not contemplate if it might really start at 10.00 or 10:10; what they know is that they should be there around 10.00. The pragmatic meaning is more relevant to real-life communications.

Item 4 in Table 2.1 is a case of ambiguity from the semantic point of view, where *glasses* ('for drinking' or 'for wearing') is semantically ambiguous, but precise from the pragmatic point of view when the utterance is considered in context. Item 2 is consistent in both views, and is irrelevant to this study as there is no vagueness involved. Items 1 and 3 are vague cases: the former is vague both semantically and pragmatically; but the latter is vague in the pragmatic sense only.

Semantic vagueness is less relevant in real-life communication, as language users usually can handle vague referential boundaries well in communication. Popper states:

> We are always conscious that our terms are a little vague (since we have learned to use them only in practical applications) and we reach precision not by reducing their penumbra of vagueness, but rather by keeping well within it, by carefully phrasing our sentences in such a way that the possible shades of meaning of our terms do not matter. This is how we avoid quarrelling about words. (Popper 1966: 19)

Popper suggests that VL is actually a matter of pragmatics. VL focuses primarily on the pragmatic side of vagueness in language use (Janney 2002: 463). VL purposively conveys intrinsic uncertainty by rendering one proposition with more than one expression (Channell 1994: 20). Speakers use VL to refer to people and things deliberately 'in a non-specific, imprecise way' (Carter and McCarthy 2006: 928). VL does not need to be made precise,

2.1 Vagueness and vague language

because the possible shades of semantic meaning, the referential application of words, are not a concern when we actually interact. Similarly, Deese (1974: 72) argues that 'ordinary situations demand that we place only the loosest of interpretations upon some linguistic utterance we hear'. It seems a misconception that precise language is needed more than VL, and the opposite may be more likely: that is, VL is usually sufficient in communication.

VL is a manifestation of uncertainty (Rowland 2007: 82), but that is not all VL represents. Often the speaker may be perfectly certain about something but still use VL to achieve strategic functions. I use the term 'vague-work', referring to 'work in which VL is strategically manipulated in communication. It is a way of vague-ing language to fit a situation' (Zhang 2011: 573). Understanding how vague-work operates is a key for a comprehensive and rigorous account of language use.

At one end of the spectrum is the narrow definition of VL (e.g. Channell 1994; Ruzaitė 2007), including conventional types of vague quantity (e.g. *about 20*, *many*), vague category indicators (e.g. *and things like that*), placeholders and totally vague words (e.g. *thingy*). At the other end of the spectrum is the definition with a wider range (e.g. Prince, Frader and Bosk 1982), including epistemic markers (e.g. *I think*, *seems*) in addition to the conventional types. This, the 'broadest definition' (Trappes-Lomax 2007: 122), is adopted in this study because terms such as *I think* and *seems* express uncertainty and play an important role in communication. However, if the scope of enquiry is too broad, we run the risk of allowing virtually all linguistic units to be classified as vague in some sense, and consequently there would be little difference between studies of VL and of precise language. To avoid VL becoming so broad that it may render analysis pointless, this study takes the position of Cheng (2007: 162) that VL is a closed set of identifiable items. It consists of a closed lexical category, judged by language use. The linguistic realisation of VL includes a range of linguistic units that vary in their degree and type of vagueness involved.

There are three characteristic types of linguistic vagueness: intrinsic (Channell 1994), context-dependable, and context-irresolvable. The intrinsically vague nature of VL makes it fluid and variable, which leads to a 'highly context-dependent language' (Ruzaitė 2007: 53). The understanding of VL is closely linked to the context in question. The characteristic of context-irresolvability sets VL apart from other linguistic phenomena such as ambiguity, in that it is not only context-dependable but also contextually irresolvable (Cheng and Warren 2001; Zhang 1998).

VL is intentional and purposive in the sense that it is used deliberately to serve certain purposes (e.g. Channell 1994), and speakers may not be fully aware that words have a vague referential boundary. There are two types of vagueness: active and passive vagueness (Zhang 2011: 573–4). The former is when VL is used on purpose ('choose to'), including situations where the speaker does not have to use VL but chooses to do so. The latter is that VL is used when a speaker has no other alternatives ('have to'), including lack of knowledge and information, cognitive or linguistic void, or lack of language competence; in such cases, where there is no precise information available the speaker has no choice but to use VL. For example, an L2 speaker might resort to VL when s/he does not know a word. Trappes-Lomax (2007: 122) argues that VL must be purposive, and defines VL as 'any purposive choice of language designed to make the degree of accuracy, preciseness, certainty or clarity with which a referent or situation (event, state, process) is described less than it might have been'. His definition seems to exclude 'have to' vagueness arising from a lack of exact information or the inability to describe something in a precise manner. While this study involves both active ('choose to', purposive) and passive ('have to', forced) VL, the active use will get the majority of attention, because most interlocutors are competent speakers, and the situations where VL must be used are less frequent than those where it is chosen for its strategic qualities. Even so, both active and passive vagueness may be strategic: for example, if one uses VL because of a lack of precise information, then eliciting the right amount of information becomes a strategy.

From the perspective of intended meaning, Brown and Levinson (1987: 225) describe vagueness as the speaker's communicated intent remaining ill-defined. VL is also termed an 'approximation' (Prince et al. 1982: 85). Cheng and Warren (2003: 394–5) find that participants interpret VL based on an understanding of what the speaker is indicating: that what is said is not to be interpreted precisely. They argue that given that a precise meaning cannot be retrieved by the hearer, the successful use of VL requires both parties in a discourse to have a shared understanding of the relative status of a particular set of vague terms. This view is shared by Koester (2010: 158), who points out that VL implies that 'you and I both know what we are talking about' and signals a certain degree of similarity and informality between interlocutors.

VL is context-dependent (Burnett 2012; Carter and McCarthy 1997; Channell 1994; Gassner 2012; Powell 1985; Prince et al. 1982; Ruzaitė 2007; Williamson 1994b). Hatch and Brown (1995: 58) state that 'the meanings are conventional, arrived at through consensus and context, and very "fuzzy"'. For example, while terms for basic colours (red, yellow, green, blue, black and white) are fairly consistent across people and language, when we mix two or more colours, boundaries blur and our judgements become inconsistent; vagueness occurs when we try to distinguish various shades of red in flowers. Compare 'there were *few* people in the classroom' and 'there were *few* people in Times Square': given the different sizes of a classroom and Times Square, *few* in the first sentence refers to fewer people than in the second sentence, and the much bigger size of Times Square influences the expectations of the

Table 2.2 *Differences between vagueness and VL*

Criterion	Vagueness	VL
Semantics or pragmatics	semantics	pragmatics
Conventional or conversational	conventional	conversational
Context-dependable or not	non-context-dependable	context-dependable
Literal or implicature	literal	implicature
Referential or inferential	referential	inferential

hearers. Warren (2007), examining the discourse intonation that manifests the meaning of VL, argues that intonation patterns are an important resource contributing to context-specific meaning of VL.

The approach of frame semantics (Fillmore 1982) seems relevant in interpreting VL. 'Frame' refers to what is going on in reality when language is used. For example, to interpret the word *many*, one needs to have world knowledge about the quantifier and anything relevant to it: the norm of *many*, the item being modified by *many*, the discourse of *many*, the speaker and the hearer, and so on. When a word is used, it activates the frame and often determines a certain perspective from which the frame is viewed; without access to encyclopaedic knowledge relating to that word, it would be difficult to understand it appropriately (Geeraerts 2006a: 15–16). There is a close relationship between world knowledge and the knowledge of language meaning.

VL is strategic. The existence of vagueness in language is hardly noticed until pointed out specifically: that is, VL is taken for granted and unnoticed (Channell 1994: 4). However, this unawareness relates only to its fluid referential boundary, and does not necessarily apply to its strategic role. We tend to use VL strategically (Channell 1994: 20; Ruzaitė 2007: 53), and Jucker et al. (2003: 1739) find that depending on the exploitation of common ground,[3] speakers strategically choose to be vague and will vary the level of vagueness to carry out a communicative task; and the kind and degree of vagueness may guide the hearer to work out the implications. Table 2.2 lists five major differences between vagueness (truth-conditional) and VL.

As shown in Table 2.2, vagueness is semantic-oriented, looking at literal meaning in a conventional manner. It focuses on referential applications of a concept without involving context. VL is a matter of pragmatics, which focuses on conversational meaning, involving inferential meaning and implicature in context.

---

[3] Common ground refers to the interlocutors' shared background assumptions about the world (Jucker et al. 2003: 1742).

In terms of causal factors of VL, three have been discussed: problems facing speakers (e.g. lack of precise information at the time of speaking, memory loss); the features of language (e.g. the generic character of words, context-bound meanings, no suitable exact word); and communicative needs (e.g. no need for precision, maintaining an atmosphere) (Crystal and Davy 1979; Jucker et al. 2003; Ullman 1962). This study focuses on the speaker's need to use VL strategically to achieve various goals.

Does VL hinder communication? It is anticipated that when using VL the speaker expects the hearers to be able to construe meaning by resorting to prior knowledge and contextual clues, although the constructed meaning may not be exactly the same as the meaning intended by the speaker. As Ruzaitė (2007: 2) points out, 'vague language is a natural and pervasive phenomenon, which usually does not cause any malfunctioning in conversation but functions as a useful communicative strategy' (see Section 9.5 for detailed discussion).

2.2   Vague language, hedging and others

There is a rich literature on the phenomenon of hedging, but less attention has been paid to distinctions between hedging, VL and other related phenomena. This section clarifies the distinctions.

2.2.1   Vague language and hedging

Hedge and hedging are closely linked but not the same: a hedge performs hedging but also has other functions. Various definitions of a hedge have different focuses. One is semantic, and is similar to a vague expression defined in a semantic framework. For example, a hedge 'is a particle, word, or phrase that modifies the degree of membership of a predicate or noun phrase in a set'; that is, a 'hedged' membership is *partial*, or true only in certain respects, or that it is *more* true and complete than perhaps might be expected' (Brown and Levinson 1987: 145). Kay (2004: 691) confirms that 'hedges can affect truth conditions'. A pragmatic focus, similar to a vague expression defined in a pragmatic framework, produces a different definition. In this case, hedges are 'expressions through which the speaker eschews categorical overtones and signals non-commitment, being thus related to the epistemic expressions without clearly belonging to the scale of epistemic modality' (Preisler 1986: 104–5). This study adopts the pragmatic definition of a hedge, in line with its main focus.

In a semantic focus, the concept of vagueness is quite different from hedging. The former primarily concerns the referential fluidity of an expression, but the latter is usually seen as a pragmatic phenomenon overlapping VL. Lakoff (1973) draws attention to 'the theoretical importance of the hedge

2.2 Vague language, hedging and others

phenomenon' (Brown and Levinson 1987: 145), defining a hedge as something 'whose meaning implicitly involves fuzziness – words whose job is to make things fuzzier or less fuzzy' (1973: 471). Hedging refers to 'the use of words or expressions which encode the speaker/writer's degree of commitment to the truth of what follows' (Channell 1994: 218). For example, in 'he is <u>sort of</u> an expert in language education', *sort of* makes the interpretation blurry and the utterance indeterminate; it also shows the somewhat uncertain attitude of the speaker. In '<u>strictly speaking</u> he is an expert in Chinese language, not applied linguistics', *strictly speaking* makes the utterance less blurry. Significant works include, among others, Hyland's (1998b) study of hedging in the written discourses of scientific research articles, and a recent book edited by Kaltenböck, Mihatsch and Schneider (2010) on hedging in relation to VL.

Rowland (2007: 82) lists two types of hedge: those like *sort of*, *about* and *approximately* 'have the effect of blurring category boundaries or otherwise precise measures'; and those like *I think*, *maybe* and *perhaps* 'hedge the commitment of the speaker to that which she or he asserts'. O'Keeffe, McCarthy and Carter (2007: 175) offer four types of hedge: modal verbs (*I think*, *I guess*), stance adverbs (*sort of*), restrictive adverbs (*just*), and features of onlineness (the cognitive processing requirements of real-time speech, including repetition and fillers such as *er*, *em*, *you know*, *well*). To avoid being overbroad and fractured, this study classifies the last category of 'features of onlineness' as discourse markers rather than hedges. They are useful indicators when discussing the clustering of vague expressions in Chapters 5–8.

Hedging conveys intended meaning through epistemic modality (Hyland 1998b: 44), generally expressing a tentative attitude adopted to achieve strategically communicative goals. Crystal (2008: 227) considers a hedge to represent a notion of imprecision or qualification, expressing a general sense of evasiveness: for example, in 'this book is <u>kind of</u> good', the speaker's commitment is not as strong as in 'this book is good'. Hedges mitigate potential face threats (Carter and McCarthy 2006; Hyland 1998c; Koester 2006, 2010), and 'lessen the degree of certainty and assertiveness of utterances' (Handford 2010: 166). These functions make hedges useful in business negotiations, especially in disagreements where there is a need to make suggestions or criticism (2010: 256). Hedging is also useful in day-to-day discourse, where it is needed for politeness and the like.

VL and hedging may serve similar functions and purposes, but hedging can use language forms in addition to VL, while VL is not just about hedging but has many other functions. For example, 'I don't know' in colloquial American English increasingly has become a mitigator to politely decline a request (Bybee 2004: 618), a form of hedging. Similarly, the cluster 'I don't know if' can do hedging work (Handford 2010: 121), although neither 'I don't know' nor 'I don't know if' is a conventional vague expression, showing that hedging can use non-VL. Meanwhile, VL can hedge, but it can also emphasise; see Chapter 6 for details.

While there is a somewhat negative connotation associated with VL, hedging is commonly perceived as a positive strategy. Handford (2010: 162) observes that 'while certain traditional perspectives on language that prioritise the written form may cast vague language and other types of indeterminacy in a negative light, an interpersonal and interactive perspective that considers discursive practices and speaker goals does not'. It is one of the tasks of this book to show that VL is a powerful language, as powerful as hedging if not more, and deserving to be part of mainstream language study rather than a marginal component.

Regardless of these differences, hedge may be used interchangeably with vague, and so act as both hedging and VL (Drave 2002: 26). Given that hedging is a common feature of business communication, Handford (2010: 166) states that it is a type of 'fuzzy' language, 'pragmatically and sometimes lexically related to vague language', whose function is to negotiate power and mitigate potential face threats. These functions can be performed through VL as well.

Generally speaking, vague expressions and hedges are pragmatic and strategically focused, while fuzzy expressions are semantically focused. Vague expressions consist of more lexical items than hedges: *many, a few, about 20* are typical elements of VL, but are not hedges. A basic distinction is that VL is a language, but hedging refers to a pragmatic function. The two interconnect in terms of lexical forms and functions but are not equivalent. VL performs more functions than hedging. Hedges are a subset of vague expressions, and thus a subset of VL.

2.2.2 Vague language and others

In addition to hedging, other concepts overlap with vagueness in language. For example, the terms 'vague' and 'imprecise' are often interchangeable (Crystal and Davy 1979; Koester 2007). Cheng and Warren (2001, 2003) view VL as different from implicit language, but Cutting (2000: 39) and Gassner (2012: 8–9) see little difference between the two. Another near-synonym is *loose talk* (Sperber and Wilson 1985/86, 1995 [1986]; see Section 3.1 for details). VL differentiates and interconnects with six concepts: ambiguity, implicitness, inexplicitness, indirectness, implicature, and generality.

Vague language and ambiguity VL differs from ambiguity in two aspects. Firstly, a vague word has no distinct meaning, but an ambiguous word has (Zhang 1998): *many* is vague because there is no clearly defined cut-off point between what is and isn't *many*. *Present* is ambiguous because it has two distinct meanings: *gift* or *current time* (Birner 2013: 11). Secondly, vagueness is not context-resolvable, but ambiguity is (Clark 2013; Zhang 1998). Ambiguity is sometimes considered part of vagueness (e.g. Huang 2012: 319), a position that is not adopted in this study as the phenomena are clearly different in these two aspects.

Vague language and inexplicitness Inexplicitness manifests as substitution, deixis, and reference (Cheng and Warren 2003). Cheng and Warren state that without resorting to context items of reference cannot stand alone: items of reference (e.g. *that* and *it*) gain meaning when constructed by the participants to correspond to a particular context. Vagueness differs from inexplicitness in that while contexts certainly contribute to the interpretation of vague expressions, vagueness remains unsolvable (i.e. remains vague) with or without the help of context. Context plays different roles in constructing meaning for the two types of expression.

Vague language and implicitness These two concepts have an intersection: covert and fluid. VL can manifest as surface features of language, but implicitness always has underlying meaning:

Studies of VL look at language that is inherently and intentionally imprecise, describing lexical and grammatical surface features themselves that may refer either to specific entities or to nothing in particular. Studies of implicitness mention whole bodies of underlying meaning, and language dependent on the context, based on unspoken assumptions and unstated meaning. Implicitness can be expressed with VL and other language features; VL can express implicit meaning but it can be taken at its face value. (Cutting 2007: 4)

Cutting asserts that implicit meaning is an integrated part of VL, but as VL is not the only language form in realising implicitness, the two are not equivalent. Vagueness may be implicit but is not necessarily so, as it can be explicit but still be vague. In cases of implicitness the speaker often wants hearers to get the implied information; this is not always the case in VL use.

Implicitness is seen as a social divider (Fairclough 1989) which requires language users with similar backgrounds to construe the 'unverbalised and context-bound presuppositions in communication' (Gumperz 1982: 131). Without this co-construction between speaker and hearer, successful communication fails to be realised. Wodak (1996: 2) claims that implicit language used by speakers in a position of power can separate 'insiders from outsiders, members of institutions from clients of those institutions, and elites from the normal citizen uninitiated in the arcana of bureaucratic language and life'. This may or may not be applicable to VL, as depending on specific circumstances VL can be a social healer as well as social divider.

Vague language and indirectness Indirect language refers to utterances that are veiled. 'Is it a bit cold here?' expresses 'proposition indirectness' (Preisler 1986: 82): the indirect message is to ask the hearer to turn on the heating or close the window. A speaker of indirect language usually hopes the veiled intention will be inferred by the hearer. Speakers of VL, on the other hand, do not necessarily want the hearer to know their true intent. Brown and Levinson (1987) state that 'would you mind ...', 'if it's okay with you ...' are indirect speech acts. While indirect language could use VL, they don't always have to be vague, and meaning can be inferred if the hearer has access to both language and context (Cheng and Warren 2003). While the meaning of indirect expressions may be successfully resolved with the help of context, this is often not the case for VL.

Vague language and implicature There are two kinds of meaning, literal and implied; implicature is a type of implied meaning. In 'you are Chinese, aren't you?' the tag question implies that you are indeed Chinese, and asks for confirmation. The implicature of such 'reversal tags' conveys 'hedged assertions' (Lakoff 1987: 475). If A asks 'what do you think of your new teacher?' and B (hesitantly) says 'well ...', the answer implies that B does not quite like to criticise the new teacher, avoiding full responsibility for his/her opinion (Clark 2013: 205). Implicature is a pervasive phenomenon and serves a unique function in communication. A contextual trigger is generally required to create an implicature, which is 'only generated when prompted by the context' (Larrivée and Duffley 2014: 543).

Grice's (1975) model of implicature assumes that conversation is a cooperative venture and that speakers adhere to what he calls cooperative maxims. Speakers more often break than follow these maxims, and when this happens specific effects are created for the hearers – what Grice calls implicatures. They manifest the speaker's intended meaning and possess indeterminacy with various possible explanations (1975: 58). Conversational implicature is 'the indirect, unstated meaning of an utterance, additional to what is said' (Cutting 2007: 5). Expressions tend to have a stable semantic core, with a set of implicatures as 'an unstable, context-specific pragmatic overlay' (Levinson 1983: 99). Implicature is not 'what is said', and does not follow logically from 'what is said' (Cruse 2006: 85); by its nature it is unsaid but implied, while VL may be said but in an unspecific way.

Both VL and implicature are forms of indeterminacy (Grice 1975: 58; Handford 2010: 162), and the two phenomena may overlap in some cases but are not equivalent. Like VL, implicature helps to maintain face (Wilson 1990: 21) and is an intentional rather than accidental act (Fowler 1985: 74). Brown and Levinson (1987: 57) use the terms 'indirect expression' and 'implicature' interchangeably.

Vague language and generality Vagueness may include generality of meaning (Crystal 2008: 23). There are two types of general expression: one is context-resolvable and the other is not. For example, *things* is a general word, usually referring to a vague inferential meaning and not context-resolvable. The pronoun *she* is also general, but once it is put in 'she is John's wife, and her

Table 2.3 *Differences between VL and related concepts*

Criterion	Implied meaning	Context-resolvable	Non-mitigation function	May withhold some information
VL	yes/no	no	yes	yes
Hedging	yes/no	no	no	yes
Ambiguity	no	yes	yes	no
Inexplicitness	no	yes	yes	no
Implicitness	yes	no	yes	yes
Indirectness	yes	yes	yes	yes
Implicature	yes	yes/no	yes	yes
Generality	yes/no	yes/no	yes	yes

name is Jane', the unspecified meaning is contextually resolved. *Things* is both general and vague; *she* is general but not necessarily vague.

As Table 2.3 shows, VL overlaps with other concepts. Ambiguity and inexplicitness involve no implied meaning, but implicitness, indirectness and implicature do. VL, hedging and generality employ both literal and implied meanings. VL, hedging and implicitness are not context-resolvable, but ambiguity, inexplicitness and indirectness can be made clear in context. Implicature and generality can be resolved through context in some cases, but not always. Except for hedging, all categories can perform not only a mitigating function but other functions as well. In terms of whether or not the speaker may withhold some information from the hearer, the answer for VL, hedging, implicitness, indirectness, implicature and generality is yes; for ambiguity and inexplicitness it is no. Among the eight concepts, the boundary between VL and ambiguity/inexplicitness is more clear-cut than between the rest of the categories, and there is more overlapping between VL, hedging, implicitness, indirectness, implicature and generality.

While this clarifies the boundary of VL, it also shows that VL overlaps other concepts. Cheng (2007: 162) indicates that VL consists of 'a closed set of identifiable items', but Channell (1994: 5) argues that the list of vague terms grows ever longer, so we can hardly call it limited. This study follows Cheng, distinguishing VL from phenomena that do not have specific linguistic categories and make meaning entirely in context (e.g. implicature). While VL is context-dependable, it has its own linguistic categories for the linguistic realisation of VL.

2.3   Linguistic categories

The forms of EL realisation that underpin this study have been developed from an overview of VL categories in the existing literature. Adolphs et al. (2007: 62) observe that 'the lexico-grammatical realisations and categories associated with VL vary considerably between researchers'. There are three general types in Channell's (1994: 18) work. The first is 'vague additives': 'a word or phrase ... added to what would otherwise be a precise statement, to result in a vague reading'. Such additives include approximators (e.g. *around*) and vague category identifiers (e.g. *and things like that*). The second type is 'vague words', including placeholders (e.g. *whatsit, thingummy*) and quantifiers (e.g. *loads of, heaps of*). The third type is 'implicature': 'this is where an apparently precise sentence can be used and understood to have a vague meaning' (1994: 18). This permits even exact numbers to be interpreted as vague quantities in actual communication (Hurford 1987; Moxey and Sanford 1993; Rosch 1975), making it different from other two in that it is a case of precision. For example, a husband calls his wife to say, 'I'll be home at 7 p.m.' The wife understands 7 p.m. as an approximation, and if her husband arrives at 7.10 p.m., she will not be surprised. The husband may arrive at 7 p.m. exactly (precise) or thereabouts (vague by implicature). This type of VL is not the focus of this study as it can be problematic for a researcher to know if 'vague by implicature' actually applies in a particular context. Focus remains on the other two types of vague expression.

Utterances involving measurements of time, duration, age and round numbers can be seen as 'inherent approximations' (Wachtel 1980: 204). According to Channell (1994: 94), round numbers are used as cognitive reference points, and some reference-point numbers are culturally determined as well. For example, *ten thousand* is likely to be more significant in Chinese, where it is one of the basic numeric units in the number system, than in English, where it is not. Inherent approximations involve both a literal and a loose meaning, according to Jucker et al. (2003: 1760); words (e.g. *like, about*) 'make the loose use of "inherent approximations" (a round number) explicit' and have 'additional conversational effects'. For example, in *about 10 minutes*, *10 minutes* is a round number, and *about* adds an inherent vagueness, creating a loose meaning. There could be another explanation of *about 10 minutes*, treating *10 minutes* as an exact number and *about* as making it vague and creating an imprecise use.

The conventional approach considers vague quantifiers and vague category identifiers and the like (e.g. Channell 1994; Ruzaitė 2007). The liberal approach considers vague quantifiers, vague category identifiers, epistemic markers (*I think*), and the like (Brown and Levinson 1987; Kaltenböck et al. 2010; Prince et al. 1982). This study adopts the liberal approach, as the conventional category alone may be a less representative, somewhat 'restrictive view of VL' (Trappes-Lomax 2007: 122–3). The liberal approach is particularly important in terms of a comprehensive picture of VL in communication.

Table 2.4 shows some consistency among the top four categories, although naming varies to some degree. Some individual words are treated quite

2.3 Linguistic categories

Table 2.4 *Taxonomy of VL*

Channell (1994); Ruzaitė (2007)	Crystal and Davy (1979)	Jucker et al. (2003)	Prince et al. (1982)
Approximator (*about 10*)	approximate quantities	approximator	approximator 1 adaptor (*sort of, a little*) 2 rounder (*about, essentially*)
Quantifier (*many, thousands, a couple of*)		quantifier	
Tag and vague category identifier (Channell), general extender (Ruzaitė) (*and everything*)	summarising lexical item	vague category identifier	
Placeholder (*thingummy*)	placeholder	placeholder	
		vague adverb of frequency and likelihood (*maybe, probably*)	shield 1 plausibility (*I think, seem to*) 2 attribution (*according to her estimates, presumably*)
	vague generic term and collective noun (*heaps*)	downtoner (*a bit*)	
	words with suffix *~ish* (*twentyish*)	hedge (*sort of*)	

differently among researchers. For example, *sort of* is an approximator in Prince et al., a hedge in Jucker et al., and irrelevant in other works. Prince et al.'s categories are either located inside the proposition to modify it and make it vaguer (approximator), or located outside the proposition to comment on it (shield) (Rowland 2007: 83). What follows is an overview of six major VL categories in the existing literature: approximator and vague quantifiers, vague category indicators, vague general terms, intensifiers, softeners, and stance markers.

2.3.1 Approximators and vague quantifiers

Approximators and vague quantifiers both refer to approximations that are unspecified numbers and quantities (Carter and McCarthy 2006; Crystal and

28 Theoretical foundations

Table 2.5 *Approximators*

Item (approximator + exemplar number)	Example
Smaller or bigger than the exemplar number: *about, around, round, approximately, roughly, ~ish, n or m*	*about 20, approximately 20, twentyish, 20 or 30*
Bigger than the exemplar number: *odd, over, or so, at least*	*20 or so, at least 20, over 20*
Smaller than the exemplar number: *almost, nearly, at the most*	*almost 20, nearly 20, less than 20*

Davy 1979), and answer the question 'how much?' (Ruzaitė 2007: 41). Channell (1994), Cheng and O'Keeffe (2014), Jucker et al. (2003), and Wachtel (1980), among others, employ a pragmatic approach where approximators and vague quantifiers are studied in context, including their pragmatic functions.

Approximators, exemplified by *about 20*, bring a vague reading in the form of approximator + exemplar number (Channell 1994: 75), they refer vaguely to amounts, times and dates (Koester 2007: 52). Channell observes that vagueness is more salient around the peripheral members of an interval representing an approximation, and the size and form of the exemplar number and the nature of the item being modified (e.g. *about 20 buttons* vs *about 20 elephants*) all affect how VL is understood.

Table 2.5 lists three categories of approximators. The second and third may be combined into one category called 'partial specifiers' (Channell 1994; Wachtel 1981). They have a seemingly exact cut-off point where the second category specifies a lower limit and the third an upper limit. Wierzbicka (1986: 597) calls *just, at least, only, merely* and *at the most* 'approximatives'. Channell's (1994: 68) data show that partial specifiers and non-partial specifiers (the first type in Table 2.5) behave similarly. This trend is confirmed by Ruzaitė (2007: 165), whose study of the approximators *about, around, approximately, roughly,* and *round* finds that they are almost equally used. While *about* occurs more in spoken language, it is interchangeable with *around*; and the exemplar number tends to be round, acting as a vague numerical reference point (Channell 1994: 78). Approximators are purposely and unabashedly inaccurate (Sadock 1977: 434), and used when precise numbers are not needed or not available.

Vague quantifiers refer to non-numerical quantities (Channell 1994: 99; Ruzaitė 2007: 41), exemplified by *several* and *a lot*. They are also called 'indefinite pronouns' or 'determiners' in Carter and McCarthy (2006: 389), referring to things in a general and open way. Like approximators, vague quantifiers are used when speakers have no need to be precise or have no precise information to offer. The function of generalising 'can be observed in a

2.3 Linguistic categories 29

Table 2.6 *Vague quantifiers*

Item	Function
Multal: *many, much, lots of, loads of, masses of, bags of, a mass of, a lot of, a load of, numbers of, heaps of, tons of, a good/great deal of, a number of*	booster, intensifier in assertive context
Paucal: *a bit of, a scrap of, a touch of, a little bit of, a little, a bit*	downtoner, diminisher in assertive/ negative context
Negative: *few, little*	minimiser in negative context
Neutral: *some, several, a couple of, a few*	assertive/negative context

huge number of utterances containing quantifiers' (Ruzaitė 2007: 98). VL tends to be used more frequently in two parts of academic writing, introductions and conclusions, because of the important role it plays in topic generalisation (Channell 1990; Swales 1990). For example, *many* signals the importance of a study area, *few*, *little* or *very few* implies a gap the study may fill. This type of VL, according to Channell (1994), assists to create implicature and thus avoid flouting Grice's (1975) maxim of quantity ('don't say more than required').

Of the two general types of vague quantifier, one is broad, modifying noun, verb, adjective and adverb, and exemplified by *much* and *more* (Quirk, Greenbaum, Leech and Svartvik 1985); the other is narrower, modifying noun only, and exemplified by *many* and *some* (Biber, Johansson, Leech, Conrad and Finegan 2010).

Table 2.6 is based on Quirk et al.'s (1985) and Ruzaitė's (2007: 81) works. There are four categories of vague quantifier: multal ones as boosters in assertive contexts, paucal ones as downtoners in both assertive and negative contexts, negative ones as minimisers (Cotterill 2007: 111) in negative contexts, and neutral ones in both assertive and negative contexts. The multal and paucal quantifiers 'differ in their communicative function' (Ruzaitė 2007: 39). For example, paucal quantifiers are hedges as 'a means of diminishing precision' (Dubois 1987: 531), while multal quantifiers are boosters strengthening the force of speech.

Vague quantifiers are used dynamically in responding to different situations. For example, *a little bit* occurs in negative contexts more in British English than in American English (Mauranen 2004; Ruzaitė 2007); *a bit* and *a little* are found to be similar in frequency by Bolinger (1972), but not by Ruzaitė (2007) who finds *a little* appears more in assertive contexts. *Some* has a non-identified referent, indicating a less-than-expected quantity (Duffley and Larrivée 2012).

From the perspective of psycholinguistics, Moxey and Sanford (1993) find, *few* (negative context) and *many* (assertive context) have different attention focuses. For example, in 'few students attended class; they went to a movie instead', *they* refers to the group who did not attend class. In 'many students attended class; they enjoyed it', *they* refers to the group who did attend class. The attention focus adds a new dimension to the analysis of vague quantifiers.

Approximators and vague quantifiers can be manipulated effectively and persuasively in communication (Channell 1994; Jucker et al. 2003; Pocheptsov 1992; Ruzaitė 2007). For example, *most people* is more impressive and persuasive than an exact number like 70%. Approximations feature four aspects: (1) being understood as loose uses of language, not literal use; (2) remaining vague about a certain quantity; (3) making conversational contributions more economical and hence more relevant; and (4) carrying additional implications (Jucker et al. 2003: 1761). Approximators and vague quantifiers are a conventional part of the study of VL, and there is little controversy on the status of this category as a prototype of VL.

2.3.2 Vague category indicators

Like approximators and vague quantifiers, vague category indicators are also a traditional and commonly agreed part of VL studies. An example is 'I bought books and things like that', where *book* is a good example of the category indicated by *books and things like that*. *And things like that* is a tag referring vaguely to a category prototyped by *book*, so the tag is called a 'vague category identifier' (Channell 1994: 143).

The naming of this category is diverse: '(terminal) tags' (Aijmer 1985; Biber et al. 2010; Channell 1994; Dines 1980; Macaulay 1991; Ward and Birner 1992), (general) extenders (Aijmer 2013; Overstreet 1995, 1999; Ruzaitė 2007; Terraschke and Holmes 2007), 'extension particles' (Dubois 1993), 'generalisers' and 'vagueness markers' (Simpson 2004), 'vague category markers' (Evison, McCarthy and O'Keeffe 2007; Koester 2006), 'vague category identifiers' (Channell 1994; Jucker et al. 2003; O'Keeffe 2002; Shirato and Stapleton 2007), 'generalised list completers' (Jefferson 1990); and 'summarizing lexical items' (Crystal and Davy 1979). This study uses 'vague category indicator' to highlight the core function: to indicate a category vaguely.

Two basic types of vague category indicators are those with a clear prototype (overt), and those without (covert) (Channell 1994: 143). The overt type is exemplified by *fish and something like that*, where *fish* is an overt and clear exemplar, and *and something like that* is a tag. The covert type is exemplified by *things Mary brought back from China*, called 'covert categories' by Cruse (1986). It overlaps with the category of 'general terms' in this study: hence only the first type is recognised here, and the covert category is classified under 'general terms' (see Section 2.3.3 for details).

According to Channell (1994: 142), there are three levels of exemplar: 'He bought furniture/a chair/a kitchen chair or something.' She considers *furniture*

2.3 Linguistic categories

Table 2.7 *Vague category indicators with* and/or

and	or
apple and something	*apple or something*
apple and something like that	*apple or something like that*
apple and stuff like that	*apple or stuff like that*
apple and all that	*apple or all that*
apple and things like that	*apple or things like that*

too general and therefore uninformative, and *kitchen chair* too specific and therefore the least suitable. The best exemplar is *chair*, which is a good exemplar for its superordinate, furniture. There may be one or more exemplars, termed 'binomials' by Adolphs, Brown, Carter, Crawford and Sahota (2004). For example, 'He bought apples, oranges and things like that', contains two exemplars: *apple* and *orange*. Such multiple exemplars are expected to belong to the same super-category, in this case *fruit*. There are also two basic structures of vague category indicators introduced by *and/or*.

Vague category indicators designate categories either conjunctively (e.g. *and something*) or disjunctively (e.g. *or something*), as can be seen in Table 2.7. Aijmer (2002: 248–9) states that the *and*-tag can be intensifying when stressed, but the *or*-tag is always de-intensifying; both can make language efficient. Vague category indicators function for semantic reasons (e.g. lexical gaps, Channell 1994), or for pragmatic reasons (e.g. marking in-groupness, Aijmer 1985; Ediger 1995b; Overstreet and Yule 1997a).

The use of vague category indicators assumes that knowledge is shared and that the hearers are socially similar (Aijmer 2002: 248). Vague category indicators leave room for other participants to 'add their own description of the situation' (Adolphs et al. 2004: 19); that is, the interpretation is co-constructed among the interlocutors, underpinned by a shared sociocultural background (O'Keeffe 2002); it also locally bound with discourse (Overstreet and Yule 1997b). Simpson (2004) treats these indicators as part of formulaic expressions. If this is the case, then it makes sense that inferring the vague category implied in the context requires common knowledge among interlocutors.

2.3.3 General terms

General terms primarily consist of nouns and indefinite pronouns, exemplified by *things*, *something*, and *stuff*. It is VL 'by choice of vague words or phrases' (Cheng 2007), defined in Koester (2007: 45) as 'vague words used to refer to entities', and exemplified by *bit* in 'the extra bit'. Crystal and Davy (1975:

112) call this type 'totally vague'; it does not even have a core meaning. It enables the speaker 'to refer to an entity or a person without knowing exactly which "name" would be the best word to use' (Yule 1996: 18), a characteristic that sets general terms apart from other types of VL.

General terms are also called 'placeholders' for a noun or name: a close set of mostly dummy nouns for items or person names, primarily used in informal discourse (Channell 1994: 164). Channell finds that placeholders are typical features of conversational language, exemplified by *stuff*, *thing*, *things*, *thingummy*, *thingummyjig*, *thingummabob*, *whatsisname*, *whatsit*, and *what-do-you-call-it*. There are three categories of placeholder: name replacing (e.g. *whosit*), item name replacing (e.g. *whatnot*), and a combination of both (e.g. *thingy*) (1994: 157–63). In using general terms with no referential content in themselves, speakers invite the hearer to infer a referent (Clark and Wilkes-Gibbs 1986: 112), and successful communication may depend on the context in which VL occurs and the shared knowledge of the interlocutors.

A general term has multiple functions, one of which is to bring in a negative evaluation, using *thing* as a deliberate strategy for expressing a speaker's negative view (Jucker et al. 2003: 1765). General terms refer to things in an open way, helping to avoid impoliteness, create solidarity, and the like.

2.3.4 Intensifiers

An intensifier (Bradac, Mulac and Thompson 1995) strengthens vaguely the degree of a property indicated by a relative adjective or adverb (Cruse 2006: 89), exemplified by *very* and *extremely*. An intensifier is also called a booster (Holmes 1985, 1990; Hyland 1998a, 2000) or an emphasiser (Quirk and Greenbaum 1973); these terms are used interchangeably in this study.

There is some disagreement on whether *very* is a vague term. Channell (1994: 110) states that when *very* modifies adjectives it is not vague, and that other adjectives on the scale of degree, such as *a bit*, *somewhat*, *quite*, and *extremely*, are not vague either. She thinks that *very happy* is actually more precise than *happy*, because *very* gives more information and therefore makes *happy* less vague. While Channell casts *very* out, Cheng (2007: 167) reclaims it, arguing that 'all items constituting scalar implicature are vague and only understood within an assumed shared understanding of approximate parameters in a particular context'. She argues that *very* in *very important* is vague because its meaning is 'unspecified, or underspecified, in this context', and it is part of scalar implicature.

While categorising intensifiers as part of VL is yet to be widely recognised, this study supports Cheng's views and classifies *very* and the like as part of VL. This is because from a pragmatic point of view a scalar intensifier enhances the strength of an utterance in an unspecific way.

2.3.5 Softeners

A softener (Holmes 1990; Terraschke and Holmes 2007) weakens vaguely the strength of a claim represented by an utterance, as exemplified by *sort of* and *kind of*. It often indicates that the speaker is unsure about the aptness of the word or phrase that is being modified (Kay 2004: 700). The functions of an interpersonal softener are mainly to mitigate the force of an utterance, as a downtoning hedge or marker of group identity, common ground and informal style (Aijmer 2002: 173–4). Softeners perform the opposite function to intensifiers, weakening rather than enhancing.

A softener is also called a downtoner or hedge (Bradac et al. 1995; Holmes 1990; Hyland 1998a, 2000; Jucker et al. 2003; Lakoff 1973; Quaglio 2009; Quirk and Greenbaum 1973), and compromiser (Bradac et al. 1995: 94). Booster and downtoner, lexical terms which increase or decrease the illocutionary force of speech acts, are terms used in Holmes (1982). Some softeners have multiple meanings and functions; for example, instead of a softener, *sort of* may be used as a discourse particle (Aijmer 2002), contributing to discourse management. *A bit* is a softener when it modifies an adjective, such as in *a bit sleepy*; it can also be a quantifier when clustered with a noun, such as in *add a bit of salt*.

2.3.6 Epistemic stance markers

There are three types of stance marker: epistemic, attitude, and style. The first two work on the content of an utterance, while the third describes the manner of speaking (Biber et al. 2010). According to Biber et al., epistemic stance markers 'express the speaker's judgement about the certainty, reliability, and limitations of the proposition; they can also comment on the source of the information', and attitude stance markers 'convey the speaker's attitude or value judgement about the proposition's content' (2010: 854).

Utterance expresses both content and the speaker's attitude towards the content (Stubbs 1986a: 15). According to Biber et al. (2010), stance markers convey various shades of stance-making and indicate speakers' uncertainty and lack of commitment to the information provided by the speaker. As shown in Table 2.8, Biber et al.'s category of epistemic stance marker is broad. This study moves the imprecision/hedge category to 'softeners' to highlight its function of mitigating. The present analysis focuses on the doubt category which expresses a low degree of certainty and commitment, including *probably*, *might*, *would*, *could* and *I think* (Zhang 2011, 2013).

There are two basic categories of vagueness: epistemic vagueness such as *I think*, and referential vagueness such as *thing* (Gassner 2012: 6). Gassner considers that, largely, epistemic markers do not involve semantic specificity

34 Theoretical foundations

Table 2.8 *Three types of stance marker*

Epistemic stance marker	Attitude stance marker	Style stance marker
Doubt Level of certainty and doubt: *probably, perhaps, may be, most likely, very likely, quite likely, I guess, I think* **Actuality and reality** The reality and actuality of a proposition: *in fact, really, actually, in actual fact, for a fact, truly* **Source of knowledge** A proposition is based on some evidence with or without specifying the exact source: *evidently, apparently, reportedly, reputedly, according to her, as he notes* **Limitation** Limitation of utterance: *mainly, typically* **Viewpoint/perspective** Viewpoint or perspective from which the proposition is true: *in our view, from our perspective, in my opinion* **Imprecision/hedge** Imprecision: *kind of, sort of, roughly*	**Speaker's attitude towards an proposition:** *unfortunately, surprisingly, curiously, sensibly, hopefully*	**Manner of speaking:** *sincerely, honestly, frankly, simply, briefly, literally*

Source: Biber et al. (2010).

but referential vagueness does, in that expressions have low or very low semantic specificity. *Think* and *believe* are known as 'parenthetical' verbs (Hübler 1983: 137), 'private' verbs (Stubbs 1986a: 18), or 'psychological' verbs (Blakemore 1992: 98). Brown and Levinson (1987: 164) observe that *I think, I believe, I assume* are quality hedges in the sense of Grice (1975), in that they 'may suggest that the speaker is not taking full responsibility for the truth of his utterance'. Grammatically speaking, there are two basic types of stance marker: phrasal and clausal (Kärkkäinen 2010: 217). Phrasal markers refer to phrases: for example, in 'he is a smart student, who only started learning Chinese, I think two months ago', *I think* involves the phrase *two months ago* and therefore is a phrasal stance marker. On the other hand, in 'I think I should go', *I think* involves the whole clause, and so is called a clausal stance marker.

Epistemic markers are manifestations of the speaker's veiled opinion (Zhang 2011). *I think* is termed a subjectiviser, highlighting 'it is my subjective opinion' and mitigating the assertive tone (Blum-Kulka, House and Kasper 1989; Rue and Zhang 2008). Epistemic stance markers are vague expressions in their own right, but can also add to an otherwise non-vague utterance to

2.3 Linguistic categories

make it vague. They function primarily for self-protection, and are classified as 'plausibility shields' (*I think, probably, seem to*) and 'attribution shields' (*presumably, according to her estimates*) by Prince et al. (1982: 89), where 'shields' are 'expressions which explicitly encode the speaker's commitment to the truth or precision of what they are saying' (Channell 1994: 19), particularly as 'a means of offering an idea without the obligation of commitment to its truth' (Rowland 2007: 86). These shields reduce the level of speaker commitment (Fraser 1980: 348); for example, *I think* denotes 'tentative assertion', detaching the speaker from total commitment to the content of utterance (Stubbs 1986a: 18). The use of *might, would,* and *could* also indicates lack of certainty. Smith and Jucker (2014) observe that everyday expressions of likelihood (e.g. *maybe, probably*) in negotiations convey both likelihood and the perspective of the speaker.

There are primarily six categories of VL in existing literature: approximators and quantifiers, vague category indicators, general terms, vague intensifiers, softeners, and epistemic stance markers. 'Some lexemes are more vague and context-dependent than others' (Ruzaitė 2007: 37); the first three of these categories are conventional and prototypical VL, in that 'the interpretation of these categories depends largely on the hearer's framework of knowledge' and they all can be 'replaced by a more precise item' (2007: 38). Items in the first three categories have vague referential boundaries, but the latter three are different in that they are about pragmatic non-absoluteness (Prince et al. 1982). In particular, the last category communicates a speaker's stance rather than 'propositional content' (Biber et al. 2010: 966). The present study adopts most of these categories, but with different names and formats to fit the theoretical framework being used.

2.3.7 Lexical categories of elastic language in this study

Of the two approaches in VL studies, liberal and conservative, a liberal approach includes not only the six categories mentioned above but also many others, such as vague nouns (e.g. *birdness*), verbs (e.g. *run*), adjectives (e.g. *good*), metonymical proper nouns (e.g. 'How's your Shakespeare?'), clausal ellipsis, and conversational implicature (Cutting 2000). In reality this approach may lead to a situation where almost all linguistic elements are vague in some sense, making little difference between studies of VL and non-VL. A conservative approach to VL covers a limited number of categories: for example, Channell's (1994) work includes only four types of VL.

This study takes the middle ground, as a too-wide classification will lead to fractured analysis but a too-narrow classification may constrict the richness of VL. Classification here consists of content-focus (e.g. approximators) and the speaker's stance-focus (e.g. epistemic markers). A similar position has been

36 Theoretical foundations

Table 2.9 *Four lexical categories of EL*

Type	Sub-type	Example
Approximate stretcher	approximators, elastic (vague) quantifiers	*about, many, some, much, a lot, most, a few, few, a little, lots of, majority*
General stretcher	general terms, placeholders, elastic (vague) category markers	*things, stuff, something, thingy, someone, anything, somebody, anybody, and things like that, or something*
Scalar stretcher	intensifiers, softeners	*very, a bit, really, so, too, quite, kind of*
Epistemic stretcher	epistemic stance markers	*possible, maybe, I think, I guess, may, might, could, probably*

taken by researchers such as Adolphs et al. (2007). Based on the existing VL categories, especially my other works (Zhang 2011, 2013), this study develops an EL typology for the data analysis that highlights the elasticity of VL, summarised in Table 2.9.

A stretcher in this study refers to an expression that has a fluid and elastic characteristic. The six categories of VL reviewed above are streamlined into the four types of EL shown in Table 2.9, each with a different focus: an approximator stretcher conveys an inexact quantity (numerical or non-numerical); a general stretcher works on expressions with limited semantic specificity; a scalar stretcher concentrates on various scales and continua of stretchers; and an epistemic stretcher stresses a speaker's uncertain attitude and lack of commitment to the information provided. The sub-categories in Table 2.9 have specific roles: for example, placeholders are 'dummy nouns which stand for item names' (Channell 1994: 164); intensifiers function to 'intensify the tone of a speech' (Zhang 2011: 574); both intensifiers and softeners are used to qualify assertions (Bradac et al. 1995: 94); and subjectivisers can diminish an assertive or imposing tone (Blum-Kulka et al. 1989). These four closed-set categories will be used for the linguistic realisation of EL in this study for two reasons. Firstly, there are open-ended vague categories, such as vague nouns/verbs/adjectives, which would make a robust empirical analysis unlikely. Secondly, vague nouns/verbs/adjectives and the like are often used for non-pragmatic purposes; for example, in 'he is <u>tall</u> and <u>handsome</u>', *tall* and *handsome* are used in a descriptive way that has little to do with strategic moves, and therefore has limited relevance to this study of the pragmatic meaning of EL.

The four categories presented in Table 2.9 are primarily adapted from the six categories in Zhang (2011: 574; 2013: 90). In these works, approximators and vague quantifiers express an inexact amount; possibility and plausibility indicators express something that is possible or could be valid; vague category identifiers/general extenders indicate an unspecified category; intensifiers/boosters express elastically a high degree of intensity and increase the tone of speech; de-intensifiers/downtoners express a low intensity degree and decrease the tone of speech; and subjectivisers/shields express a speaker's low certainty or commitment. Possibility and plausibility indicators and subjectivisers/shields are combined into a single category, the epistemic stretcher, for this study, while intensifiers/boosters and de-intensifiers/downtoners constitute the category of scalar stretcher. Zhang (2011) also has a category of vague nouns or pronouns (Andersen 2010; Jucker et al. 2003), which are similar to the general stretchers of this study. This typology corresponds in some way with Prince et al.'s (1982) work on medical discourse, which discerns two types of hedge: shields (e.g. *I think*), which add fuzziness to the degree of the speaker's commitment, and approximators (e.g. *somewhat*), which add fuzziness to the meaning of the sentence. For example, in 'I think she is Chinese', the shield *I think* makes the speaker sounds less than committed to the statement 'she is Chinese'.

There are different forms of vagueness in language: semantic, pragmatic, syntactical and non-verbal, to name a few. Vagueness even exists in the relations between sequences (Janney 2002). This study primarily focuses on the pragmatic meaning of EL, and does not focus on vagueness in syntactic structure (e.g. in how a passive may be used for mitigation) or any other linguistic phenomena.

2.4 Pragmatic functions

VL is used for strategic purposes; as Ruzaitė (2007: 34) states, 'vague language is a versatile phenomenon and has a variety of positive effects in communication'. This section discusses functions in existing literature and identifies the ones suitable for data analysis in this study.

Table 2.10 provides a representative, rather than an exhaustive, list of VL functions, showing that VL is essentially an interactional strategy (Jucker et al. 2003: 1739) and a deliberate and purposive use of language (Channell 1994; Mortensen 1997; Zhang 2011). Of the ten functions, some are for information (*giving the right amount of information*), others are interpersonal (*politeness and face saving*). Some appear to be cooperative (*maintaining informality and atmosphere of friendliness*), others competitive and defensive (*deliberately withholding information*). Some are strategic and intentional (*mitigation and tentativeness*), but others are 'forced' (*discourse management*). The discourse management function includes lack of information, memory lapses, lexical gaps, and the like (Channell 1994; Cotterill 2007; Crystal and Davy 1979), where VL is essential.

VL creates active participation as listeners interpret a speaker's vague message (Wardhaugh 1985). This may be seen as a cooperative behaviour

Table 2.10 *Pragmatic functions of VL*

Name	Representative source
Avoidance and protection of self or others	Channell 1994; Trappes-Lomax 2007
Deliberately withholding information	Channell 1994; Drave 2002
Discourse management	Ruzaitė 2007
Emphasising or de-emphasising certain information	Drave 2002; Ruzaitė 2007
Evaluation of situation	Drave 2002
Giving the right amount of information	Channell 1994
Maintaining informality and atmosphere of friendliness	Channell 1994; Crystal and Davy 1979; Drave 2002
Mitigation and tentativeness	Drave 2002; Rowland 2007; Ruzaitė 2007
Politeness and face saving	Channell 1994; Ruzaitė 2007
Self-distancing	Ruzaitė 2007

(Tannen 1989: 17) because interlocutors have to make an effort to 'decode' the meaning, and participants find the discovering process rewarding. Competitive and defensive attitudes can occur when a speaker has specific information but won't provide it. Channell (1994: 179) considers this a violation of Grice's (1975) Maxim of Quantity, which triggers implicatures. Defensive tactics and pejorative attitudes tend to be overlooked, but this study puts them in the spotlight because they are an important part of communication.

Ruzaitė (2007: 122–3) observes the following functions of approximator and vague quantifier: (1) using language persuasively (emphasising and mitigating); (2) suggesting that more precision is impossible (generalising, guessing, expressing uncertainty, upholding the principle of academic honesty, making impromptu calculations, and displacement); (3) implying that precision is not necessary; (4) displacement; (5) discourse management; (6) correcting or monitoring oneself; (7) specifying an abstract reference; (8) saving face; and (9) encouraging. Some of these functions are discourse-dependent; for example, Ruzaitė's data take the form of teacher–student interactions, where 'encouraging' is a typical teacher tactic. Using a different type of discourse, this study does not adopt verbatim Ruzaitė's categorisation, but some of her categories remain useful and are integrated into this study, for example 'mitigating' and 'generalising'. What follows is a discussion of seven major pragmatic functions of VL in the existing literature.

2.4.1 The right amount of information

Providing the right amount of information involves presenting unspecific information in a situation (Channell 1994), where using precise language is neither possible nor necessary. For example, in 'I went shopping today, and bought a few things', *a few things* indicates that the speaker feels no need to say exactly what they are, and perhaps the hearer does not care either; so the information provided is the right amount.

The right amount of information helps a conversation go smoothly (Shirato and Stapleton 2007: 396), as 'hearers are often not aware of the lack of precise information' (Channell 1994: 194) and approximation can adjust the amount of information given (Sadock 1977; Wachtel 1981). Channell (1994: 173) states that 'one possible use of vagueness is to tailor an utterance such that the right amount of information is given', which follows Grice's (1975) Maxim of Quantity: providing the appropriate amount of information as required, no more and no less. For example, 'She is young and pretty' is good enough to meet the hearer's need to know what she looks like, and there is no need to provide an exact measurement of her height or details of her facial features unless the situation requires. When one has to talk about other individuals' beliefs and plausible reasoning, VL tends to be used to maintain scientific integrity and realistically provide 'scholarly orderliness in their representation of knowledge' (Prince et al. 1982: 96). This case also follows Grice's (1975) Maxim of Quality in that one does not give information that is not supported by evidence.

2.4.2 Mitigation

There are cases where we need to modify our speech to avoid being 'too direct, unduly authoritative or assertive' (Carter and McCarthy 2006: 202). This is because 'simply by speaking we trespass on another's space' (Thomas 1995: 176). Mitigating is perhaps the most natural and recognised function of VL, because of its nature and capacity. VL can 'minimize imposition and attenuate negative discursive moves, such as complaint or criticism' (Zhang 2011: 576). We choose to be safely vague about our own opinions so as not to be seen to disagree (Brown and Levinson 1987: 116). VL can 'help to soften what is said' (Carter 2003: 11); for example, in 'she does not like him' vs 'she *sort of* does not like him', *sort of* reduces the bluntness of the overtly direct utterance.

Focusing on quantifiers, Ruzaitė (2007: 183) points out that 'mitigating quantifiers can mitigate not only a quantity, but also the force of requests, apologies, advice, instructions and criticism'. In addition to the vague expressions themselves, their syntactic position is relevant in performing mitigation: for example, *I think* can be put in the position of clause initial, middle or final. It is the clause final *I think*, as in 'I need to go now, I think', most often doing the mitigating (Biber et al. 2010: 972). VL mitigates by blurring the speaker's intent (Brown and Levinson 1987: 117): for example, in 'she *sort of* loves him', *sort of* leaves the interpretation to the hearer, which assumes some degree of common ground between speaker and hearer, so that the latter is able to infer the former's intent.

VL can mitigate in various discourses. For example, in a tension-prone context it acts as a 'tension management device' (Trappes-Lomax 2007: 134). In an academic setting, Ruzaitė classifies mitigating as part of 'using language persuasively', using paucal quantifiers with small quantities, e.g. *a little bit*, as in 'this may look a little bit confusing' (2007: 94). In a medical context, Adolphs et al. (2007: 69) find that VL is used as a 'softening device to tone down the alarming nature of possible medical diagnoses', as when the nurse is extremely cautious in discussing with the patient a possible worst case scenario.

2.4.3   Politeness and face

VL is a strategy for politeness (Channell 1994; Stubbs 1996), intended to avoid conflict and offence (Brown and Levinson 1987; Lakoff 1990; Leech 1983). The notion of *face* involves self-image in relation to other people, and face-threatening acts are 'those that might be seen as a threat to the hearer's self-image'; linguistic politeness involves the recognition of 'much subtler threats to the self-image that a person presents publicly' (Birner 2013: 201). VL is often used to prevent face-threatening acts from eventuating, or to reduce their impact. Koester (2007: 53) states that VL is used to mitigate potentially face-threatening acts, most evident in service encounters, where general extenders are 'noticeably frequent, most occurring during a meeting between a supplier and customer', and 'the cost of performing a face-threatening act is extremely high – the supplier may lose the customer's business'. That is, VL serves for politeness and face-saving, which is important in successful communication.

VL increases 'the relative politeness of expressions' (Brown and Levinson 1987: 143). VL minimises face threats in criticism (Mey 2001), decreases the negativity of impolite utterances (Caffi 1999; Fraser 1980), and reduces the force of confrontation (Terraschke and Holmes 2007). VL attends to the face needs of both the speaker and others (Ruzaitė 2007; Trappes-Lomax 2007). Current literature focuses on self-protection, but protection of others deserves more attention. VL can avoid three kinds of trouble in attending to face needs: personal (self), interpersonal (others), and interactional (misunderstandings and misalignments) (Trappes-Lomax 2007). VL is the most efficient form of polite communication (Jucker et al. 2003), serving politeness and face-wants.

2.4.4   Informality and solidarity

VL leads to building of informality, intimacy and solidarity. VL maintains interpersonal relationships between speaker and hearer (Brown and Levinson

1987; Ruzaitė 2007). For example, vague category markers serve to show group membership (Ediger 1995a; Overstreet and Yule 1997a), as in 'at the meeting, the HoD talked about ASL and stuff like that', where *and stuff like that* assumes a shared background between speaker and hearer, including knowledge of the acronyms HoD (Head of Department) and ASL (Academic Study Leave). The speaker marks group membership and creates an informal and intimate atmosphere using vague category markers, as 'for the speaker to have listed every possible item in the set would have been at best pedantic and at worst absurd' (Evison et al. 2007: 139). VL can be a marker of in-groupness (Carter and McCarthy 2006; Cutting 2000) where a 'social group sharing interests and knowledge employs non-specificity in talking about their shared interest' (Channell 1994: 193). Along similar lines, Cutting (2007: 15) states that VL is used mostly with 'a socially cohesive function as a high-involvement strategy for asserting in-groupness'. VL is a social action to enhance solidarity between speaker and hearer.

VL is often associated with informal conversational settings (Carter and McCarthy 1997; Channell 1994; Crystal and Davy 1979; Jucker et al. 2003), and the 'level of formality and giving the right amount of information are closely related' (Channell 1994: 192). VL is used more in informal than in formal settings, but as Rowland (2007) demonstrates, this does not mean that the latter is devoid of it.

Shared knowledge is often required in VL communication (Brown and Levinson 1987; Overstreet 1999), with both parties successfully negotiating expectations about what the other party knows within the social space (Vygotsky 1978). Channell confirms that 'any social group sharing interests and knowledge employs non-specificity in talking about their shared interest' (1994: 193). Terraschke and Holmes (2007), basing their findings on a corpus of informal dyadic interactions among Germans and New Zealanders, comment that general extenders (e.g. *and something like that*) are pragmatic devices used interpersonally, to build rapport. The interpretation of VL is based on an assumption of shared background knowledge and rapport management (Spencer-Oatey 2000). This type of VL 'emphasizes the collaborative nature of vague category projection' (Evison et al. 2007: 153), which tends to lead to the convergence of the social groups.

2.4.5 Strengthening

The strengthening function of VL is not widely recognised. Exemplified by *very* and *quite a lot*, vague expressions are used to enhance the degree or strength of an utterance, and to increase its illocutionary force (Zhang 2011: 575). Intensifiers typically carry out the function of strengthening. For example, *very* in 'it is very hot today' strengthens the degree of hotness, but in a vague fashion. Similarly, the function occurs in written discourse, where words such as *clearly, obviously* and *of course* 'allow writers to express conviction' (Hyland 2000: 179).

In addition to intensifiers, other types of vague expression can carry out the function of strengthening. For example, multal quantifiers (*a lot, many*) highlight a large quantity or long periods of time, as in 'yeah, cost me <u>a lot</u>, cost me <u>a great deal of</u> money', where the quantifiers 'do not simply refer to an amount of certain objects, but put a special emphasis on the hugeness of the amount under discussion' (Ruzaitė 2007: 87). The degree can be further strengthened by repeating the same quantifier: 'he has <u>many</u>, <u>many</u> friends'. VL is also persuasive (Channell 1994: 179–80), when approximations are used to maximise the persuasion power. General extenders are also found to be emphatic (Ediger 1995a; Overstreet 1999). In this study, the function of 'strengthening' also includes 'persuasive' and 'emphatic'.

Gender may play some role in the use of intensifiers. Women tend to use intensifiers more than men, according to Wright and Hosman (1983), and similar findings appear in Bradac et al. (1995), who note that women use intensifiers (or hedges) depending upon whom they talk to: more intensifiers when talking to other women, but more hedges when talking to men. That is, women are more emphatic when dealing with women, but less assertive when dealing with men.

2.4.6 Self-protection

VL is often used for self-protection or the protection of others. Protecting others is primarily about politeness and face-saving (see Section 2.4.3 for details). Self-protection functions to cushion the speaker from being challenged and refuted (Channell 1994; Jucker et al. 2003; Trappes-Lomax 2007; Zhang 2011). In particular, VL is used by a speaker to avoid being compromised by a statement that turns out to be wrong (Matthews 1997): for example, in 'she <u>might be</u> John's wife' the speaker's tone of uncertainty shows a defensive attitude.

A similar term to self-protection is self-distancing, used by Ruzaitė, where VL suggests 'a lower degree of the speaker's commitment to the truth of the claim', and conveys 'the speaker's stance and his/her attempt to distance him/herself' (2007: 158). The linguistic realisation of 'self-distancing' in Ruzaitė's work is wide ranging, including various types of hedge (*I suspect, perhaps, might, sort of*), discourse markers (*you know*), general extenders, repetitions, pauses with or without fillers (*erm*), imprecise quantities (*more or less, some*), tag questions, and general incoherence (2007: 158, 161). Among the devices of self-protection, epistemic shields (marking the speaker's commitment) are widely recognised (Kärkkäinen 2007). Avoidance is also a form of self-protection, according to Trappes-Lomax (2007: 135), who states that self-protective motives can avert conflicts and manage tensions strategically.

The main reason for self-protection is often the speaker's uncertainty, and may manifest in two different ways: as a plausibility shield to express doubt; or as an attribution shield through which the speaker attributes a belief to someone else (Prince et al. 1982). VL is called 'tentative language' (e.g. *maybe, perhaps, guess*) in Tausczik and Pennebaker (2010: 36), as it tends to be used when a speaker is less than certain about what is being said. We don't speak directly, so if things go wrong the existing relationship can be maintained, face can be saved, and both sides are comfortable (Pinker 2011). Pinker argues that implicit language can keep awkwardness at bay, but once explicit language is out there, we cannot take it back. VL is preferred because one can use it to self-protect and avoid being on the record as wrong; precise language cannot be 'unsaid', and backs the speaker into a corner.

2.4.7 Withholding information

VL can be used to withhold information deliberately (Channell 1994: 4). Different from all other functions of VL, withholding information is often viewed negatively. This brings out the issue of the nature of VL: cooperative or competitive? Previous works concentrate on cooperative VL, and its other nature is less explored. In my other work, I highlight the uncooperative nature of VL and define it as a negative attitude and divergent language move, describing two competitive categories: confronting, with a non-accommodating tone and used as a social divider, and evading, where the speaker 'deliberately avoids conveying correct/accurate information to manipulate the situation to the speaker's advantage' (Zhang 2011: 577). Ruzaitė (2007: 31) states that 'too much evasiveness due to the excessive use of vague language can be confusing and non-informative', but this is only to the hearer; for the speaker, evasiveness may be a useful weapon to achieve a communicative goal. Deception may be the ultimate uncooperative use of VL, implying a lack of honesty and consideration (Tannen 1996). This function is particularly relevant to this study, which is based on adversarial discourse in a situation where a less than cooperative attitude is not a rare phenomenon.

Ruzaitė finds that 'vague expressions are frequently employed when speakers want to manipulate the amount of information they provide' (2007: 48). She cites an example from Chase (1950: 202), who found that during exams, students employed VL to cover their lack of knowledge and minimise the risk of mark deduction. VL 'is useful when speakers want to hide their ignorance and to distance themselves from the information they provide in order not to make categorical assertions' (2007: 48); that is, VL functions as a device to evade some sort of unfavourable situation the speakers find themselves in.

44   Theoretical foundations

Table 2.11 *Categories of EL pragmatic function in this study*

Name	Definition	Example
1 Just-right elastic	used to provide unspecific and right-amount information when precise information is not needed or unavailable	She has some students.
2 Rapport elastic	used to elicit rapport between speaker and hearer, and to mark in-groupness	Do you want me to buy you a drink or something?
3 Mitigating elastic	used to soften the claim of an utterance, to convey politeness and the like	She is sort of shy.
4 Intensifying elastic	used to strengthen the claim of an utterance or the intensity of an argument	I'm afraid this is a very serious issue.
5 Self-protection elastic	used to express a cautious and uncommitted attitude to a claim the speaker makes, to shield self from vulnerability and being wrong	I think it is probably okay to do that, but you'd better double check with the boss.
6 Evasive elastic	used to withhold information inappropriately, sometimes bordering on deception	He might or might not know this.

Source: Channell (1994), Ruzaitė (2007), and Zhang (2011).

In addition to the seven functions discussed previously, VL has other less recognised functions. It can be used for evaluative purposes, such as *I think* (Bucholtz and Hall 2005; Powell 1985; Zhang 2013), or vague quantifiers that 'evaluate a quantity and convey the speaker's interpretation of its significance' (Ruzaitė 2007: 213). VL is used for discourse management (Aijmer 1997; Holmes 1990; Kaltenböck 2013; Kärkkäinen 2003; Preisler 1986; Zhang 2013). To help hearers capture the intended meaning, speakers may convey not only representational meaning but also procedural meaning (Blakemore 1992: 150). VL conveys ironic and humorous effects as well (Channell 1994: 171–3; Cutting 2007: 3).

VL can be used for a combination of purposes, practical (e.g. presenting the right amount of information) and interpersonal (e.g. building solidarity). In my co-authored work (Zhao and Zhang 2012) studying Chinese business negotiations, we find that the dominant VL purpose is practical. What is discussed in this section lays a good foundation to inform the classification of EL pragmatic functions for this study, shown in Table 2.11.

2.4.8   Pragmatic functions of elastic language in this study

Words such as *sort of* and *a bit* convey 'imprecision and make statements less assertive and less open to challenge or refutation' (Shirato and Stapleton 2007: 396). One way to avoid face-threatening or offensive situations is to resort to loose use of language (Brown and Levinson 1987). The six functions listed in Table 2.11 serve different purposes. For example, just-right elastic is used to provide an appropriate amount of information where the speaker does not have precise information or thinks that it is not important. This includes the traditional function of expressing 'uncertainty' or 'tentativeness', which is a 'default' usage of VL. Channell (1994: 186) states that 'speakers use vague expressions when there is uncertainty about what they want to say. Two situations in which speakers are often uncertain is where they are talking about the past, or the future.' She calls this function 'displacement'. Ruzaitė (2007: 109) also mentions displacement, in that quantifiers are abundantly employed to talk about past, future or hypothetical situations in her British and American corpora, when a speaker does not have precise information and follows Grice's Maxim of Quantity to present the right amount of information (vague information). Mitigating elastic tends to be used in a situation infused with some kind of negativity, such as a criticism or unfavourable evaluation. Evasive elastic may be adopted when the speaker is uncooperative.

This study does not list 'uncertainty' or 'tentativeness' as separate categories, because by its very nature EL expresses uncertainty and tentativeness, a fundamental implicature of elastic expressions. All categories in Table 2.11 rely on the characteristic of EL being uncertain and tentative. For example, the speaker employs *sort of* with an implicature of tentativeness to perform a mitigating function; without it there will be no mitigation. The speaker can also use the uncertain nature of *sort of* to evade a question. There seems little point in presenting the default functions of uncertainty or tentativeness as independent and separate.

2.5 Vague language and institutional discourses

Existing works on VL cover a wide range of discourses, from everyday to institutional life. This study is set in an institutional context. It sits within five relevant institutional discourses where VL plays an important role.

Medical discourse Prince et al. (1982) investigate the interactions between doctors in an intensive care unit. The findings show that VL is frequently present in doctors' conversations, between 150 and 450 hedges per hour. VL typically serves as an appropriate device in representing knowledge, and when the interactants have to describe 'other individuals' beliefs' and 'plausible reasoning' (1982: 96). Prince et al.'s findings are supported by Adolphs et al.'s work in a different health-care context, where VL is 'particularly appropriate in the health-professional–patient interaction, in order to provide the patient with an account of their illness which is understandable' (2007: 63). Adolphs et al. find some tensions concerning the appropriateness of using VL in healthcare communication, illustrating the difficulty the healthcare professional faces in judging how best to deliver information about a patient's health. They must meet the institutional requirements of providing precise and clear information about a patient's medical problems and gaining precise understanding of a patient's symptoms, while at the same time they must elicit and deliver such medical information in a way that the patient can understand and not find unduly alarming. (Adolphs et al. 2007: 63)

Adolphs et al. affirm that VL is less intimidating and threatening in describing illness to patients; it is found to build trustworthy relationships between health professionals and patients, enabling effective communication.

Classroom discourse Rowland (2007) investigates VL in mathematics classrooms from primary school to university. He finds that presenting end calculation results has to be precise, but hedges such as *about*, *maybe* and *I think* exist when predictions and generalisations are made in enquiry-based and problem-solving activities. Language in the mathematics classroom utilises a number of forms of vagueness, and utterances are often tentative and provisional (2007: 81). Cognitive uncertainty, Rowland states, is to be expected and is a valid response to a mathematical challenge.

Conference discourse Trappes-Lomax (2007) looks at presenters at medical conferences. He discusses the 'hazards' we expose ourselves to in speaking and writing, and the kinds of VL we use to shield ourselves from losing face, whether as addressor or addressee.

Courtroom discourse Cotterill (2007) draws on data of British trials to examine the use and abuse of VL in witnesses' responses to lawyers' questions. She concludes that contrary to the traditional view that precision and directness should be used and vagueness is inappropriate in the courtroom, VL does play a role and is necessary in examination and cross-examination.

Business negotiation discourse Based on the corpus of the Cambridge and Nottingham Business English Corpus (containing about one million words of spoken naturally occurring data), Handford (2010: 162) finds that in competitive win–lose negotiations, VL is used to obfuscate personal and professional commitment and responsibility. Zhao and Zhang (2012) investigate VL based on real-life data of Chinese business negotiations and find that social factors (gender, age, power status, and social distance) influence the use of VL.

A common finding in all five general sites of discourse is that VL plays an important role that cannot be filled by precise language. Different functions of VL are highlighted in different discourses: building trustworthy relationships in medical discourse, problem-solving in classroom discourse, and face-saving in conference discourse; all these are important in achieving successful communication. The last two discourses (courtroom and business) are similar in that there is some degree of conflict of interest in the context, and VL is used to protect speakers from total commitment to their claims. This is in contrast with a win–win, cooperative context, where VL is often used for solidarity. Like these two, the data of this study are tension-prone as well.

The degree of sensitivity in discourse impacts on the use of VL. My collaborator and I find that vague expressions (e.g. *I think, some, or something*) are used more in sensitive discourse than in everyday conversation (Zhang 2013; Zhang and Feng 2013). There is a positive correlation between the level of sensitivity, VL frequency, and specific VL items. Similarly, Linell and Bredmar (1996: 366) find that in sensitive medical talk vague expressions are used to ward off face threats and avoid embarrassment. This empirically verifies vagueness and incompleteness as face-preserving techniques (Brown and Levinson 1987). Koester (2007: 45) finds that during a university staff meeting, vague referents (e.g. *this thing*) are used to shield the speaker from saying something inappropriate when discussing a sensitive topic. Similar behaviours are also found in chaplain–patient and nurse–patient talks in hospital (Adolphs et al. 2007: 74–6), and in intercultural interactions (Terraschke and Holmes 2007: 214). The severity of cases may have some impact on the use of EL, a consideration relevant to the current study.

2.6 Summary

This chapter provides an overview of the major issues surrounding VL communication, laying the foundation for a framework of EL that consolidates past research and charts new directions.

The review of existing literature provides a way to conceptualise EL and categorise its forms and pragmatic functions. The conceptual difference between vagueness and VL is that vagueness traditionally focuses on semantic, referential and literal meaning, and VL on pragmatics, inference and implicature. Vagueness looks at conventional sentences independent of context; VL investigates conversational and contextualised utterances. There are differences and similarities between VL and the related notions of hedging, ambiguity, inexplicitness, implicitness, indirectness, implicature and generality, which can be revealed by using four criteria: 'implied meaning', 'context-resolvable', 'non-mitigation function', and 'withholding information'; these help to make the boundaries of VL clear enough. VL and hedging, for example, are both implied meanings, not context-resolvable, and withhold information; the difference is that VL serves functions of both mitigation and non-mitigation, but hedging is for mitigation only.

This study intends to consider EL systematically to overcome the lack of a systematic analysis and avoid the overproduction of ad hoc categories and functions. Based on the literature, EL in this study is realised through the four linguistic categories of approximate, general, scalar and epistemic stretchers, and is analysed through six pragmatic functions: just-right, rapport, mitigating, intensifying, self-protection, and evasive elastic.

VL is influenced by the nature of the discourse. In win–win discourse it tends to be used cooperatively; but in win–lose discourse it has a competitive purpose. As conflicting discourse and the competitive functions of VL are less explored, they will be addressed in this study, one of few attempts to look at both cooperative and competitive functions in adversative institutional discourse.

Three major weak aspects of current scholarship exist: an overarching theoretical account of VL, an explication of the competitive nature of VL as it is manifested in the function of evasiveness, and the impact of social and speech factors on VL. These will be addressed in the following chapters.

3 Elasticity theory

The behaviour of EL can be explained from a pragmatic perspective using a theory of elasticity that will be developed here and tested in the later chapters, providing empirical evidence for the manifestation of elasticity in actual language.

3.1 Cooperative Principle and Relevance Theory

A critical review of the Cooperative Principle (Grice 1975) and Relevance Theory (Sperber and Wilson 1995 [1986]) will highlight the theoretical foundation and advantages of developing elasticity theory.

3.1.1 Grice's maxims and conversational implicature

Grice (1975) proposes the Cooperative Principle to explain conversational implicature. The principle is manifested by four maxims: quality (be truthful), quantity (be as informative as is required), relevance (be relevant) and manner (be clear, brief and orderly):

> if I am asked what time I expect to be home from work, and if I genuinely do not know, because I cannot anticipate workload or traffic, then my most truthful reply, that for which I have evidence, could be 'about six o'clock'. From this, the hearer would infer that I could not say exactly. (Channell 1994: 33)

Channell argues that in this example VL observes the Maxim of Quality when precise information is unavailable. Grice's maxims provide some support for the use of VL; for example, precision 'usually leads to loss of clarity, and to waste of time and effort on preliminaries which often turn out to be useless, because they are bypassed by the real advance of the subject: one should never try to be more precise than the problem situation demands' (Popper 1992: 24). This statement supports the Maxim of Quantity: do not say more than you need to say. VL can be more appropriate than precise language when the situation suits.

VL may also violate the maxims. When speakers mitigate or evade, they may not be truthful. In real-world language there are cases where language use is not truthful, but appropriate to its context. According to Grice, when the maxims are flouted there will be some implications/implicatures. In that case, as Sperber and Wilson (1986: 154–5) state, 'the hearer will assume that the maxim is being observed on another level, and will try to recover as an implicature some related proposition which a speaker observing the maxims might have wanted to convey'. When the maxims are not observed by the speaker, the hearer tends to look for conversational implicatures.

Conversational implicature is not what is said, but is a meaning inferred by the hearer, based on the understanding of the speaker's intended meaning. As Grice puts it, 'the implicature is not carried by what is said, but only by the saying of what is said, or by "putting it that way", and there is an indeterminacy in working out which implicature it actually is from a list of possible implicatures' (1975: 58). The notion of conversational implicature 'offers illuminating insights' into the semantics associated with VL (Rowland 2007: 83), which differs from implicature in that it is a combination of what is said and what is not said.

While the use of VL flouts the Maxims of Manner or Quantity, it may enable a speaker to observe the Maxim of Quality (Rowland 2007: 84). The flouting, Rowland argues, implies a lack of either information or commitment from the speaker. A woman who says her age is 'in the 30s' does so to avoid giving her precise age. Brown and Levinson (1987: 225) confirm the view that VL violates the Maxim of Manner, because the speaker chooses to 'go off record by being vague ... in such a way that his communicated intent remains ill-defined', but 'by using what is technically indirectness' the speaker minimises the threat of face-threatening acts. Overstreet (1995, 1999) notes that general extenders are often used in apologising, violating Grice's maxims by indicating mitigation and evasion.

Grice's framework has met with some criticism. Wilson and Sperber (2012: 56) consider it leaves some issues unexplained, such as the phenomenon that VL is not strictly and literally true and passes 'unattended and undetected in the normal flow of discourse'. Grice has also been questioned for not taking cultural factors into consideration, because 'different cultures, countries and communities have their own ways of observing and expressing [and violating [Cutting's brackets]] maxims for particular situations' (Cutting 2008: 40). Cutting points out that the boundaries between Grice's maxims are not clear-cut, and there could be multiple maxims operating at once. This may not be isolated to Grice's maxims, as categorisations, such as the pragmatic functions of VL, often overlap; it would be problematic to claim that there is a categorical boundary.

The notion of conversational implicature is relevant to VL use. When we talk to each other, according to Grice, speaker and hearer each assume the other is using VL cooperatively. If John does not know how many students are in his class, he may say 'about X' to adhere to the maxims. However, we may not always follow the maxims, and when we flout them there may be an effect of implicature. If John does know the student numbers but still uses 'about X', the implied message could be that he wants to hide something. While conversational implicature can explain VL to some degree, the two are not the same. Grice's framework may not provide an adequate account of VL, as the maxims offer 'a possible set of principles for a theory, but do not constitute in themselves such a theory' (Channell 1994: 32).

3.1.2 Relevance theory and loose talk

Relevance Theory (Sperber and Wilson 1995 [1986]) is about implicature, cognition, and communication, affirming that human cognition requires maximal relevance with regard to communication. It incorporates Grice's Maxim of Relevance, but reduces the four maxims to one principle of relevance, enough on its own to 'explain how linguistic structure and background knowledge interact to determine verbal communication' (1986: 161). The principle has two sub-principles: the cognitive principle of relevance and the communicative principle of relevance (that is, simply by speaking, speakers imply their belief that their speech is optimally relevant). Human processes 'are geared to achieving the greatest possible cognitive effect for the smallest possible processing effort' (1995: vii): hearers expect a high level of relevance to warrant their attending to the stimulus, while the level is the best the speaker can achieve given particular means and goals (1995: 270). If someone in the street asks 'what time is it?' if it is 11.01 a.m., do you say *11 a.m.* or *11.01 a.m.*? The first is good enough to adhere to the general principle of relevance theory, as it serves the purpose and costs both speaker and hearer the minimal production or processing effort. The second answer is more truthful but less relevant.

Expressions such as *11 a.m.* are called 'loose use' of language or 'loose talk' in Relevance Theory. Loose use is an approximate use of language; one form of loose use is to choose shorter forms of language where appropriate. For example, compare 'the meeting starts at 9 a.m.' (approximation, because meetings rarely start exactly at a said time) and 'the meeting starts at or shortly after 9 a.m.' In most cases the hearer will not be misled by the first, and the latter is longer and does not provide more valuable information; the shorter approximation is preferable (Wilson and Sperber 2012: 55).

In some cases, words have both a strict and a general sense (Wilson and Sperber 2012: 19). For example, 9 a.m. has a strict/literal sense (not a second more, not a second less), and a general/non-literal sense (about 9 a.m.). Loose uses are non-literal, interpretive, and based on resemblance relations among representations (Sperber and Wilson 1991: 546). Loose use of language is of two types: approximation and category extension. Approximation is exemplified by 'Holland is flat', where *flat* is used in a broad sense because the Netherlands is not completely flat: there are hills. Approximation broadens a word with a relatively strict sense to a 'penumbra of items' which 'strictly speaking fall outside its linguistically specified denotation' (Wilson and Sperber 2012: 106). Along the same lines, category extension is exemplified by phrases such as (on a picnic, pointing to a flattish rock) 'that's a table!' As Wilson and Sperber note, the rock is not a table, but on this occasion it resembles a table, and may be temporarily included in that category. When broadening, the literal meaning of a loose use is not preserved: Holland is not literally flat and a rock is not literally a table.

Vague use and loose use differ, depending on whether there is a continuum or a sharp conceptual boundary. Wilson and Sperber (2012) argue that vague terms have no sharp boundary but a continuum; loose use retains a sharp boundary but there is no continuum. For example, in 'it is very late, I have to run to catch the bus', no continuum exists: there is a sharp discontinuity between running and walking. Running might be loosely used to indicate the activity of going on foot at a speed more typical of running. However, 'walking at different speeds is not equivalent to running relative to different standards of precision', and loose-use expressions 'have sharp conceptual boundaries, frequent loose interpretations' (2012: 20). It appears that, conceptually, 'running' and 'walking' are not vague, but can be 'loosely' interpreted in context.

In the framework of Relevance Theory, propositions such as 'Holland is flat' are treated as representing a literal truth-condition rather than being 'approximately true'. While Grice's Maxim of Quality is an inferential model of human communication, Sperber and Wilson state that Relevance Theory treats utterances with expectations of relevance rather than truthfulness, and the interpretation of utterances is arrived at by satisfying the hearer's expectations of relevance: 'Sometimes, the only way of satisfying these expectations is to understand the utterance as literally true. But just as an utterance can be understood as an approximation without being recognised and categorised as such, so it can be literally understood without being recognised and categorised as such' (Wilson and Sperber 2012: 61). These statements seem to suggest that vague use and loose use can differ in language form. For example, when a daughter calls her mother and says, 'I'll be home at 8 p.m.' rather than 'I'll be home about 8 p.m.', *at 8 p.m.* may be a loose use, a seemingly precise expression interpreted as an approximation and categorised as such. *About 8 p.m.* is a vague form, and naturally is inferred as one and categorised as such. Such loose use, according to Wilson and Sperber, refers to an expression with a precise, strict sense but a loosely interpreted meaning. A vague use, on the other hand, refers to an expression with a vague strict sense and a vaguely interpreted meaning.

3.1 Cooperative Principle and Relevance Theory

Loose use is about the relationship between the utterance and the speaker's thought, and 'any utterance is only an approximation to the thought the speaker has in mind. The degree of resemblance between this thought and the utterance varies' (Jucker et al. 2003: 1746). In this view, a downtoner is a loose use in the sense that it indicates that 'the degree of interpretive resemblance is not as close as the hearer might otherwise expect. The truth-conditions of a sentence containing a downtoner remain unchanged' (2003: 1746). Loose talks mark 'a discrepancy between an utterance and a thought the speaker has in mind. The marker indicates to the hearer that he should not process the utterance in the most literal sense' (2003: 1766): that is, 'the meaning the speaker wants to convey is not sufficiently covered by an available word' (2003: 1748). When our language is not 'good enough' to represent our thought, loose talk occurs. This is not the case for VL, however, as it can be used deliberately when the speaker could be precise but chooses not to be.

VL is used effortlessly without much notice (Ruzaitė 2007: 33). It is preferred over precise language as 'in relevance-theoretic terms, the vaguely formulated utterance may provide access to more relevant contextual assumptions for the hearer ... more efficient in the sense that it yields the same contextual assumptions for lower processing cost' (Jucker et al. 2003: 1765). It takes more effort to perceive and remember exact numbers than non-exact numbers (Moxey and Sanford 1993, 1997). VL seems 'to be easier to process and makes fewer demands on the hearer; it is probably also the case that a speaker may choose to use a greater amount of vague language to make the discourse easier for the hearer(s) to understand' (Cheng and Warren 2001: 93). These views are challenged by Wardhaugh (1985) and Tannen (1989), who argue that interlocutors have to make more effort to 'decode' the meaning of vague expressions. Mortensen (1997) also asserts that VL is non-specific and non-committal due to lack of competence or deficient social skills, and hence may require more effort to interpret. Empirical evidence is needed to confirm if VL demands more effort to process. Even if it does, its use may be justified if it can achieve particular cognitive effects –or contextual assumptions, in Jucker's terms.

Unlike Grice's maxims, Sperber and Wilson's principles are not intended to be treated as rules (1995: 271). Developed from Gricean pragmatics, Relevance Theory involves human cognition, and its cognitive and communicative principles differ from Grice's socially acquired cooperation principles. Grice considers that both speaker and hearer observe and adhere to cooperative principles in conversations; they share a common goal and are expected to work together to achieve it. Sperber and Wilson doubt that these assumptions are always the case, apart from the common goal to make sure no misunderstanding between speaker and hearer occurs (1995: 268). In reality competing and conflicting goals are not rare, and are particularly evident in adversarial situations. It would be no surprise if uncooperativeness appeared in such conversations, often mixed with cooperative tactics.

There are some questions about Relevance Theory. Cutting (2008: 42) states that, like Grice's Cooperative Principle, Relevance Theory runs short of observing the influences of cultural and social dimensions (age, gender, status, and nationality), and that each country or culture might possess unique ways of abiding by or demonstrating the relevance principle. I argue that when relevance principles and cultural protocols clash, the latter tend to prevail (Zhang 2005). These points are echoed in Aijmer:

> Relevance theory does not take 'an integrated view' on how utterance meaning is achieved and is therefore less adequate to describe what is going on in talk-in-interaction. In particular, it does not explain how pragmatic markers can change over time or in different text types. We need also to consider politeness principles and appropriateness conditions which are less general than the relevance principle but specific to a particular culture or society, region, social situation, historical period, etc. (Aijmer 2013: 11–12)

Although Relevance Theory can explain certain features of VL and is helpful in considering looseness (and vagueness) in its theoretical framework, it is a cognitive paradigm of language use. This study has a primarily pragmatic orientation and focuses on language behaviours rather than on human cognition. There is a need to develop a new model of VL for a comprehensive explanation of the system of VL and its use.

3.1.3 Cooperative and competitive

Assuming that people always interact cooperatively is somewhat idealistic, yet cooperative interactions have been the focus of language studies for years. Prior to the 1980s, discourses studied in research were primarily of the everyday, orderly and cooperative type; then a focus shift occurred, and from 1980 onwards more hostile and competitive discourses were looked at, focusing more attention on conflictive communication (Briggs 1997). Nevertheless, as I argue in other work, there is a need for 'a more realistic, non-idealised account of language use' (Zhang 2011: 596) that includes research on competitive and confrontational interactions and discourses.

Cooperation is 'a joint effort from interlocutors for a common communicative purpose, involving positive and collaborative linguistic behaviours' (Zhang 2011: 576). The working definition of competitiveness or non-cooperation is that these terms refer to diverging interactions involving negative and confrontational linguistic behaviours, with little likelihood of reaching a common goal. Cooperation typically includes pragmatic strategies of just-right elastic, mitigation elastic and rapport elastic; non-cooperation typically includes evasive elastic.

The phenomenon of competitiveness has been acknowledged. Mey (1993) notes that people who have conflicting interests, or even are at war with one another, are not likely to observe cooperative principles. Based on empirical evidence drawn from tension-prone situations, I have found that people communicate uncooperatively, especially in adverse and confrontational situations (Zhang 2011). Competitiveness or potential competitiveness exists in adversarial discourses as well as in everyday discourse. Brown and Levinson (1987: 145) state that 'ordinary communicative intentions are often potential threats to cooperative interaction'. For example, making a request presupposes that the hearer can and is willing to fulfil it but has not yet done so; it runs the risk of becoming an uncooperative exchange.

Cooperative and competitive communication may be intertwined to serve different purposes. Goffman's (1974: 222) notion of 'collaboration between opponents' assumes limited competitive exchanges in communication. For example, quarrelling is viewed as cooperative, because when people quarrel, they 'listen to each other, take turns yelling, maintain a degree of coherence, and so forth' (Pratt 1981: 13). Holdcroft (1979: 135) believes that 'cooperation for a limited purpose against a background of conflict and general suspicion is surely intelligible. Indeed, the background conflict may provide a more powerful motive to talk, as the only way of breaking a deadlock, than a background of amicable agreement.' 'Even in fierce arguments and hard bargaining each participant needs to understand what the other means, and the bitterest disputants must agree to disagree' (Martinich 1980: 215). There is cooperativeness in competitive discourse, and vice versa. However, while there may be elements of cooperation in an adversarial discourse, the uncooperative elements are expected to be the focus, especially for participants who quarrel and argue for divergent purposes.

Cooperative and competitive functions play different roles in communication. Different situations have different interactional needs, so while cooperative maxims may apply in one situation, uncooperative maxims may apply in another. Uncooperative interactions are as intriguing as cooperative ones, if not more so; and each intention plays out by interacting with and complementing the other.

3.2 Zhang's seminal work on elasticity of vague language

The seminal work on the elasticity of VL carried out in my other work (Zhang 2011) highlights the positive and effective characteristics of VL. I use the metaphor of a slingshot to describe the way in which VL stretches in response to the needs of communication:

VL features strategic elasticity, which can be stretched and negotiated to suit the moment-to-moment communicative needs. The elasticity refers to the interpretation of

VL that is not specified, and is dependent upon context and communicative purpose. The interlocutors in interaction co-construct the understanding of VL; that is, VL is stretchable and negotiable. (Zhang 2011: 573)

Based on the concept of elasticity, I propose a main maxim ('stretch language elastically in discursive negotiations to achieve communicative goals') and four specific maxims: go just-right ('provide the right amount of information'), go general ('speak in general terms'), go hypothetical ('speak in hypothetical terms'), and go subjective ('speak in subjective terms') (Zhang 2011: 578–9). The maxims encapsulate the strategic dimensions of VL use, which are empirically explained via institutional data (encounters between Australian Customs officers and passengers).

These findings, according to Zhang (2011), show the interconnection between VL's pragmatic functions, linguistic realisations and pragmatic maxims, the dominant factors of the communicative goal, and versatile pragmatic strategies based on a continuum of polarities (soft and tough, firm and flexible, cooperative and uncooperative). The important contribution concerns non-cooperation types, confronting and evading, which until now have been largely overlooked. VL elasticity emphasises its interactive nature and response to negotiating processes, where communicative goals must be adjusted constantly when working towards an agreeable solution.

Similarly, Channell (1994: 201) states that flexibility (reflecting vagueness) is a valuable component of a fully useful and effective language describing all forms of human experience, and Glinert finds that stretching words in Chinese–English translations in political apologia during two Sino-American crises played a crucial role in their resolution. The negotiation process is described in the image of 'stretching the rubber band between Western and Oriental cultures' (Glinert 2010: 57–8). This is a useful example of EL informing linguistic behaviours and practices.

The notion of elasticity has been adopted in some specific linguistic studies. For example, Parvaresh and Tayebi (2014) apply the concept in their study of VL based on Persian data. In my recent work (Zhang 2014), I use institutional data to investigate the pragmatic functions of *I think* through the lens of elasticity. I find that elasticity manifests in two forms, multi-trajectory and fluidity, between the functions of *I think*. Multi-trajectory refers to the speaker's ability to choose any function and stretch it in any direction; fluidity refers to the non-discrete boundary of the pragmatic functions of *I think*. The two forms overlap. On similar lines, my collaborative work (Zhang and Sabet, in press) adopts the elasticity concept to bring together three characteristics of *I think* (frequency, position, and cluster), based on a corpus of classroom interactions between L1 and L2 speakers of English. The findings show that elasticity is manifested through three stretchable, non-discrete and fluid continua: frequency, position, and cluster. L1 and L2 speakers stretch to variable degrees and stop at variable points along all three continua. It is not appropriate to assume 'over-use' or 'under-use' when L1 and L2 speakers use different frequencies in language use, as these may simply be the result of different focuses and preferences, confirmed by Zhang and Sabet (in press). Sabet and Zhang's (in press) extensive study also shows how the elasticity theory is manifested in academic discourse.

Based on the conceptual work in my 2011 publication, this study develops a fully fledged theory of elasticity in EL, taking into consideration the principles of elasticity, its boundaries, properties, structures, and the processes and mechanisms through which elasticity is realised.

3.3 Elasticity theory

Elasticity theory asserts that, governed by principles of fluidity, stretchability and strategy, speakers deliberately stretch EL in a 'more-or-less' fashion to achieve communicative goals. EL is inherently, purposely, and strategically fluid and stretchable. The word 'stretchable' is a metaphor to indicate that when an elastic expression is used, its interpretation can be extended in one way or another; for instance, the set of *many students* can be stretched by *many* upward to a large number; *few* in *few students* can stretch the set of students downward to a small number. Such stretch work serves an important role in effective communication.

3.3.1 Principles of elasticity

There are three principles in elasticity theory.

> **Fluidity principle** The meanings of utterances are non-discrete, overlapping, context-dependent but context-irresolvable: that is, elasticity is a matter of degree, and EL stretching is gradual rather than abrupt.
> **Stretchability principle** Utterances can be stretched in various ways, and how far to stretch is governed by communicative needs. Appropriate stretching assures effective communication.
> **Strategy principle** Fluid utterances are employed primarily to serve strategic purposes, performed through their pragmatic functions.

The principles are interconnected and complementary. Fluidity indicates that language itself is rubber-band-like elastic. If language were not fluid, the other two principles would not exist. Stretchability enables speakers to realise their communicative goals: in other words, strategy is the purpose of stretchability. Without a purpose it would be pointless for speakers to stretch language, and indeed all speech has a purpose. In general, fluidity is the basis, stretchability is the means, and strategy is the end. Combined, they make EL an indispensable part of effective communication.

Elasticity is pragmatically and intentionally indexed through EL. Linguistic meaning is perspectival, dynamic, flexible, non-autonomous, and encyclopaedic (Geeraerts 2006b), and lays an essential foundation for language to have room to elasticise. Speakers can exploit the inherent vagueness of language for particular communicative purposes (Channell 1994: 97). Whether or not and how much a speaker stretches EL depends on the situation and how strategic the speaker needs or wants to be. Stretching an elastic band too far breaks it; similarly, an utterance may be overstretched (Zhang and Sabet, in press), as when EL is used for deception. There are situations where utterances are stretched not by choice because the speaker may lack precise information and is uncertain about the situation in question, but most stretch work is done by choice, as a means to achieve a communicative goal.

Elasticity is characterised by three features.

1 Elasticity is co-constructed through negotiation between speaker and hearer, based on their shared knowledge.
2 The manifestation of elasticity is influenced by factors such as social background and speech.
3 Elasticity is universal in the sense that it exists in wide-ranging linguistic phenomena and there are some common EL elements across languages and cultures, but specific in the sense that there may be some cross-linguistic and cross-cultural EL discrepancies.

The meaning of EL is co-constructed, and elasticity provides space for communicators to achieve this. Interpretations of EL are expected to be different and approximate due to contextual factors, but good enough to carry on communicating. Elasticity is universal in the sense that it is expected to exist everywhere and in every form (Zhang 2011), and there are certain EL phenomena common to many languages and cultures. On the other hand, elasticity is specific in terms of how it is manifested over different contexts, communicative goals, languages, cultures, and social impacts. Given that elasticity is a multi-faceted phenomenon, a combination of similarities (universality) and variations (specificity) is expected.

Some elastic expressions have a relatively stable core meaning but unstable peripheral meanings: the core meaning of *many* is 'a significant number' (Moxey and Sanford 1993), which is invariant, but its application is variant from context to context. Some other elastic expressions have no stable core meaning, like *things*, which is interpreted entirely by context.

Elastic expressions tend to have some kind of implicature: in 'few students attend her classes'; the implicature is that she is not a popular teacher.

Expressions can have a 'meaning potential', which is 'a rich meaning representation where the meanings are related to each other in different ways'; it is 'a fairly abstract representation' of the speaker's knowledge about the meanings of an expression (Aijmer 2013: 149). The meaning potential has 'a specifiable set of formal and functional features' (e.g. co-occurrences) which constrains (although not completely) the actual functions an expression performs, and should also be able to 'describe its indexical ties to a particular activity' (2013: 149): that is, elasticity can be manifested through stable core meaning, dynamic meaning potential, and the like.

3.3.2 Boundaries of elasticity

Elasticity refers to the fluidity, stretchability and strategy of EL, and requires all three to be present. For example, elasticity excludes an utterance that is fluid but not strategic, or strategic but not fluid. While irony may be used as a strategic move, it may not be part of elasticity, because it does not quite meet the requirements of fluidity and stretchability. Elasticity manifests through a continuum involving the fluidity of utterances themselves (local elasticity) and the global level of overlapping between the utterances (see Section 3.3.3 for details).

The boundaries of elasticity relate to meaning types. Literal meaning is a basic and default meaning ('take hold of' for *grasp*, rather than 'understand'), and non-literal meaning (e.g. implicature) refers to something intended and unsaid (Cruse 2006: 85, 96–7). Loose talk is seen as a non-literal use of language (Sperber and Wilson 1991). In this study, EL is a combination of literal meaning and non-literal meaning, because it contains both 'what is said' and 'what is not said'. Implicature is perceived as an intended meaning that the speaker is willing to get across to the hearer. In the case of EL, there could be another type of meaning: hidden meaning. The speaker does not necessarily want the hearer to know the hidden meaning, although the hearer may be able to infer it.

Elasticity theory has a different explanatory power in relation to other relevant theories such as gradience theory (Bolinger 1961), prototype theory (e.g. Geeraerts 1989), and fuzzy set theory (Zadeh 1965). Gradience theory, also known as categorical indeterminacy, focuses on the indeterminacy of blurred boundaries between two linguistic elements or categories on a gradual scale. Bolinger finds that non-discrete scales are not exceptional in various linguistic fields, where particular items can occur at various stages on a scale. The prototype theory and fuzzy set theory explain a less clear category by degree of resemblance or membership. For example, Zadeh uses an interval from 0 to 1 to indicate how closely an item belongs to a set. The membership of *about 20* is illustrated in Table 3.1, showing that the numbers of *about 20*

Table 3.1 *Membership of* about 20

Number	17	18	19	20	21	22	23
Membership	0.4	0.6	0.8	1	0.8	0.6	0.4

are mostly not in the 100% category but indicate a degree of belonging: for example, number 18 belongs to *about 20* 60%, and number 23 has less membership of *about 20* than number 19.

Gradience, prototype and fuzzy set theories adopt a formal and static approach to the blurry boundaries of linguistic categories. They are primarily semantic and logic-oriented, and context-independent. Elasticity theory instead adopts a pragmatic approach, looking at the fluidity of language from the perspective of strategic stretching, and taking context into consideration.

3.3.3 Properties of elasticity

The basic property of elasticity exists in the three signature properties: fluidity, stretchability and strategy. There are another three related properties of elasticity (Zhang 2011: 579). The first is an interconnection between linguistic categories, maxims and pragmatic functions; for example, epistemic markers tend to conform to the 'go epistemic' maxim and perform a self-distancing function. The second, communicative purpose, determines how elasticity is executed. The third, versatile pragmatic strategies, which are capable of functioning along continua with opposite ends, such as soft and tough, firm and flexible, cooperative and uncooperative moves. EL is gradual along a continuum, in a more-or-less fashion rather than all-or-none. At any point, the elasticity of EL shows a degree of appropriateness to the categories represented by the ends. For example, a degree of intensity may be indicated on a continuum between boosting or softening, and a degree of certainty on a continuum between confident or doubtful, assertive or unassertive. This suggests a dialectic relationship between elasticity and the continuum it sits in.

Elasticity is context-dependent. It is interactional and co-constructed in social actions. Its pragmatic meaning goes hand in hand with context. Language meaning is never homogeneous, always context-bound (Ullman 1962: 118). Co-text and context (interactional, situational, and extra-situational) (in the sense of Janney 2002) are the keys to interpreting the elasticity of VL. The interpretation of VL, such as approximators, is sensitive to contextual information, because VL is purposely and unabashedly inaccurate and has to be accounted for within a pragmatic analysis (Sadock 1977: 434). Vague utterances express indeterminate meaning; the intended illocutionary force is 'often

3.3 Elasticity theory

not fully specified' and implicatures are 'not linguistically encoded at all' (Sperber and Wilson 1986: 161). EL, including intended illocutionary force and implicature, is fluid, and the understanding of EL resorts to context.

The relativity of stretching positions is another property of elasticity: the unmarked/non-stretched position vs the marked/stretched position. In the continuum of tallness (*a bit tall*, *tall*, *very tall*), *tall* is the unmarked position and the other two are marked. Elastic expressions stretch from the unmarked position; like a slingshot, they can 'stretch out' as well as 'bounce back' to the original position. For example, someone may be described as *a bit tall* (stretched position) first, and later as just *tall* (non-stretched position). In real speech 'stretch out' and 'bounce back' need not both be present unless context demands it. For example, someone may be described as *very tall* ('stretch out'), but never as *tall* ('bounce back').

3.3.4 Structures of elasticity

Elasticity is structured at local and global levels. In my (2014) concept of global and local elasticity, the local level refers to individual non-discreteness. An individual utterance has an unspecific meaning, which is itself elastic. The global level refers to a collective non-discreteness between utterances, in that the boundaries of meanings overlap. Local and global elasticity are complementary: local fluidity makes up the global fluidity, and both determine the working of fluidity. As EL has a meaning potential, it can construct a 'good/close enough' meaning at any level to serve discursive tasks.

The collocation of vague expressions takes three forms: pre-vague (e.g. *about 20*), middle vague (e.g. *many*) and post-vague (e.g. *20 or so*) (Zhao and Zhang 2012). Similarly, there are three constructions with elastic expressions in different positions: preceding, middle, and succeeding stretchers. Preceding stretchers include phrasal stretchers (e.g. *nearly 20*) and clausal stretchers (e.g. 'I think she is a smart girl'). Middle stretchers include phrasal stretchers (e.g. *20 or 30*) and clausal stretchers (e.g. 'He will be back, I think, in the end of this year'). Succeeding stretchers include phrasal stretchers (e.g. *apple and something like that*, *20-ish*) and clausal stretchers (e.g. 'She is a smart girl, I think'). Preceding and succeeding stretchers display different trajectories, the first stretching forwards from the stretcher (*nearly 20* elasticises towards 20) and the second stretching backwards (*20-ish* elasticises back to 20).

The structure of elasticity of EL consists of lexical category and pragmatic strategy. For the analysis of elasticity, this study devises four lexical categories (see Table 2.9): approximate stretchers (e.g. *a few*), general stretchers (e.g. *things*), scalar stretchers (e.g. *very*, *a bit*), and epistemic stretchers (e.g. *possible*, *I think*). EL's six categories of pragmatic function, listed in

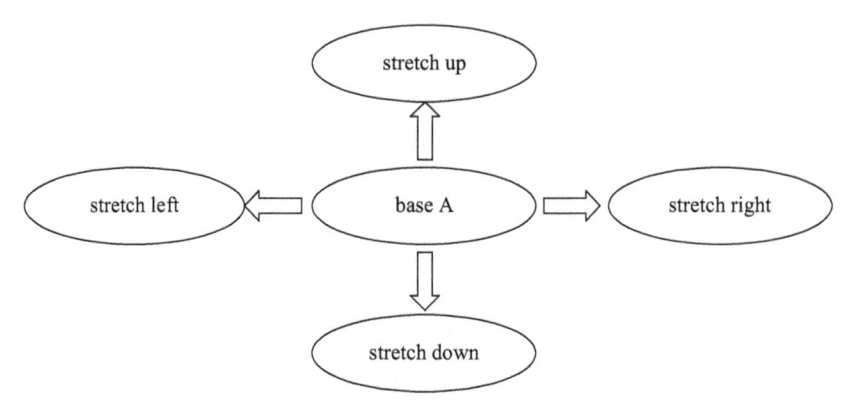

Figure 3.1 Stretching in multi-directions

Table 2.11, are just-right elastic, mitigating elastic, rapport elastic, intensifying elastic, self-protection elastic, and evasive elastic. These are not meant to be categorical: they may overlap, and play more than one role depending on context.

3.3.5 Processes and mechanisms of elasticity

The process of elasticity (elasticisation) is in line with that of 'schematic framework', defined in the sense of Langacker (1986): a structure of different but interconnected levels, where the bottom level presents more specific elements and higher levels offer more general patterns. Schematisation takes place when moving from a specific to a more general level (Geeraerts 2006a: 10). For example, people may go from *the* to *a/whatever*, or from *some* to *any*; that is, from a specific to a schematic level. The 'go general' maxim (Zhang 2011) seems to be one of the elasticisation or schematisation processes.

The mechanism of elasticisation consists of 'input' (utterance), 'input stretching' (elasticising the input), and 'output' (stretched utterance). VL stretching can be in all directions (Zhang 2011): 'this is very important' stretches upward, 'this is a bit embarrassing' moves downward, and 'There are about 20 students in the classroom' shifts left and right, or horizontally. These stretch works are displayed in Figure 3.1.

As Figure 3.1 shows, elasticity is stretchable vertically or horizontally. The model is: let A be a base (input in an unmarked position). Stretcher S functions on A, so the possible outputs are S + A = S/A+, S − A = S/A−, S +/− A = S/A+/−.
(3.1)

A: He is tall.
S/A+:   He is *very* tall.
S/A−:   He is *kind of* tall.

(3.2)

A: He is 20 years old.
S/A+/–: He is *about* 20 years old.

In (3.1), *very* acts on *tall* by stretching it upwards to intensify the degree of *tallness*. In opposition, *kind of* stretches the degree of *tallness* downwards to soften it. In (3.2), *about* stretches the boundary of 20 by expanding it horizontally to the left and right.

Four maxims are proposed as a form of mechanism of elasticity: 'go just-right', 'go general', 'go hypothetical', and 'go subjective' (Zhang 2011). These four maxims demonstrate how elasticisation works. This study adopts the category of 'go general', and combines 'go subjective' and 'go hypothetical' into one maxim, 'go epistemic', because subjective and hypothetical maxims can be covered by a single epistemic maxim. 'Go just-right' is split into two maxims, 'go approximate' and 'go scalar', to define its functions more clearly; 'go just-right' is somewhat too general to be effective as it stands.

Table 3.2 shows the four maxims used in this study. Take 'go general' as an example: *thing* and *stuff* are general words, widely used in spoken discourse (Carter and McCarthy 1997: 16–19). Linell and Bredmar (1996: 366) refer to the general use of VL as 'abstract' expression, to mitigate, ward off face threats and avoid embarrassment. Crystal and Davy (1969: 211) state that 'there are many words and phrases which are useful in law simply because they are so general'. The 'go general' maxim is often seen in day-to-day communication. For example, in China some people are proud of coming from bigger places, and tend to stretch their words when being asked where they are from. Someone from a small city in *Liaoning* province might say 'I'm from Liaoning', rather than specify the city, using the general term *Liaoning* to hide behind without having to disclose that he or she comes from a smaller city. This type of elasticisation is also illustrated in Janney's (2002) work, drawn on data from court testimony during the O. J. Simpson civil trial in 1996. In excerpt (6.11) of this book, the encounter is between plaintiffs' attorney Daniel Petrocelli and Simpson concerning telephone calls made from Chicago to Los Angeles the day after the murders. Petrocelli wants a proper name to be

Table 3.2 *Four maxims*

Name	Definition	Example
1 Go approximate	elasticise in approximate form	*many, a few, about 20*
2 Go general	elasticise in general form	*and stuff like that, thing, stuff*
3 Go scalar	elasticise in scalar form	*very, a bit, many, few*
4 Go epistemic	elasticise in hypothetical and subjective form	*possible, could, might, I think*

confirmed, but Simpson purposely replaces it with an indefinite pronoun. In this way, Simpson appears to evade the question, using the strategy of 'go general'.

The maxim 'go general' can be seen in expressions such as *things* or *something like that*. This 'go general' differs from employing other types of generalised term, such as moving from *dog* to its hyperonymy of *animal*. The maxim refers to a strategic move using an elastic stretcher, but *dog* and *animal* form a semantic relationship between a subset member and its superordinate set.

While the 'go general' maxim may follow a schematisation process, the maxims proposed in this book are not meant to be something that everyone has to follow when they use EL in communication. They are generalisations about linguistic behaviours in EL use. While we are not required to obey these maxims, they provide a mechanism or guidance for using particular strategies in EL.

3.4   Summary

Since there is no well-developed theory of VL (Ruzaitė 2007: 13), this chapter develops the elasticity theory of EL after reviewing Grice's (1975) Cooperative Principle and Sperber and Wilson's (1995 [1986]) Relevance Theory. While Grice's maxims and Sperber and Wilson's 'loose talk' are relevant to EL issues, Grice's focus on implicature ('what is not said') differs from that of elasticity theory ('what is said' as well as 'what is not said'). There are some questions about Relevance Theory, one of which is its lack of cultural and social dimensions. To adequately account for EL, elasticity theory must take account of sociocultural effects. There has been disproportionate attention to cooperative behaviour (positive and collaborative attitudes) and inadequate consideration of competitive behaviour (negative and confrontational attitudes), although the two interact and complement each other.

The elasticity theory developed in this study states that EL is a springy language guided by three principles of fluidity, stretchability and strategy. The theory highlights several characteristics of elasticity: (1) elasticity is co-constructed as a result of interactional negotiation between speaker and hearer; (2) its manifestation is influenced by social and speech factors and the like; (3) elasticity is both universal (similar among languages and cultures) and specific (showing cross-linguistic and cross-cultural discrepancies).

The boundaries of elasticity relate to meaning types: EL is a combination of literal, non-literal meaning (implicature), and hidden meaning. A distinctive feature is that the speaker may not necessarily want the hearer to know everything. Elasticity has several properties: EL is gradual along a continuum in a more-or-less fashion, rather than all-or-none. Elasticity is context-dependent,

3.4 Summary

stretching between marked and unmarked positions. EL may be 'stretching out' to a marked position and/or 'bouncing back' to the unmarked position.

The structure of elasticity has both global (collective) and local (individual) levels. There are three different constructions: preceding stretcher (e.g. *nearly 20*), succeeding stretcher (e.g. *apple and something like that*), and middle stretcher (e.g. 'there seems to be something inside the box'). Elasticity is informed by lexical realisation and pragmatic strategies. Its lexical categories include approximate stretchers (e.g. *a few*), general stretchers (e.g. *things*), scalar stretchers (e.g. *very*, *a bit*), and epistemic stretchers (e.g. *possible*, *I think*). Pragmatic functions include just-right elastic, mitigating elastic, rapport elastic, intensifying elastic, self-protection elastic, and evasive elastic. These categories are, paradoxically, non-categorical: an utterance may play more than one role depending on context.

Processes and mechanisms of elasticity involve elasticisation, which consists of 'input' (utterance), 'input stretching' (elasticising the input), and 'output' (stretched utterance). Elasticity is stretchable vertically (upward or downward) or horizontally (left or right). The mechanism of elasticity also involves four maxims: 'go approximate', 'go general', 'go scalar', and 'go epistemic'. These maxims are not rules; rather they are tendencies, offering guidance in terms of possible EL strategies.

While existing literature tends to view vagueness in language negatively, this study, continuing my previous (2011) work, turns attention to the positive and effective role of EL. To show measurable notions, empirical evidence is brought in to illustrate elasticity theory. Through the examination of linguistic interactions, the following chapters show how the theory is tested and supported in real-life linguistic practices. The corpus has an important function: to fine-tune and elevate work-in-progress theory to a more robust account.

4 Methodology

This study resorts to a corpus of institutional data to evaluate elasticity theory and empirically establish its rigour, using mixed methods research. The corpus is spoken and naturally occurring, because EL is particularly prevalent in spoken language (Biber et al. 2010; Carter and McCarthy 1997) and natural language is typically representative of EL patterns. The analysis focuses on how and why elasticity is manifested, to reveal what interlocutors do with EL and how words are stretched to deal with situations elastically. Specific methods are designed to explore the research questions (stated in Section 1.3) by looking at the interconnected aspects of EL frequency, clusters, pragmatic functions, social factors, and impacts of speech elements. Such a multi-faceted analysis will achieve a robust, rich picture of EL, which is important to ensure the validity of the claims made in this study.

4.1 A mixed methods research

A mixed research design combines both qualitative and quantitative approaches (Creswell 2009). Multi-methodological pluralism in linguistic research is adopted to take advantage of the triangulation of a variety of methods, maximising the best parts of each to strengthen and validate research outcomes (Jick 1979; Schönefeld 2011; Stubbs 1986b). The three points to triangulate are 'the two sources of the data and the phenomenon', and triangulation refers to the enquirer being able 'to improve his investigation by collecting and integrating various kinds of data on the same phenomenon' (Creswell 2008: 553). Blending the advantages of qualitative and quantitative studies of EL cross-confirms the validity of findings, permitting 'greater confidence in the generalisation of results' and offering a context by which the numerical findings can be further explained (2008: 554–5). Exhaustive evidence can be obtained by utilising a broad range of methods (Lakoff and Johnson 1999), and this study aims to achieve as much credible empirical evidence as possible to support the claims made.

The advantages of mixed methods research offset the disadvantages of quantitative and qualitative research (Creswell and Plano Clark 2007) by heightening, expanding and complementing them (Morse 1991). A quantitative approach tends to provide macro patterns based on a large population, offering little micro or detailed analysis that takes into account context or speakers' roles, so its findings must be treated with caution. A qualitative approach is limited in the ability to generate an overall pattern without a reasonable size of population, but can provide in-depth analysis and rich contextual information. Combining the two permits an investigation of both the frequency (quantitative) and pragmatic functions (qualitative) of EL.

This is not a matter of piling up qualitative and quantitative methods: the two kinds of data and analyses should be integrated. Creswell (2009) insists that the researcher must compare the two data sets for potential discrepancies and provide explanations for them, and this procedure guides the analysis here. To know how EL is used, we need to know what forms of EL are used where; to know why, we need to look at the context in which it is used. The combination of investigations of EL frequency, forms and functions warrants a mixed methods research.

This study is an equivalent status design, where quantitative and the qualitative approaches are used equally to understand the phenomena under study (Creswell 1994: 177). Both forms of data are collected simultaneously, and the researcher gives equal weight to each. The dominant quantitative approach, presented in Chapter 5, is a frequency discussion which provides a general picture of how EL, as single words and as clusters, is used. Chapter 6 contains the qualitative approach and considers pragmatic functions, providing contextualised information on why EL is used, something a quantitative method is not able to offer. The qualitative analysis looks into the ongoing process of construction and negotiation between participants. Chapters 7 and 8 consist of both quantitative and qualitative analyses of data, deriving language patterns as well as the useful contextual clues to adequately explain the patterns.

4.2   Data and rationales

The corpus is naturally occurring, institutional, video spoken data, which is most suitable for the objectives of this study.

4.2.1   Data

The corpus consists of video recordings, primarily taken at international airports and international mail handling centres throughout Australia, and offers real-life spoken language, a typical discourse type for VL (Channell 1994: 197). The recordings were screened as a TV documentary series entitled *Border Security*: *Australia's Front Line* on Channel 7 (Australia) from 2008 onwards. Written consent to use the data was obtained.

68   Methodology

The settings of these data are formal and institutional, rather than informal and private. Institutional data differ from daily conversations, particularly in that in this corpus the institutional investigation directs the course of the interchanges. In courtroom discourse, 'conversational concessions are available to neither defendant nor lawyer; in order for due process to be seen to be done, these topics must be explored exhaustively' (Cotterill 2007: 108). The setting of this study is similar to a courtroom setting in that neither officer nor passenger has much choice but to carry out the necessary interrogation.

The corpus has 255,851 words, of which 201,444 were officers' and 54,407 were passengers'. This word count covers what was actually said by the participants; the narrator's voice-over and all tags (names of speakers, coding numbers for speaking turns) are excluded. The narrative voice-over is a prepared monologue, not naturally occurring, and therefore not a good fit with the spontaneous data. In this study, monologue specifically refers to narrator's talk, and dialogue refers to interactions between participants. The size of the corpus is enough to ensure empirical credibility, with EL presented in sufficient quantity to make the analysis meaningful.

Transcription of data was primarily (93%) completed by professional transcribers, the remainder by well-educated individuals (the 7% was proofread by others). To ensure transcriber agreement, I prepared transcription guidelines and a sample file for all transcribers. Transcription was done in conventional orthography, which was sufficient to serve the purpose of the analysis, and included actual speech plus basic non-verbal activities such as pausing, latching in speech, and salient body language; a summary of conventions is provided. The non-verbal activities were used in analysis to help interpret the intentions of participants. To cross-check accuracy, I transcribed 3% of the total data; the agreement between the two versions was 99.5%.

The data mostly comprise interactions between officer and passenger, or officer and officer. Sometimes participants, mostly officers, talked directly to the camera (to the TV audience). This occurred mainly when they were checking international post, on their way to compliance operations, putting suspected goods through X-ray machines and the like, when they explained to the TV audience what was going on. These talks were spontaneous and an integral part of discourse, and so are included as part of the data. They differ from the narrator's voice-overs: both provide background information for the audience to enable them to follow the unfolding action, but the voice-over narration is postpared (created after the data were collected) and non-spontaneous, making it quite distinct from the spontaneous interactions between participants.

The dynamics of the televisual documentary setting are represented not only by the interactions among the participants: the audience are ratified participants or 'encircling hearers', covertly in the background of 'display' talk (Cotterill

4.2 Data and rationales 69

2007: 100; Goffman 1981: 137). The TV audience were intended addressees, constantly in the background, and most talking to camera was conducted to brief them on what was happening, explaining the reasons behind decision making and maintaining the flow of interaction.

(4.1)

Data: Episode 4, from turn 4:2:1 to turn 4:2:2, one speaker, over two speaking turns.
Context: At Sydney's International Mail Centre, customs officer Kane (male in his late 20s) has just made a shocking discovery in two packages from Thailand, having spotted oddly shaped organic matter on the x-ray.

(Officer Kane looking at x-ray and talking to camera)
4:2:1[1] KANE: I've just run it back through the x-ray (pause) and what were just clumps of organic material (pause) now clearly you can see a ... what looks like a snake.
4:2:2 KANE: You can see the discernable head (pause) and the tail. And it's (pause) kind of ... you can actually make out where it's attempted to get out of the box and ... and made a break for its freedom. (pause) Our responsibility is to (pause) get them looked after as quickly as possible, so I'll refer this to our investigations unit who will have it seen to by a vet. (slight left shrug)

(4.2)

Data: Episode 1, from turn 1:1:24 to 1:1:30 and 1:1:121 to 1:1:122, three speakers, over nine speaking turns.
Context: Encounter between officer Lee (male in his 40s) and passenger (Canadian male in his 30s). Lee is questioning the passenger about prohibited narcotics. Later, a conversation occurs between Lee and another officer (male in his 40s).

1:1:24 LEE: Ah that's just a metal detector to see if you've got metal on ya ... (pause) weapons, or anything like that. I'm not looking for that. I'm looking for drugs to see if you have drugs.
1:1:25 PASSENGER: I don't have drugs, sir.
1:1:26 LEE: A simple pat down search to see if you have any =
1:1:27 PASSENGER: =No. No.
(Officer Lee talking to camera)

---

[1] 1:1:24 stands for episode 1, extract 1, speaking turn 24, hereafter.

(4.2) (*cont.*)	
1:1:28 LEE:	So at the moment we're detaining him for a 219 frisk search. He's er refused that, (pause) so er we're looking to er upgrade it to an external search, which involves taking all his clothes off. (turns to the passenger) So your only objection is the principle of it?
1:1:29 PASSENGER:	Yes, because this gentleman (indicates someone off screen) is doing ... doing his job very well.
1:1:30 LEE:	Yeah.
......	
	(Officer Lee talking to camera)
1:1:121 LEE:	So that's the package that he had in his groin. Erm, (pause) we're just going to gimlet a er bit of the powder out of it ... er assuming it's powder inside ... and er test it in a field er narcotic test, to see what's inside.
1:1:122 OFFICER:	Yes, it's a white powder, as you can see. (pause) So you have to be careful getting it out, because you don't want to flick it. This could be potentially very toxic, so you don't want to inhale any of it.

In excerpt (4.1), Kane is working on his own, explaining what he is doing to the TV audience. In excerpt (4.2), the first part of the conversation, Lee is talking to a passenger. In the middle of the interaction he turns to the camera to explain to the TV audience what is going on, then goes back to the conversation. This 'talking to camera' is an embedded part of the interaction, especially in turn 1:1:121 where Lee is talking to the TV audience while his colleague is present. This study does not separate the talking-to-camera data from other data, as the dual audience justifies its inclusion.

The data are in English, very occasionally in a foreign language that is translated on screen.

The participants primarily form two groups: Australian Customs officers (quarantine, immigration officers) and passengers. Recording took place at various Australian Customs workplaces, including international airports/mail centres (95%), and other places (5%, cargo/container examination facilities, farms and workshops, seaports and Australian waters where compliance operations were conducted). The data mainly come from two major international airports in Sydney and Melbourne. Most international mail centres were in the precincts of international airports. Officers were L1 (or near-L1) speakers of English, and a mix of gender, age and rank. Passengers were L1 or L2 speakers; some spoke little English. They too were a mix of gender and age, arriving in Australia from various countries and for various purposes. The interrogations took place in cases of suspected drug trafficking, work permit violations, false passports, fake tourism, quarantine issues, etc. The officers' task was to detect and deter unlawful activities and illegal movement of goods into Australia.

4.2.2 The rationales

The advantages of naturally recorded data in this study are naturalness, and contextualised, accurate phonological features (Channell 1994). A pragmatic analysis, an integral part of this study, traces dynamic meaning-generating processes in actual instances of discourse. Invented linguistic data can be misleading (Sinclair 1991), because a sentence may be grammatical but not necessarily acceptable and natural in actual language use (Channell 1994: 38). Discourse Completion Tests and role-play data involve to a greater or lesser extent 'decontextualised examples in a non-natural setting ... they are at best indicative of the understandings which may arise in natural settings' (1994: 76). Channell argues that linguists' intuitions do not appear 'very empirically valid', so using real data for a '*post hoc* analysis of meanings, if it is carried out with rigorous attention to seeking justification within the structure of the conversation, is currently the only reasonable way to study meaning' (1994: 39). Naturally occurring data are far superior to invented examples because they are natural.

On-screen documentary data, such as those in this study, are naturally occurring. Although the interlocutors are aware of the cameras, the situation is in line with other types of naturally recorded data where participants are aware that they are to be observed and recorded (Zhang 2011: 584). Nowadays almost all researchers are required to inform participants if they are involved in any data collection, which impacts the level of spontaneity and results in the impossibility of ethically collecting data without participants being aware and possibly adjusting their speech. On-screen or off-screen, both are naturally occurring data (see Section 4.4 for more discussion on this issue).

The term 'naturally occurring' is challenged by Labov (1972, on the observer's paradox) and Speer (2002). Gassner (2012: 16) comments that 'the notion of naturally occurring data is in itself problematic, given that this type of data is also not entirely "natural", because research participants will be aware that a study is taking place as consent forms have to be signed or recording devices will have to be installed which influences the data's naturalness'. While this point is taken, these types of data are the closest possible to real-life communication.

The use of video data enables replaying and reviewing to check and double-check the fine details of EL uses and the dynamic situations that produce them, capturing both sound and image, verbal and non-verbal activities. Video recording is currently the optimal way to catch fine details of talk-in-interaction.

Its reliability is excellent; it permits rechecking to enhance accuracy. It offers a wealth of natural discourse features, a particularly useful one being the preservation of the sequence of talk, which is important for qualitative analysis. Audio recordings alone 'inevitably lose some information, for example nonverbal cues such as eye movements, facial expressions or gestures' (Dörnyei 2007: 139); and while non-verbal aspects are generally beyond the scope of this investigation, they are analysed as part of the EL cluster where relevant. Video data show demographic information about participants, which helps the analysis of the impact of social factors such as power status and gender.

The value of video data is that they offer a way 'to gain access to the thoughts, feelings, concerns, interpretations, reactions, etc.' of the participants (Pomerantz 2005: 96). Pomerantz suggests that video data, as recall practice, may offer hints for further analysis to clarify any information in question. Video is favoured by researchers such as Adolphs (2006) for its flexibility and dynamics at the time of recording, and its versatility in all types of current and future studies. However, Dörnyei (2007: 139) warns that 'although video data is obviously richer than audio recordings, the video recording process is much more difficult and obstructive than switching on a small Dictaphone, and analysing video is not an easy task either'. Dörnyei recognises the workload of the researcher faced with interpreting visual and audio data, and indeed data handling is an immensely time-consuming process. However, the difficulties are outweighed by the overwhelming advantages video data offer, especially where visual information of contexts and participants is needed to enrich analysis.

The selection of institutional data in this study provides insights into the study of EL, particularly through the new data concerning how participants behave in confrontational situations. In institutional discourse, professionals need to find ways of carrying out their professional tasks. The Australian Customs officers' primary task is to get the truth out of a suspect passenger; the relationship between officer and passenger can easily turn into confrontation between accuser and accusee or the authority figure and the target/ victim. These encounters require considerable skill to negotiate, and EL is one of the most important elements in achieving this. At the same time, the passengers are in a dire situation and need to defend themselves. EL again is a crucial weapon to help get them out of trouble. The selection of such data helps to achieve the goal of this study: to reveal how elasticity is manifested in institutional discourse with implications for other types of language discourse.

4.3 Data analysis

In order to answer the research questions raised in Section 1.3, the data were analysed quantitatively and qualitatively. Chapter 5 is mostly a quantitative analysis, in the form of EL types, clusters, and frequency distribution, using

4.3 Data analysis 73

the taxonomy provided in Table 2.9. Chapter 6 is a qualitative analysis on EL strategic functions, using the categories in Table 2.11. There are also analyses of social and speech factors (Chapters 7 and 8), investigating both EL distribution and pragmatic functions.

This contextualised analysis focuses on verbal activities, strengthened by relevant anecdotal and ad hoc discussions. Non-verbal activities can help to interpret implicature: facial expressions, such as a nervous look, may confirm a certain interpretation of the speaker's intended meaning. Excerpts from the corpus used in the qualitative analysis are prefaced by brief background information to contextualise them. Many participants' first names, mainly of officers, were conveniently provided in the corpus. Since the names are already in the public record, there is no need to code them in this study.

As the elasticity of EL involves all levels of linguistic analysis, this analysis focuses on two major levels. At the lexical level, types and clusters of elastic terms and their frequency are analysed to demonstrate how EL is realised. At the discoursal level, EL is analysed to demonstrate its stretchability and strategic functions.

4.3.1 Lexical analysis

As presented in Table 2.9, EL can be realised in four types: approximate stretcher, general stretcher, scalar stretcher, and epistemic stretcher. For this analysis, individual forms and their frequencies were generated automatically by WordSmith Tools (Mike Scott 2010, version 6.0), an analytical software package. Relevant words and their clusters were rank-ordered, with the help of the concordance tool in the package, as evidence of EL formations and speakers' lexical-pragmatic choices. The automatically generated list could have contained inaccuracies because contextual clues are not considered to clarify items that have multiple meanings and uses. For example, *about* is an approximator in *about 20*, but a preposition in *talk about* (not an elastic word), therefore, the lists were checked manually by me to make sure of the accuracy of the data.

The validity of the findings was measured and confirmed by a chi-square test on the statistical significance of the distributional difference in the use of EL. Significance was tested using chi-square calculation (Preacher 2010–2015). The *p*-value (p stands for probability) represents a significance level. In this study, when $p < 0.01$ the difference is statistically significant and representative of its population.

4.3.2 Discoursal analysis

At the discoursal level, the data were analysed for the strategic functions EL performs and how social and speech factors impact on the elasticity of EL.

EL is strategically utilised for certain communicative needs and power plays in conflict-filled talk-in-interactions. The data reveal how interlocutors manage and negotiate their discursive moves and ultimately resolve the situation in question. This analysis follows the six pragmatic functions of EL listed in Table 2.11: just-right elastic, mitigating elastic, rapport elastic, intensifying elastic, self-protection elastic, and evasive elastic. The study looks at speaker and hearer, their interactions and discursive moves.

At discoursal level, the analysis is predominantly qualitative, 'systematically accounting for the shape, structure and function of the associated utterance, that is, viewing the utterance as a whole as performing some discourse function or constituting some action' (Kärkkäinen 2012: 2194). A sequential analysis reveals moves where participants deliberately stretch EL to negotiate preferred outcomes. Social and speech factors are also investigated, as the interrelatedness of EL and such factors may shed light on the linguistic behaviour of EL.

Body language and facial expressions help identify the pragmatic functions of EL. For example, gesture is an integral part of constructive and manipulatory language; it effectively performs descriptive, indicative and pragmatic functions (Kendon 2004) and is valuable in revealing not only how participants use EL but also the complex contexts that trigger its use.

Excerpts from the data have been selected to illustrate how EL is used. The criterion is that the excerpts contain EL that illustrates a point in question, allowing examination of the linguistic behaviours of EL. The selected data need to be able to show how speakers resort to elasticity and interact with hearers. It is the intent that all excerpts provide a sufficient amount of background information to illustrate how the stretch work unfolds. Avoiding the common mistake of overlooking responses from the hearer, the discoursal level analysis focuses on the speaker–hearer interaction, which helps to reveal the illocutionary force of the speaker.

4.4 Limitation of research

There are some potential shortcomings of this study, although it is hoped that certain measures put in place may overcome or at least minimise possible weaknesses. TV documentaries provide naturally occurring encounters, but they are often edited down from lengthy footage before being aired, perhaps to pick the most interesting bits or to fit a time-slot. In this respect they differ from traditional linguistic data collection where researchers record and transcribe data verbatim, with no editing. The difference between traditional research data and on-screen documentaries may influence the ways in which EL is represented in the data, but the impact 'should be in limited capacity' (Zhang 2011: 584), and thus should not affect the validity of the findings

4.4 Limitation of research

derived from the documentaries. While it is possible that on-screen data are edited before it is aired, the data in this study show no visible sign of editing; there is no reason to doubt their credibility.

The corpus in this study is adversarial in nature: how representative is it? While it may not be the most common form of everyday interaction, adversarial types of communication, in varying degrees, are not rare. As an integral part of communication, adversarial discourse has been overlooked in existing literature, and this study rectifies this lack.

This study is based on institutional data: so how much can be claimed? Institutional talks display adaptations and variations of ordinary conversations (Atkinson and Heritage 1984; Drew and Heritage 1992), so the patterns observed may not be representative of all types of talk. This study claims no more than the data can support, and recognises that it is important to be cautious with any generalisation. As Cheng and Tsui (2009: 2367) point out, the findings observed from a particular data set are tendencies situated in 'specific contexts of interaction'; they are not 'laws and general principles', but 'clues and guidelines'. It is possible that patterns emerging from this study are applicable to other types of discourse, but any such generalisation needs to be validly made.

Classifying a specific function of EL is never straightforward, as nobody is a mind-reader of another's intentions and 'pragmatic inferences are not always clear' (Shuy 2014: 22). Cotterill (2007) warns that caution is needed in any attempt to interpret a speaker's motivation in producing VL. In this study, the officer–passenger encounters occur in contexts where the possibility of deliberate evasion and deception is relatively high. Since the participants could not be contacted to elicit their personal reflections, it can never be known for certain if, for example, EL was used 'to take linguistic shortcuts' (O'Keeffe 2003: 9), or to be 'deliberately and unresolvably vague' (Powell 1985: 31). On the other hand, as Levinson (1983: 53) notes, participants have the ability to infer 'the purposes for which utterances are being used'. The participants include the television audience as well in this study. What we do as researchers is to speculate. We may never be absolutely sure, but we have a pretty good idea about what utterances are intended for: 'While interpreting participants' intentions is always difficult, the status of "insider" helps: we can use our knowledge of language to exemplify and illuminate how and why language is used' (Holmes 1995: 40). In addition to employing inside knowledge, researchers can use discursive clues and any other evidential signs. Contextual triggers can also be used as diagnostics to identify the implicature of EL. It is not just the immediate environment that may determine the function of EL, but the bigger discourse segment. What the speaker says as well as what the hearer responds provide contextual clues; in particular, hearers' responses may be useful because 'they are more open to empirical observation than information

76   Methodology

about speakers' intentions' (Channell 1994: 26). An effort to take all available empirical evidence into consideration maximises the validity of the analysis of EL pragmatic functions. Even so, it needs to be clear that the pragmatic functions of EL are a 'best guess' and can never be categorical.

4.5   Summary

This study provides empirical evidence to evaluate and confirm the proposed elasticity theory of EL based on a comparative analysis of EL form, function and context. It adopts a mixed methods approach, combining qualitative and quantitative methods to blend the advantages and maximise the best elements of both. The method is not a simple addition: the two kinds of data and analyses (e.g. frequency, forms and functions) are integrated to strengthen the robustness of the study and validate the research outcomes.

The corpus consists of spoken data recorded in Australia, primarily at international airports and international mail centres. The video recordings were screened as a TV documentary series entitled *Border Security: Australia's Front Line* on Channel 7 (Australia) from 2008 onwards. The data consist of 255,851 words, a corpus substantial enough to ensure the empirical credibility of this study. The data are in English, with very occasional data in a foreign language. The participants are in two groups: Australian Customs officers and passengers. Their interactions involve suspected cases, such as drug trafficking, work permit violations, false passports, fake tourists, and quarantine issues.

The chosen corpus is naturally occurring, video-recorded, institutional data, which are most suited to the objectives of this study. The rationale for using naturally occurring data is its naturalness and rich interactions. Documentaries are naturally occurring whether on-screen or off-screen, although participants are aware that they are being observed and recorded. Institutional data broaden the analysis of EL into adversarial contexts and offer the most useful examples of how the elasticity of EL manifests in negotiations. Video is one of the best ways to catch the fine details of talk-in-interaction. It enables replaying and reviewing to check and double-check details of manipulation of EL and the dynamic situations that produce them, via sound and image, verbal and non-verbal activities. Video data offer a wealth of natural discourse features, especially preserving the sequence of talk, which is important for qualitative analysis. They also offer demographic information about the participants, which helps analysis of the impact of social and speech factors such as power status and gender.

The data analysis focuses on two levels. At a lexical level, types, clusters of elastic items, and their frequency are analysed to demonstrate how EL is realised. The validity of the findings is measured and confirmed by chi-square

4.5 Summary

tests, regarding the statistical significance of difference in the use of EL. At discoursal level, EL is analysed to demonstrate why EL is used, by looking at its strategic functions and the impact of social and speech factors on it.

There are some limitations to this study, but certain measures may overcome or minimise their impact. The documentaries may have been edited before being aired, although there are no visible signs of editing and therefore no reason to doubt the credibility of the data.

5 Linguistic realisation of elastic language

The linguistic realisation of EL is derived by looking at frequency distributions overall as well as of each of the individual stretchers: approximate, general, scalar and epistemic. The first three are stretchers whose job is to introduce elasticity to the utterances they work on, and the last one is to add elasticity to the degree of speakers' commitment to their claim and epistemic stance. The qualitative analysis uncovers any tendencies of stretchers to cluster, revealing lexical patterns of EL use in combinations. It shows which stretchers or types of stretcher tend to co-occur, and with which other expressions, demonstrating the linguistic behaviour of EL at a different level from the analysis of the stretchers themselves.

Frequency analysis identifies what and how much is desirable or acceptable for certain expressions. While this provides a general and useful picture of EL use, it is not enough merely to present quantitative numbers; thus, this chapter also contextualises the stretchers and their clusters, taking account of the settings in which they are spoken.

5.1 Overall lexical pattern

The analysis in this study focuses on high-frequency stretchers, because low-frequency stretchers provide insufficient examples for a satisfactory analysis.

Table 5.1 lists the 20 most frequent stretchers in the data. Raw frequency is based on the corpus of a quarter of a million words. The last column lists standardised frequency per 10,000 words, to provide comparable information for this book and for other researchers. Of the top 20 elastic words selected here, the total occurrence is 4,938, and the density is 192.9 elastic words per 10,000 words.

Among the top 20 stretchers, *very* is most frequent, with a density of 26.3 per 10,000 words. The least dense, *or something*, has four occurrences per 10,000 words, seven times less frequent than *very*. The top ten terms with more density are *very, some, anything, something, lot*, quite, things, a bit, much*, and *probably*. Cheng's (2007: 165) list of the top 10 most frequent vague

5.1 Overall lexical pattern

Table 5.1 *Twenty most frequent stretchers*

Rank	Item	Raw frequency (n = 255,851)	Normalised frequency[1] (per 10,000 words)
1	*very*	674	26.3
2	*some*	570	22.3
3	*anything*	564	22.0
4	*something*	450	17.6
5	*lot**	290	11.3
6	*quite*	242	9.5
7	*things*	220	8.6
8	*a bit*	208	8.1
9	*much*	182	7.1
10	*probably*	178	7.0
11	*sort of*	167	6.5
12	*could be*	162	6.3
13	*about*	160	6.3
14	*possib**	143	5.6
15	*maybe*	141	5.5
16	*stuff*	126	4.9
17	*a little bit*	124	4.8
18	*too*	120	4.7
19	*so*	114	4.5
20	*or something*	103	4.0
	Total	**4,938**	**192.9**

*Note: lot** includes *a lot, a lot of*, and *lots of*; *possib**: includes *possible* and *possibly*. These abbreviations apply throughout.

terms, based on a corpus of spoken English in Hong Kong, includes *very, about, some, more, much, something, many, quite, things*, and *most*. Cheng's corpus consists of 920,000 words, with 230,000 words each from academic, business, conversational and public subcorpora. Six of the ten are the same as in this study, showing a reasonable degree of similarity. The other three are *about* (ranked 13 in this study), *most* (ranked 23), and *many* (ranked 25). The discrepancy may be attributed to a number of factors, such as the different types of spoken English, speaker, or setting. The word *more* is not classified as vague in this study because it is used primarily in a comparative and relational sense, rather than to express an unspecified meaning.

Table 5.1 mostly consists of single words. Based on the CANCODE corpus (five million words), Carter and McCarthy (2004) find top 20 three-word clusters, of which three are elastic terms (#2 *a lot of*, #14 *a bit of*, #18 *a couple*

---

[1] This study uses a normalised frequency throughout, necessary when comparing findings from different sized data sets. It is also convenient for potential comparisons between this and any other studies.

80   Linguistic realisation of elastic language

Table 5.2 *Twenty most frequent stretchers by category*

Approximate stretcher	General stretcher	Scalar stretcher	Epistemic stretcher
about (13)	*anything* (3)	*very* (1)	*probably* (10)
some (2)⁺	*something* (4)	*quite* (6)	*sort of* (11)
*lot** (5)⁺	*things* (7)	*too* (18)	*could be* (12)
a bit (8)⁺	*stuff* (16)	*so* (19)	*possib** (14)
much (9)⁺	*or something* (20)		*maybe* (15)
a little bit (17)⁺			

Note: (13) stands for 'rank 13th' in Table 5.1; ⁺ stands for items with multiple categories.

Table 5.3 *Eight stretchers to be analysed*

Approximate stretcher	General stretcher	Scalar stretcher	Epistemic stretcher
about (13)	*anything* (3)	*very* (1)	*probably* (10)
some (2)⁺	*something* (4)	*quite* (6)	*sort of* (11)

of). The order of ranking for the clusters is slightly different in this study: *a lot of* (213 occurrences), *a couple of* (83 occurrences), and *a bit of* (73 occurrences): the last two items swap places. Of the top 20 five-word clusters in Carter and McCarthy's study, four elastic clusters make the list: #8 *this, that and the other*, #10 *all the rest of it*, #14 *and that sort of thing*, and #18 *all that sort of thing*. Each of these occurred only once or twice in this study, quite different from Carter and McCarthy's data.

In Table 5.2, items are listed according to four stretcher categories, then according to frequency within each category, except for the first column. The first column consists of two types: *about*, at the top, is a typical approximate stretcher; the following ones belong to more than one category. *Some* could overlap between approximate and general stretchers, while *lot**, *a bit*, *much*, and *a little bit* could overlap between approximate and scalar stretchers. The overlap is an example of global elasticity, as discussed in Chapter 3. While overlapping happens between the first three categories, the epistemic category is less collaborative. Overall, the items in the first two categories rank higher than the ones in the last two: on average approximate stretchers rank 9, general stretchers rank 10, scalar stretchers rank 11, and epistemic stretchers rank 12.

In the following sections the top eight items of the 20 most frequent stretchers are analysed, as shown in Table 5.3. The pattern of analysis is quantitative followed by qualitative; the qualitative analysis is to elaborate the quantitative findings.

5.2 Approximate stretchers 81

In Table 5.3 each category has two words, the most frequent in their respective categories. An analysis of the most frequent words in each category will show how the elastic slingshot is implemented, and how the speakers follow the four maxims 'go approximate', 'go general', 'go scalar' and 'go epistemic'.

5.2 Approximate stretchers

The category 'approximate stretcher' consists of two subsets: approximator and quantifier. This category is similar to what Channell (1994) calls 'approximating qualities' and Ruzaitė (2007) calls 'quantifiers and approximators'. *About* is a typical approximator, and *some* represents elastic quantifiers.

5.2.1 *About* and its clusters

The word *about* has various usages, one of which is to modify a quantity and imply elasticity, for instance *about 20*. In line with what was found by Cheng (2007: 173) of 954 instances of *about*, 160 (16.8%) worked as approximators. In 'he talked about the party', *about* is not an approximator but a preposition to bring in the noun *party*. *About* in *be about to* is not treated as an approximator either, as it is an integrated part of the idiomatic meaning of 'something soon to take place' (e.g. 'the train is about to leave'). This idiom, found 90 times in this study, focuses on imminence, unlike the *about* in *about 20*, an approximation.

In terms of structure, *about* is a preceding stretcher. It functions on the item being modified to make an approximation. Approximators such as *about* in *about 20* might appear pointless as 20 by itself can be understood as a round number, but approximators make the vagueness explicit (Jucker et al. 2003: 1759). There are other ways to make an approximation: 'we were in the zoo for like two hours' uses *like* as a casual form of approximator.

Table 5.4 shows that of the total 160 instances of *about*, 81.3% of which follow the '*about* + number' pattern expressing an approximation of people, money, time, weight, etc., 13.8% follow the pattern '*about* + a/an + quantity/period of time', where a/an is interchangeable with *one*. There are other less

Table 5.4 *Frequency of* about *clusters*

	about + number	*about* + a/an + quantity/period of time
Raw frequency (n = 255,851)	130	22
Normalised frequency (per 10,000 words)	5.1	0.9

frequent *about* clusters: '*about* + *another* + number' (... *about another 20 or 30 to go* ..., ... *about another thousand dollars* ...). The findings of '*about* + number' (5.1) vs '*about* + *a/an* + quantity/period of time' (0.9) in this study support Cheng's (2007: 174–5) results (4.0 vs 0.28), where the frequency of '*about* + number' is much greater than the second pattern. Overall, participants use more *about* clusters than those in Cheng's study. An explanation may be that one quarter of Cheng's data are of academic discourse which makes less use of *about* clusters; Ruzaitė (2007: 174) finds that approximators occur infrequently in spoken academic discourse. The following excerpts show how *about* clusters are used in officer–passenger interactions.

(5.1)

Data: Episode 26, from turn 26:2:9 to 26:2:14, two speakers, over six speaking turns.
Context: Encounter between officer Paramjit (male in his 40s) and a passenger (British male in his 20s). The two are discussing the finance of the passenger.

(Officer searching passenger's bag)
26:2:9 PARAMJIT: How much do you have in your bank account?
26:2:10 PASSENGER: My bank? **About £2,200**, maybe a bit more. I get paid tomorrow as well. I get paid another 570 tomorrow, so it's **about 2,700** in total.
26:2:11 PARAMJIT: And you have a credit card?
26:2:12 PASSENGER: I've got a credit card and it's got **about £100** on it but I've got people at home, my mum and my dad are also ...
26:2:13 PARAMJIT: Do they support you?
26:2:14 PASSENGER: They can support me, yes. And my girlfriend's got plenty of cash.

In turn 26:2:10, when asked about his savings, the passenger uses *about £2,200*. He may not remember the exact amount, as is suggested by his subsequent use of the elastic expression *maybe a bit more*. Then he says that because he'll get £570 tomorrow, the total amount should be *about £2,700*. Later, in turn 26:2:12, when asked about his credit card account, he again uses *about £100*. The passenger mentions 570 without adding *about*; it could be that he remembers his salary amount clearly. The repeated use of the '*about* + number' cluster suggests that the passenger cannot recall the exact amount, perhaps indicating uncertainty. In the circumstances an exact amount is not necessarily required, or after the first use of approximation the officer would have asked for a precise figure. Based on the reaction of the officer, the passenger re-uses *about* clusters.

5.2 Approximate stretchers

There is an interesting use of '*about* + round number'. 2,200 + 570 is 2,770, which is simple addition and could have been easily said; however the passenger uses 2,700 instead. It may be that the speaker believes that approximation (2,700) is better than a precise number (2,770). Another possible reason is that the speaker prefers '*about* + round number' over a precise number. *About* tends to be used with round numbers (Channell 1994; Ruzaitė 2007), and in excerpt (5.1), 2,200, 2,700 and 100 are all round numbers. The passenger is consistent in stretching numbers using *about*, *about* + 2,200, 2,700, 100, and especially in choosing *about* 2,700 over 2,770. The approximate stretcher *about* brings out the elasticity of quantity expressions.

The passenger in excerpt (5.1) adopts the 'go approximate' maxim to serve his communicative goal of expressing numbers in a non-precise fashion. This can only be carried out when his interactant, the officer, understands and accepts the expressions: the elastic meaning is co-constructed by both parties. The approximation can also be explained via the principles of Relevance Theory (Sperber and Wilson 1995 [1986]), where the speaker thinks that exact information is irrelevant and an approximation may lessen the hearer's processing effort. There is a less likely possibility that the passenger knows his exact saving amount, say £2,150, but uses *about* £2,200 to make the amount look a bit more: but if it was his intention to use approximation that way, he should not have used 2,700 later but gone for 2,800. This last possibility is not supported by the evidence in the data.

(5.2)

Data: Episode 71, from turn 77:1:39 to 77:1:46, two speakers, over eight speaking turns.

Context: Encounter between an officer (male in his 30s) and passenger Bobby (American male in his 30s). The officer is questioning nervous Bobby about his mystery internet romance to determine if he is indeed in Australia for love.

71:1:39	OFFICER:	How are you doing, sir?
71:1:40	BOBBY:	Just fine.
71:1:41	OFFICER:	Alright, so what brings you to Australia on this occasion?
71:1:42	BOBBY:	I just met someone over the internet.
71:1:43	OFFICER:	You met this lady on the internet how long ago?
71:1:44	BOBBY:	It's been **about a year**.
71:1:45	OFFICER:	**About a year**? Are you staying with her or are you going to the hotel? Which one is it?
71:1:46	BOBBY:	That's what I don't know. I'm going to check with her. I'm wanting to go and stay with her, but if I don't see her, I'll have to get a motel until I find her.

In excerpt (5.2), the cluster is '*about* + *a* + period of time', less frequent than '*about* + number' used in excerpt (5.1). In turn 71:1:42, Bobby mentions that he just met someone over the internet, prompting the officer to clarify the length of their online dating. Bobby says *about a year* in turn 71:1:44. The officer responds with a rhetorical question, and seems satisfied with the approximation without further pursuing an exact period of time. It would be unusual for Bobby to give a more precise answer, such as *one year three days and two minutes*, unless he wants to show some sort of attitude.

Excerpt (5.2) raises a question: How far can an expression stretch? It may depend on the item being modified by *about*. Channell's (1994: 76–7) survey of '*about* + exemplar number' finds that the intervals represented by *about* approximations can go on either side of the exemplar number. In this study, '*about* + number' can stretch horizontally to both sides of the number being modified.

The length of the interval can also be influenced by the size or form of the number. For example, *about 20* clearly has a smaller range to stretch than *about 20,000*, but Channell (1994) finds that *about* 31 and *about* 30 have different intervals, and a round number like 30 generates a longer interval. She states that the nature of the item being approximated (e.g. discrete vs non-discrete, man vs ants) affects the length of the interval. Other contextual factors such as the setting play an important role in how far the *about* approximation can spring. For example, *about 10 people* in a sitting room may be interpreted to have smaller range than in a park, because the latter is a much larger setting than the former. In the same way, *about a year* may stretch further than *about a day* because *a year* is longer than *a day*. There appears to be a positive correlation between the length of interval of an *about* approximation and the size of the exemplar number being modified by *about*.[2]

5.2.2   *Some* and its clusters

Traditionally, the lower-bounded implicature of *some* is 'at least *n*' (Gazdar 1979, Horn 1972), and the upper-bounded implicature is 'not all' (Chierchia 2004, Levinson 2000).

Based on their corpus findings, Larrivée and Duffley challenge the default and decontextualised interpretation of 'some and not all' for the upper-bounded reading of *some*, as only 38% of the stressed uses of *some* were observed to have the upper-bounded reading (2014: 544). The scalar implicatures of *some* are produced when required by context, and the diagnostics used in their study to identify the implicature of *some* are the possibility of inserting a scalar modifier (e.g. *only some, at most some, at least some*), an adjoined

---

[2] Channell (1994) finds that '*n* or *m*' ('20 or 30') has a larger interval than '*n* or so' ('20 or so'), and '*n* or so' has a larger interval than 'about *n*'.

5.2 Approximate stretchers

scalar phrase (*and no more, but not all, and maybe more, and possibly all, must*), or *some* performing an adversative function or with a negation. They also note that implicatures only arise in *some* + plural noun or non-countable noun, which enables quantitative variation in the referent of the noun phrase or evokes an unspecified quantity that is neither the whole (upper-bounded) nor none (lower-bounded) of the referent (2014: 543).

In this study, the meaning of *some* is multi-faceted. As a quantifier, *some* typically refers to an unspecified quantity: for example, *some books*. The quantity represented is typically moderate, but *some* can indicate a greater amount: 'he has not seen his daughter for some years'. It is also an indefinite pronoun: 'some like his new book, and others don't'. *Some* can be a synonym of *about* or *approximately*, as in 'some thirty people attended his birthday party'. *Some* modifies both quantity and quality (Anderson 1973; Duffley and Larrivée 2012). It is also a general stretcher when referring to someone or something that is unknown or unspecified: 'I saw some young man walking into the bookshop just a moment ago'. *Some* is not unspecific, though, when it expresses 'remarkable', as in 'that was some speech!'

The pragmatic function of *some* is multiple. For example, Schick (2014) observes that the indefinite determiner *some* as in *some people* acts as a robust resource for socialising in indexically and pragmatically complex ways. The referential vagueness inherent in *some* contributes fundamentally to the usefulness of *some people* as a language socialisation resource (2014: 243). The primary function of *some* is to mitigate; for example, as Schick demonstrates, it can be used to reduce the impact of negative assessments.

Some is the second most frequent stretcher in this study. The finding largely supports the work of Ruzaitė (2007: 161), where *some* is most frequent in academic settings in Britain and the United States. As shown in Table 5.2, approximators (*about*) are far less frequent than quantifiers (*some*), as is also found in Ruzaitė (2007: 165). Her data reveal that the frequency of approximators is very low, while quantifiers occur much more. Koester (2007: 51) also finds that approximators are less frequent in her data, at 24 out of 34,000 words (7 in every 10,000). In this study, *about* occurs 6.3 times per 10,000 words, but *some* is 22.3, close to four times more than *about*.

As noted in Table 5.1, the total occurrence of *some* in these data is 570. Of these, as Table 5.5 shows, 73.7% (420) are in the form of '*some* + noun/noun phrase', 9.3% (53) in the cluster *some sort of* and 7.7% (44) in *some of*. The remaining types are infrequent, including *some kind of* (similar to *some sort of*), *some are* (plural) and *some is* (singular). The nouns in these data are often plural, which supports the findings in Larrivée and Duffley (2014).

Approximately three-fourths of *some* are used as a quantifier to modify following nouns or noun phrases. That is, *some* + noun/noun phrase is about eight times more frequent than *some sort of* and ten times more than *some of*.

86   Linguistic realisation of elastic language

Table 5.5 *Frequency of* some *clusters*

	some + noun /noun phrase	*some sort of*	*some of*
Raw frequency (n = 255,851)	420	53	44
Normalised frequency (per 10,000 words)	16.4	2.1	1.7

In this study, *some* is flexible enough to go with various noun types, such as a countable noun (*some people*), or a non-countable noun (*some money*).

(5.3)

Data: Episode 35, from turn 35:3:18 to 35:3:21, two speakers, over four speaking turns.
Context: Encounter between officer Andrew (male in his 30s) and a passenger (Chinese male in his 60s). Andrew is asking about undeclared food.

35:3:18 ANDREW: It's not looking good because, first of all, you obviously understand the rules, yeah. I've asked if you have any food, you've declared no food on your card and you have it hidden in your bag. Just wait here for one second, thank you. (to camera) I just got **some** non-declared dried spices and that, **some of** which is not permitted into Australia. For example, there's lily bulb and **some** non-commercial vegetable as well in a jar. (to passenger) It's very important that you declare all your food items.
35:3:19 PASSENGER: Okay, yes.
35:3:20 ANDREW: You need to declare it so that we can inspect it.
35:3:21 PASSENGER: All right.

In excerpt (5.3), *some* in *some non-declared dried spices* and *some non-commercial vegetable* is a common use of *some* in turn 35:3:18: a quantifier in the form of *some* + noun phrase, the most frequent pattern. The noun *species* in the first instance is a countable plural noun, while *some* in *some non-commercial vegetable* is a mass and singular form. *Some* in the partitive *some of* is an indefinite pronoun. *Which* following *of* denotes the whole (non-declared dried species), and the *some* cluster here indicates a contrast between the part evoked by *some* and the whole denoted by *which* (Larrivée and Duffley 2014: 540). All three *some* imply an unspecified amount; they stretch the quantity in question around the moderate scale of quantity.

5.2 Approximate stretchers 87

Andrew uses *some* and its clusters probably because precise information is not available. He could count the items or weigh them to obtain exact information, but apparently does not think precise numbers are warranted; imprecise quantity is just as good, if not more effective, in this case. As far as the hearers (the passenger and TV audience) are concerned, all they need to know is that undeclared food has been found and the case is under investigation. Exact quantities seem unimportant in excerpt (5.3). In many situations, exact number is un-reportable and irrelevant (Jucker et al. 2003: 1755).

Vague quantifiers are effective in communication, where they 'often convey meaning that is different from, and more relevant than a precise expression would. That is, they help guide the hearer towards the best interpretation of the speaker's intention' (Jucker et al. 2003: 1766). Readability can be diminished by too many precise numbers (Channell 1990; Moxey and Sanford 1993). The examples in excerpt (5.3) illustrate the effectiveness and relevance of the use of elastic quantifiers.

(5.4)

Data: Episode 31, from turn 31:4:1 to 31:4:9, two speakers, over five speaking turns.
Context: Officer 1 (male in his 20s) and officer 2 (female in her 40s) are examining sealed packages of flavoured drink powder, on the lookout for prohibited items.

31:4:1 OFFICER 1:	Looks like it might be **some sort of** powder.
31:4:2 OFFICER 2:	Yeah. Declared that there's, um, **some kind of** drink powder. (indicating scan of mail items on screen) Definitely worth a look. Um, definitely the blocks. We've certainly had detections of similar consistency and of similar declarations so it's certainly worth taking one step further at this stage.
...... (31:4:3 to 31:4:6 are omitted as less relevant)	
31:4:7 OFFICER 1:	So that one is blackcurrant flavoured, is that right?
31:4:8 OFFICER 2:	Yeah, this is the blackcurrant.
31:4:9 OFFICER 1:	So we should probably be looking at **some sort of** purply powder. That's interesting (packet contains pink granules).

In excerpt (5.4), *some* is used differently from *some* in excerpt (5.3); the latter highlights an unspecific quantity where the former does not. The cluster *some sort of* is not quite a quantity stretcher, but more of a quality/general stretcher, indicating some unknown person or unrevealed item in question. In turn 31:4:1, when officer 1 says, 'looks like it might be some sort of powder', he is unsure of what is in the packet. The officers are watching the screen of a scan machine; without opening the actual packet they cannot determine its contents. *Some sort of* is an indicator of uncertainty; the co-occurrence of the other elastic expressions *looks like* and *might be* is evidence reinforcing the speakers' tentativeness.

The response from officer 2 in the next turn echoes the uncertainty of officer 1 by using *some kind of drink powder*. In the last turn, 31:4:9, officer 1 again uses *some sort of* in 'So we should probably be looking at some sort of purply powder', coupled with *probably* to strengthen the sense of dubiousness. The hedging function of *some sort of* (or *some kind of*) in (5.4) shows that *some* has versatile roles: it can express not only fluid quantity, but also qualified certainty, perhaps to minimise the risk of being wrong.

Ruzaitė (2007: 150) finds that quantifiers have a strong tendency to quantify generic lexemes, particularly *some, a lot, many* (+ *people, things, stuff, ways, cases,* and *instances*). She stresses that 'collocating lexemes are of special importance as they are the evidence for the salience of the generalising function of quantifiers' (2007: 150). This study goes further: that *some* can also be used as a general stretcher, as illustrated in excerpt (5.4), where it functions in kind more than in number.

The maxims of 'go approximate' and 'go general' are adopted regularly by the participants in using *about* and *some*, and their clusters as shown in excerpts (5.1) to (5.4). The clusters are used to express uncertainty, to mitigate, to do self-protection, and the like.

5.3   General stretchers

VL is defined by Carter and McCarthy as

words or phrases with very general meanings (*thing, stuff, or whatever, sort of, or something, or anything*) which deliberately refer to people and things in a non-specific, imprecise way. Purposefully vague language is very common in informal spoken language. (Carter and McCarthy 2006: 928)

The category of general stretchers includes stretchers with general meaning. The two most frequent in these data are *anything* and *something*, and the two major types of general stretcher are indefinite pronouns and general extenders (e.g. Overstreet and Yule 1997a, b; Parvaresh, Tavangar, Rasekh and Izadi 2012; they are called 'chunks' by Evison et al. 2007: 143). *Thing* and the like are called an 'ideal proform' with poor 'semantic content' (Fronek 1982: 636–7). It can be 'saturated' (Gassner 2012: 11) by items from the immediate linguistic 'co-text' or from the wider extra-linguistic 'con-text' (Halliday and Hasan 1985: 10); sometimes inference is needed for construction of the content of *thing* and other general stretchers.

5.3 General stretchers

General extenders include expressions such as *and stuff like that*, *and that sort of thing*, *and everything (else)*, *and all that*, *or something like that*, *or anything*, *or anything like that*, *or whatever*. General extenders are normally clause final, consisting of a conjunction/disjunction and a noun phrase. They tend to indicate an 'insider' group, and aid in fluency as they 'buy' the speaker time to plan a speech (Aijmer 2013). Channell (1994) states that *the servers and things like that* is made up of an exemplar (*the servers*) + a vague tag (*and things like that*), where the exemplar is meant to allow the hearer to identify the category referred to. The indefinite pronouns tend to consist of a quantifier (e.g. *some*, *any*) and a noun of broad semantic scope (e.g. *thing*, *one*), and are often used to refer to things that the interlocutor cannot or does not want to specify (Biber, Johansson, Leech, Conrad and Finegan 1999: 351ff). Dines (1980: 19) calls general extenders 'terminal tags as qualifying elements', which are salient 'as elements which qualify the content of the utterance'. The following are examples extracted from the data.

... yeah like a cheese or something for our traditional taster ...
... just trying to trick him in his answering and stuff ...
... the ones that went through emails and agencies and all that ...
There are little bits of seed and things like that ...
... any knives, razors, any sharp objects or things like that ...
... so you're not aware of any criminal convictions or anything that he might have ...
... just in case there's a storm or rain or whatever come on ...

In these examples, the general extenders elicit a general category rather than an exhaustive list of terms. They are effective and good enough to serve the discourse needs without requiring too much effort from speaker or hearer.

5.3.1 *Anything* and its clusters

The meaning of *anything* refers to any indefinite entity or state of affair, with a wide and elastic range. It ranks third on the most frequent list (Table 5.2), occurring 564 times in these data.

Table 5.6 shows that the cluster *there's anything* is more frequent than the other two clusters. In addition to the three listed, less frequent clusters

Table 5.6 *Frequency of* anything *clusters*

	there's anything[a]	*anything else*	*or anything*
Raw frequency (n = 255,851)	58	38	36
Normalised frequency (per 10,000 words)	2.3	1.5	1.4

[a] Includes two other forms: *there is anything* and *is there anything*.

included *or anything like that* (0.7 per 10,000 words, 19 raw occurrences) and *anything at all* (0.4 per 10,000 words, nine raw occurrences). *Anything* was also part of the cautionary statement read to passengers in serious situations: 'You do not have to say or do <u>anything</u>, but <u>anything</u> you do say or do may be used in evidence'. The frequency of this cluster was 1.0 per 10,000 words (26 raw occurrences), which is special to this particular data set.

(5.5)

Data: Episode 50, from turn 50:4:40 to 50:4:44, two speakers, over five speaking turns.
Context: Exchanges between officer Lee (male in his 30s) and passenger Phac (Vietnamese male in his 20s). Lee is finding out what's inside Phac's pictures.

50:5:40 LEE:	How about I drill also right there. Okay, I'll just make a little drill hole and make sure if there's **anything** in there.
50:5:41 PHAC:	(nodding vigorously) Yeah, yeah.
50:5:42 LEE:	(to camera) When we swabbed it before we got results for ephedrine. Ephedrine is evident in cold and flu tablets and they also use it for the manufacture of ecstasy. Apart from seeing the segments in the wood, his halted manner means he's very nervous, he's clenching his fists a lot. (drilling into picture)
50:5:43 LEE:	(to camera) There shouldn't be any colour produced there. If I break the right ampoule now, if there's **anything** in there it should go blue in colour. (no colour change takes place) There's nothing there.
50:5:44 LEE:	(to camera) Well, we've got readings, we've got really good readings and we've drilled it, we've checked it – there's absolutely nothing in the picture. So we've still got those drug readings, so I think we're going to need to do a body search – just a frisk – just to see if he's got **anything** on his body. (to Phac) I've got some concerns.

The two *there's anything* in turn 50:5:40 and 50:5:43 are both used in a conditional clause. Of 58 *there's anything* occurrences, 30 (more than half) are combined with an *if* clause, indicating that the speaker prefers using an *anything* cluster to describe something conjectural or unknown at the time of speaking. The same function appears in 'just to see if he's got <u>anything</u> on his body' in turn 50:5:44. The elasticity of *anything* gives the speaker space to accommodate any eventuality. For example, in turn 50:5:43, by using '*if* + *there's anything*' Lee suggests that the situation is unpredictable; here

5.3 General stretchers

anything indicates an indefinite situation. In the end it turns out that there is nothing in the picture, an outcome that is covered by the elasticity of *anything*. The general nature of *anything* makes it suitable to act as a protector for the speaker to discuss a future or unknown event with safety.

(5.6)

Data: Episode 42, from turn 42:1:73 to 42:1:87, two speakers, over nine speaking turns.

Context: Encounters between an officer (male in his 30s) and a passenger (Asian/Latino American in his 30s). The officer is asking about illegal drugs.

42:1:73 OFFICER:	I'm going to give you the chance now to basically, if you have **anything**, either on your body or in your bag, let us know now. Do you have **anything**?
42:1:74 PASSENGER:	No. I'm not... I don't got **anything** on me. (shrugs)
42:1:75 OFFICER:	Okay. You said before obviously you've used cannabis. When was the last time?
42:1:76 PASSENGER:	(rolls eyes and head) Oh my gosh, I'd say a day ago or so I smoked some bud, yeah.
...... (42:1:77 to 42:1:82 are omitted as less relevant)	
42:1:83 OFFICER:	And did you smoke all of it?
42:1:84 PASSENGER:	No, I left, like, a roach or something like that.
42:1:85 OFFICER:	And was that in your belongings with you?
42:1:86 PASSENGER:	You know what, can I look in here real quick to make sure it's not in my cigarettes or anything like that?
42:1:87 OFFICER:	Sure.

In excerpt (5.6), the officer's goal is to find out if the passenger possesses any illegal drugs. He starts in 42:1:73 by questioning in a broad sense: *anything* serves the purpose well. He first uses a conditional clause, 'if you have <u>anything</u>', to be somewhat indirect, then poses the same question again but a bit more directly in 'do you have <u>anything</u>'. This could be a strategy to press the passenger for a truthful answer. The passenger answers the question with a clear denial, using 'I don't got <u>anything</u> on me' in turn 42:1:74. He also uses *cigarettes or anything like that* in 42:1:86, to avoid an exhaustive list of the items in his bag. The passenger employs other similar elastic expressions, such as *a roach or something like that* (general extender) in 42:1:84, *a day ago or so* (approximator) and *some bud* (general term) in 42:1:76. The frequent use of EL, coupled with his body language (shrug, roll eyes and head), suggests that he is either lacking precise information or deliberately avoiding providing it. (After a frisk search the passenger was cleared and free to go.)

5.3.2 *Something* and its clusters

Unspecific pronouns refer to indefinite reference 'made to some entity or entities, but the identity of the referent(s) is either not known or not relevant to the message being conveyed' (Cruse 2006: 86–7), or the speaker does not want to name it for some reason. The meaning of *something* refers to an undetermined entity or notion in a general sense: in 'there is something in the box', *something* is an object unspecified. *Anything* has a larger set of possibilities, and so is more general than *something*. For example, *anything else* could mean *whatever*, but *something else* cannot. When speakers use *something*, they are more certain than when they choose *anything*: in 'do you want to say something' the speaker expects 'you' to say something; in 'do you want to say anything', the speaker does not necessarily expect 'you' to say anything.

(5.7)

Data: Episode 37, from turn 37:1:13 to 37:1:14, two speakers, over two speaking turns.
Context: Officer Asa (female supervisor in her 40s) and officer Stephanie (female in her 30s) are discussing a possible case of someone concealing illegal items.

37:1:13 ASA:	Did you ask if he's got **something** in his pocket or **anything** on his body?
37:1:14 STEPHANIE:	Yeah, I've asked a few times and he keeps moving. He's got **something** here, but I wasn't going to ask him to remove it, because it might be in his underwear.

In excerpt (5.7), Asa asks about the possibility of *something in his pocket* first, then *anything on his body*. This implies that Asa has a stronger expectation of something in the pocket than on the passenger's body. The general nature of *anything* prevents it from being used by Stephanie in the next turn; she is pretty sure that the passenger has something hidden, so she uses *something* instead of *anything*. Excerpt (5.7) demonstrates that the meaning of *anything* is more elastic and stretchable than that of *something*.

There are two kinds of *something*: specific indefinite and non-specific indefinite: in 'he plans to buy *something* for her birthday' vs 'he is holding *something* in his hand', the hearer is not required to identify the item referred by *something*, so both terms are indefinite. The difference is that the former does not indicate there is any specific item in mind (hence, a non-specific indefinite), but the second sentence does indicate some specific (although unnamed) item in his hand.

5.3 General stretchers

Table 5.7 *Frequency of* something *clusters*

	or something (*like that*)	*something else*	*something like*
Raw frequency (n = 255,851)	103	19	18
Normalised frequency (per 10,000 words)	4.0	0.7	0.7

Table 5.7 shows that the general extender *or something* (*like that*) is used six times more frequently than *something else* or *something like* (excluding *or something like that*). *Or something* occurs 1.1 and *something else* 0.4 per 10,000 words in Cheng (2007: 177), suggesting that on average participants in the Australian Customs institutional discourse prefer the 'go general' maxim more than those in Cheng's data (academic, business, conversational and public discourses).

(5.8)

Data: Episode 52, from turn 52:1:28 to 52:1:35, two speakers, over eight speaking turns.
Context: Encounters between officer Clarinda (female in her 40s) and passenger (Arab male in his 20s). The officer is searching the passenger's bags.

52:1:28 CLARINDA:	What is this?
52:1:29 TRAVELLER:	Am I suspect **or something**?
52:1:30 CLARINDA:	Sorry?
52:1:31 TRAVELLER:	Am I suspect **or something**?
52:1:32 CLARINDA:	No, we're just searching. We do quite a lot of searches. If you look around you, there's lots of people being searched, there's lots of people waiting in the line to be searched. So this is what you . . .?
52:1:33 TRAVELLER:	Well, these are most . . . Well, these are presents.
52:1:34 CLARINDA:	What are these tablets, mate?
52:1:35 TRAVELLER:	I've no idea what they are.

As the bag search goes on, the passenger looks increasingly nervous. In turn 52:1:29, instead of answering Clarinda's question, he asks, 'Am I suspect or something?' *Or something* is a general extender, and using its general sense tactically the passenger wants to know if he has been picked out for a search specifically. A general stretcher can also mitigate the abruptness of an otherwise blunt question: 'Am I suspect?' The officer assures him that it is just a routine check, but the passenger seems to stumble over his words in 52:1:33 and is quite nervous. In the end, the tablets turn to be banned steroids, but the passenger claims that he didn't know they were steroids because family members in Syria packed some of his bags.

(5.9)

Data: Episode 99, from turn 99:4:16 to 99:4:18, two speakers, over three speaking turns.
Context: Officer Mary (female in her 30s) and another officer (male in his 20s) are examining an old keyboard that tested positive for traces of narcotics.

99:4:16 MARY:	We're continuing more testing on these items here, but we're not, um, concerned that it's drugs anymore. It's not narcotics. So our next step is to unscrew the screws and get inside and have a look, and see if it's possibly maybe **something else** inside. All right, let's have a look. Let's see if it still works. Batteries are in there. Oh, here we go. There you go. It's all working. Oh, there's one that's not on.
99:4:17 OFFICER:	Some keys don't work?
99:4:18 MARY:	I think **something** here maybe? Oh. Let's turn it over and have a look at it.

The cluster of *something else* is used by Mary in turn 99:4:16 to refer to the fact that the keyboard was examined for hidden narcotics initially, but none were found and the officers continued their examination for other possible illegal items inside the keyboard. She combines the use of *something else* with *possibly* and *maybe*, signalling tentativeness. In turn 99:4:18, Mary uses *something* again, this time referring to a more specific but undetermined object. Around *something*, Mary uses other two elastic expressions, *I think* and *maybe*, to enforce her sense of uncertainty. Mary uses the cluster of *something* and other elastic expressions to indicate that she is not sure if there is indeed something in it, as it is only a guess based on the fact that some keys on the board do not work. (In the end the officers' persistence paid off: some ATM skimming equipment was concealed in the keyboard.)

The characteristic of being general is a distinctive feature of EL. Wierzbicka's recent list of natural semantic metalanguage (cited in Cruse 2006: 115) consists of a total of 56 primes, at least 17 (30%) of which are vague expressions of some kind: *someone, something, other, some, many, much, good, bad, big, small, a long time, a short time, far, near, very, would* and *maybe*. This is because Wierzbicka's metalanguage is itself general and non-specific. Along similar lines, we might consider that the general stretcher follows a minimalist approach, which is defined simply as 'go less' or 'go general' rather than providing specific information, in line with Relevance Theory (Sperber and Wilson 1995 [1986]) in that better interactions are those that achieve optimal cognitive effect with least processing effort. A general expression such as *and something like that* may be the most suitable choice in response to the demands of a particular context.

Clearly, general terms are useful in many ways, but this does not mean that general terms suit all situations. For example, in *The Voice* contest (19 May 2014, 8 p.m., Channel 9, Australia), a contestant said, 'I am glad someone turned around', but the mentor, Kylie Minogue, corrected him by pointing out it was not just someone: it was Kylie. Obviously, Kylie felt that *someone* was too general and she preferred a more specific mention – that providing her name was better than using an impersonal term. This indicates that language considered appropriate by one person is not considered the best choice by another.

Apart from the general terms discussed above, there are also other forms of general expression. For example, in English when one has a sensitive disease and does not want to say precisely what it is, the phrase 'a medical condition' is often used instead. This occurs in other cultures as well. In Chinese there is a new and popular expression: *ni dongde* ('I'm sure you know what I've got in mind', with a humorous touch). People use it when they don't want to be specific about something that is normally sensitive, embarrassing, or the like. The general expression offers a convenient way out of an otherwise challenging situation. It is evident that the 'go general' strategy is very much at work.

5.3.3 Stretching between *I* and *we*

In the data, an intriguing phenomenon is the stretch work that occurs between *I* and *we*. The pronouns are not usually considered elastic, but a seemingly precise meaning may become elastic from a pragmatic perspective. *We* is inclusive, stressing in-group membership and social similarity (Brown and Levinson 1987: 57). This, in principle, also applies to a strategic elasticising between *we* and *you*: when *you* should be used, the speaker may choose *we* instead to highlight buddy-membership. For example, in Chinese *you* can be replaced by *we* (*zanmen*) to show inclusiveness with an implicature of 'you and I are on same side'. Chinese reporters in particular have a tendency to use *we* instead of *you* when addressing their interviewees, to establish trust and solidarity with the people they are talking to.

The difference between *I* and *we* may also be a matter of honesty. Pennebaker (2011) argues that '*I, me* and *my*' indicate someone less affirmative but more truthful, so it is a bad sign when politicians use *we* instead. *Our* represents the robust academic vague-ism which can mitigate damage done

96   Linguistic realisation of elastic language

by speech (Trappes-Lomax 2007: 129). The strategic use of *we* by the officers in this study has a particular institutional purpose (Linell and Bredmar 1996), as a strategy for self-protection or to shorten the distance between the speaker and hearer for their corporation, as illustrated in the excerpt below.

(5.10)

Data: Episode 5, from turn 5:1:101 to 5:1:111, two speakers, over 11 speaking turns.
Context: Officer Ahmad (male in his 30s) and passenger Jason (New Zealand male in his late 30s). Ahmad is finding out why there are traces of cocaine on Jason's plane seat and laptop.

5:1:101	AHMAD:	The only explanation **I**'ve got ... (pause)=
5:1:102	JASON:	=(nods) Yes.=
5:1:103	AHMAD:	=... is either you're ... (pause) you can admit to me that you're using ... (pause)
5:1:104	JASON:	I'm not using cocaine.
5:1:105	AHMAD:	Or (pause) anything.
5:1:106	JASON:	Anything.
5:1:107	AHMAD:	Because ah **we** don't care if you do, that's your personal (pause) issue.=
5:1:108	JASON:	=Yes.=
5:1:109	AHMAD:	=But (pause) if you're carrying something through the airport, **we** need to know about it.
5:1:110	JASON:	I'm carrying nothing through the airport.
5:1:111	AHMAD:	Okay.

Jason didn't declare his past criminal convictions and there were traces of cocaine on his plane seat and laptop. Ahmad starts questioning in 5:1:101 using *I* in 'the only explanation I've got ... (pause)', at this stage he refers himself as *I*, an individual officer whose institutional task is to find out why the traces of cocaine were found. The first reason Ahmad offers is that Jason might use cocaine himself. Note that Ahmad speaks with a great deal of hesitation and padding, manifested by pauses, changes in wording ('is either you're ... you can admit ...') and the use of the general extender *or anything* to mitigate the possible negative impact of asking if Jason uses cocaine. After Jason denies that he is using cocaine in 5:1:104, Ahmad in 5:1:105 adds *or anything*, which enables him to press for an admission of possible use of drugs of any kind with less imposition.

Interestingly, in 5:1:107 Ahmad changes *I* to *we*, where *we* signals the powerful institution of the Australian government. This has two possible purposes: to distance him from the risks of being proven wrong and avoid direct confrontation, or to increase his illocutionary force because now he represents the institution. He encourages Jason to admit if he is using drugs by minimising this to a merely personal issue. Ahmad in 5:1:109 uses *we* again, this time to warn Jason that if he carries any drug it will be serious, and *we* the institution need to know. *Something* in 'if you're carrying something through the airport' is used as a general stretcher to indirectly refer to drugs. Ahmad uses *we* twice here to indicate the institutional role he plays and to put pressure on Jason to admit if he uses or carries drugs. However, Jason twice categorically states that he neither uses nor carries drugs. (A later frisk revealed nothing, and Jason was allowed to enter Australia.)

Ahmad in excerpt (5.10) uses *I* and *we* interchangeably, as if the two overlap and *I* can be upgraded to *we* to empower the authority of the speaker, in the hope of obtaining Jason's cooperation. *We* in the data contains more institutional power, more authority than *I*, and is used in a strategic move to press for truth.

While *I* and *we* are not exactly elastic expressions, the phenomenon of how they stretch is a good case of the versatile use of pronouns in the context of EL, given the somewhat fluid nature of the expressions in real-life, pragmatic use. The findings in excerpt (5.10) suggest that the pronoun *we* acts as a corporate stance maker representing authority, in line with what is found in Handford (2010: 179), where *we* plays a critical role in business negotiations. In excerpt (5.10), *we* is inclusive of speaker and peer officers, but exclusive of the hearer (the passenger). In this study, *we* and the like are treated as a special category of general stretcher to serve institutional and self-protection purposes (see Section 6.5 for details).

5.4 Scalar stretchers

The meaning of a scalar stretcher depends on other scalar stretchers on the same scale. For example, on the scale of *few – hardly – fairly – often – very – extremely*, the meaning of *very* overlaps *often* and *extremely*. Scalar stretchers are typically adverbs of degree which 'describe the extent to which a characteristic holds. They can be used to mark that the extent or degree is either greater or less than usual or than that of something else in the neighbouring discourse' (Biber et al. 2010: 554). Degree adverbs tend to answer questions such as 'how much/many?' and 'to what extent?' Some quantifiers can also be used as scalar stretchers when ranked in a scalar fashion, as in *few – a few – several – some – many – most*. In this type of quantifier, meaning is determined relationally, 'by knowing how the term in question relates to other quantifiers which indicate either more, or less' (Channell 1994: 118). A sample of stretchers is listed in Table 5.8.

Table 5.8 shows that the scalar stretchers have three loosely divided parts: lower, middle and high. Speakers use the high end to tone up their utterances

Table 5.8 *Scalar stretchers*

Lower end of scale	Middle part of scale	High end of scale
e.g. *hardly, little, a little, a little bit, a bit, few, sometimes*	e.g. *fairly, rather, somewhat, some*	e.g. *often, extremely, really, mostly, lots of, a lot of, most, quite, too, very, so, many*

and the lower end to tone them down. Of these parts, various scalar sets can be made: *a little bit – a bit – somewhat – quite – a lot*; *sometimes – often – most*. These scalar terms are fluid, their interpretation stretchable along the scale. They often occur as modifiers, mostly premodifiers such as *too hot*. The interpretation of scalar terms is determined implicitly according to a particular situation (Channell 1994: 97). Channell counts *all schools* as a vague expression, because without knowing the size of the total set it could mean 12 or 12,000 (1994: 99). While she is correct to say that the pragmatic meaning of *all schools* is vague, this study considers that the quantifier *all* is not.

Quantifiers used as scalar stretchers are weak in modifying quantity. For example, *a bit of a* in 'that was a bit of a showing off' (a negatively loaded lexeme) is not quantifying the amount of *showing off* and is better understood as a 'hedge or modalizer of speaker's attitude' (Channell 1994: 111). Scalar stretchers are used in positive or negative utterances. Ruzaitė (2007: 158) finds that negatively loaded lexemes tend to co-occur with paucal quantifiers (e.g. *a bit, a little*, and *a little bit*) which are the lower-end stretchers shown in Table 5.8. *A bit of a problem* is used because 'admitting a problem can be face-threatening. Therefore, unsurprisingly, such a phrase is mitigated with *a bit*' (2007: 152). Neutral or positively loaded lexemes tend to co-occur with *some, a lot of, many*, etc. In terms of pragmatic force, the higher end of stretchers can intensify the degree in question and create persuasive and emphatic effects (2007: 151), as in *so many*.

Scalar implicature (Channell 1994; Cheng 2007; Levinson 1983) is 'an additional meaning of the negative of any value higher on the scale than the one uttered' (Yule 1996: 134). Jucker et al. (2003: 1752) note that 'any expression from a set that can be arrayed on a scale can convey information not only about the position of an event on that scale but can also convey a scalar implicature, that is, an implication based on the part of the scale above it'. On a scale of *a few – many – most*, 'He has a few books' implies that he does not have *many* or *most* books. *A little* indicates *but not many*, and *nearly* excludes the meaning of *more than*. The traditional scalar implicature (e.g. *some* implies *not all*) is expanded in this study to include underlying messages indicated by scalar stretchers. For example, when using *a lot*, the speaker implies that something is more than expected.

5.4 Scalar stretchers   99

The scalar implicature of quantifiers is empirically explored in Moxey and Sanford's (1997) work, where speakers' focus and expectations play an important role. In a series of experiments, participants selected overlapping ranges for *few* (10–25%), *some* (25–75%), and *many* (25–90%). This suggests that 'the meaning in these expressions must not reside entirely in the proportions they convey but rather in other information that is implied' (Jucker et al. 2003: 1752). Moxey and Sanford (1993) find that *very* and *very many* differ in strength of claim rather than in number. They uncover ways that quantifiers add implicature that would not be possible with an exact number. For example, quantifiers have different focuses: *few* in 'few students came to class; they all went to a football match' highlights the people who didn't come; while *many* in 'many students came to class; they enjoyed it' focuses on the people who did attend. When speakers use *many*, they expect something significantly more than a norm; otherwise *few* would be used. Moxey and Sanford find that the speaker's belief of the hearer's expectation alters their use of quantifiers: for example, if the speaker thinks that a quantity is more than the hearer expects, *quite a few* is used; otherwise *only a few* would be used. In the same vein, Jucker et al. (2003) claim that the implicature of *many* in 'many friends came to my birthday party' is that 'I' is popular. If *many* is swapped for 20, then the exact number in '20 friends came to my party' has little implicature.

5.4.1   *Very* and its clusters

As shown in Table 5.1, *very* is the most frequent elastic word in these data, supporting the finding in Cheng (2007: 167). *Very* increases the intensity of an utterance, and is traditionally termed an amplifier or intensifier (Biber et al. 2010: 554). It tends to modify gradable adjectives and adverbs, indicating degree on a fluid scale; it can be positively or negatively loaded.

Almost all instances of *very* in these data are elastic; the few non-elastic examples include *the very person* and *at the very end of*. Like Cheng's (2007: 170), the findings in this study show that the most frequent cluster of *very* is '*very* + adjective/adverb'.

Table 5.9 shows that *very* is used mostly with adjectives, to strengthen the degree of claim upwards. The top cluster is *very good*, a positively loaded expression. There are also negatively loaded clusters (*very nervous*) and neutral clusters (*very much*). The opposite of the *very* cluster, *not very*, stretches *very* downwards to decrease its illocutionary force. The cluster '*not very* + adjective/adverb' occurs 21 times (0.8 per 10,000 words), less frequently than the *very* cluster. A possible reason is that the function of *not very* is performed by other expressions such as *a bit, somewhat, fairly*, etc.

Table 5.10 shows that there are some similarities between Cheng and Zhang: six out of ten items are the same, which makes a majority. The six

100   Linguistic realisation of elastic language

Table 5.9 *Frequency of top 10* very *clusters*

	Raw frequency ($n = 255{,}851$)	Normalised frequency (per 10,000 words)
very good	53	2.1
very much	36	1.4
very high	32	1.3
very hard	18	0.7
very nervous	16	0.6
very careful(ly)	16	0.6
very important	15	0.6
very well	14	0.5
very serious	14	0.5
very strong	12	0.5

Table 5.10 *Comparison of top 10* very *clusters in Zhang and Cheng (per 10,000 words)*

Zhang (this study)		Cheng (2007: 171)	
very good	2.1	*very good*	3.0
very much	1.4	*very very*	2.2
very high	1.3	*very important(ly)*	1.6
very hard	0.7	*very much*	1.3
very nervous	0.6	*very strong(ly)*	0.9
very careful(ly)	0.6	*very nice(ly)*	0.8
very important	0.6	*very difficult*	0.8
very well	0.5	*very well*	0.8
very serious	0.5	*very high(ly)*	0.6
very strong	0.5	*very different(ly)*	0.5

items are *very good, very much, very high, very important, very well,* and *very strong*. Table 5.10 shows that overall participants in Cheng's study use more *very* clusters than those in Zhang's, implying that the Australian Customs setting demands rather less strengthening of a claim. In Zhang's data, *very nervous* and *very serious* are indicators that the customs context is characterised by confrontation and interrogation. *Very high* often co-occurs with *risk* or *reading* (associated with drug testing), reflecting the particularity of customs discourse; it does not appear in Cheng's data. *Very very* is the second most frequent item in Cheng's data, but hardly appears in this study. In Cheng, *very* is used more in business and conversation contexts, less in academic and public speech. Ruzaitė's (2007: 193) work, based on academic data, has *very much* as the most frequent cluster. These three studies draw on different discourses, but some universality exists: for example, *very good* and *very*

5.4 Scalar stretchers

much are top frequent items. However, some discourse-specific patterns also emerge, demonstrating the relevance of context to the use of scalar stretchers.

(5.11)

Data: Episode 35, from turn 35:1:10 to 35:1:14, two speakers, over five speaking turns.
Context: An officer (female in her late 20s) and a passenger (German male in his 30s). The officer is questioning the passenger about his nervous behaviour.

35:1:10 OFFICER:	(to camera) It's come up positive for a reading for cocaine, so now that we've had a positive reading for narcotics, we will organise to conduct a frisk search, make sure that the passenger's not carrying within his body. (to passenger) Are you happier with English?
35:1:11 PASSENGER:	English is fine, yeah.
35:1:12 OFFICER:	Your English is **very** good.
35:1:13 PASSENGER:	Thank you. Must I read it all?
35:1:14 OFFICER:	Yes please, just read it all so I know that you understand.

The officer has to make sure that the passenger understands English to be able to carry out further investigations. When she asks if the passenger is happy to communicate in English, the passenger responds positively. Then in turn 35:1:12, the officer confirms that the passenger's English is *very good*. She uses it to underscore that his level of English is sufficient to express himself clearly, emphasised by *very*. The emphatic assessment rules out the need for an interpreter. (In the end heroin was found hidden in the base of the passenger's suitcase, and he was sentenced to eight years in prison.)

(5.12)

Data: Episode 32, from turn 32:4:36 to 32:4:39, two speakers, over four speaking turns.
Context: An officer (female in her 30s) and a passenger (American female in her 20s). The officer is questioning the passenger, who claims she is here to see if Sydney is the place to spend her upcoming honeymoon.

32:4:36 OFFICER:	How long have you been together?
32:4:37 PASSENGER:	About two months or so.
32:4:38 OFFICER:	**Not very** long?
32:4:39 PASSENGER:	(looking down to right) I was waiting to get a divorce from my husband. So like me and him (nods head to right) can get married.

102   Linguistic realisation of elastic language

The officer is checking if the passenger is a genuine tourist. She starts by asking how long the passenger and her boyfriend have been together. The passenger provides a vague period by using *about two months* first, then adds *or so*. The approximate stretcher *about* indicates that it could be more or less than two months. *Or so*, on the other hand, indicates an approximation that is skewed upwards from the exemplar number (Channell 1994: 62). By adding *or so*, the passenger may be trying to stretch the period of two months to something longer. In spite of the passenger's attempt, the officer's assessment is *not very long* in turn 32:4:38. *Not very long* stretches the time period downward to shrink the length, implying the suspicion of the officer that the real purpose of the passenger may be something else than looking for a place to honeymoon: as they have only been a couple for about two months, it is unlikely they are already planning marriage.

The *not very* stretcher in excerpt (5.12) performs the opposite function to *very good* in excerpt (5.11). *Not very long* sends a discouraging message to the passenger, and to convince the officer that although two months is not that long they are serious about each other, she provides further detail in turn 32:4:39: that she is waiting for a divorce so that she can remarry. Her body language indicates that she is not very focused, perhaps due to nervousness. (In the end the passenger was found carrying cocaine and sentenced to six years and three months' imprisonment.)

5.4.2   *Quite* and its clusters

Quite ranks sixth among the most frequent items listed in Table 5.1. The meaning of *quite* is somewhat more complex than that of *very*. Of its several meanings, the one relating to elasticity most is 'more than usual, rather': *quite soon*, *quite tasty*. Occasionally, *quite* also means 'to a moderate degree': *quite good but not perfect*. Other meanings without scalar implicature are not in the category of scalar stretcher, such as 'completely' ('he didn't quite make it'), 'remarkable kind' ('she is quite a lecturer'), or an interjection as an expression of agreement.

As shown in Table 5.11, the most frequent *quite* cluster is *quite* co-occurring with an adjective, and more than four times as often as '*quite* + adverb'. The following two excerpts illustrate how *quite* co-occurs with adjective and adverb.

Table 5.11 *Frequency of two major* quite *clusters*

	quite + adjective	*quite* + adverb
Raw frequency (n = 255,851)	130	31
Normalised frequency (per 10,000 words)	5.1	1.2

5.4 Scalar stretchers

(5.13)

Data: Episode 40, from turn 40:3:45 to 40:3:51, three speakers, over seven speaking turns.
Context: Officer Ann (female in her 40s) and two passengers (a couple from China in their 30s). Ann is questioning the couple about undeclared food.

40:3:45 ANN:	Okay, what I'm going to do today, I'm just going to give you a warning today ...
40:3:46 PASSENGER (MALE):	Oh, yes.
40:3:47 ANN:	All right? (looks intently at the Chinese female)
40:3:48 PASSENGER (FEMALE):	Thank you very much! Madam.
40:3:49 ANN:	I'm going to give you a written warning though, because this is **quite**, **quite** serious stuff that you've brought in today.
40:3:50 PASSENGER (FEMALE):	I fully understand. I fully understand.
40:3:51 ANN:	Yeah, okay, and all this stuff, you can't have.

The Chinese couple brought in fruits and meat without declaring them. Ann gives them a written warning, and explains her decision in turn 40:3:49, using *quite, quite serious stuff*. *Quite* as a scalar stretcher, modifying the adjective *serious*, indicates that the seriousness is more than usual. It stretches the degree of seriousness upwards to warrant a written warning, but not enough for a fine. If Ann were to issue a fine, she would use *very serious* or *extremely serious* instead. This assumes a scale of '*serious, quite serious, very serious, extremely serious*', where *quite* is positioned lower than *very*. Ann reinforces the level of more-than-usual seriousness in turn 40:3:51, hoping to deter the passengers from bringing food into Australia undeclared in future.

(5.14)

Data: Episode 88, from turn 88:4:8 to 88:4:10, two speakers, over three speaking turns.
Context: Officer Alisa (female in her 30s) and a passenger (Vietnamese male in his 20s). Alisa is examining undeclared food brought in by the passenger.

88:4:8 ALISA:	Here we have some dried squid. It's very important that we check that it's been sufficiently dried. **Quite** often we find live infestation in the fish. These are some dried fish flakes. Fish can have water fleas which we might not have here. What's this one? Wow!
88:4:9 PASSENGER:	This is a tea.

> (5.14) (cont.)
>
> 88:4:10 ALISA: This is a fresh plant leaf. This could affect the Australian export industry. It could cost the country billions in dollars in eradicating or limiting disease spread, so it's completely prohibited – restricted article.

In turn 88:4:8, Alisa explains why it is important to make sure that food brought in must be declared and checked. She uses *quite* to stretch the frequency of *often* (adverb), suggesting it happens more than usual and emphasising the need to obey quarantine rules. The scale formed in this case is *often – quite often – very often*, where *quite* sits in the middle. When Alisa finds a fresh plant leaf, to emphasise the seriousness of the matter, in turn 88:4:10 she says 'it's completely prohibited – restricted article', where the high-end scalar stretcher *completely* serves a strengthening function.

This analysis of *very* and *quite* shows that the maxim 'go scalar' plays an important role in strengthening (or mitigating when in negation form) the degree of the speaker's claim. The stretching power of *quite* is revealed as less than that of *very*. In the same way, other scalar stretchers have different degrees of stretching power, so that they occupy different positions on a scale and perform different functions to respond to the communicative goals of the moment. The distinctive feature of scalar stretchers is their overlap. Precisely how much or how little they can push the items they modify upwards (*very* and *quite*) or downwards (*a little bit, somewhat*) is underspecified, as their respective positions on a scale are relational and not precisely located. Consequently, the scalar implicature associated with such stretchers is manifested in a fluid fashion.

In a way scalar stretchers can make a meaning relatively precise: '*a bit disappointed* is more precise than just simply *disappointed*, as is *very disappointed*' (Channell 1994: 110). Channell considers the job of *very* and *a bit* here is to make the meaning of *disappointed* more precise by narrowing its semantic range. However, this does not necessarily mean that scalar stretchers themselves become precise.

5.5 Epistemic stretchers

Traditionally, linguistic analyses suffer from an 'intellectualist prejudice that language is essentially an instrument for the expression of propositional thought', and fail to see the equal importance of language representing non-propositional concepts like modality, subjectivity, or locutionary agency and their interdependence (Lyons 1981: 235–6). From an epistemological point of view, language has two basic functions: presenting factual information and the

5.5 Epistemic stretchers

stance of the speaker (Banfield 1973; Maynard 1993). As epistemic stretchers in this study refer to epistemic stance markers, expressing the speaker's judgement about certainty, reliability and so on, the speaker's stance is 'the expression of personal feelings and assessments' (Conrad and Biber 2000: 57). Epistemic stance refers to the degree of certainty and commitment to the truth of propositions and sources of information (Ochs 1996: 410). Kiesling considers stance an important interactional meaning, indicating how certain speakers are of their assertions (2009: 172). In situations where a speaker's knowledge and opinion are often expressed in the form of uncertainty or probability, epistemic stretchers can be attitudinal indicators of doubt (Parvaresh and Tayebi 2014). Such attitudes may be expressed by *might*, *could*, *should*, or *must be* (degree of certainty). These terms carry out a subjective function of language by implying a speaker's positionality.

Epistemic stretchers primarily associate with stance-taking, or 'taking up a position with respect to the form and content of one's utterance', a fundamental property of communication (Jaffe 2012: 3). It conveys different degrees of speaker stance, including ways in which speakers express their evaluation of the truth value of a proposition (Du Bois 2007; Englebretson 2007). What is distinctive about stance-taking in this particular institutional data is that often it is an institutional stance for officers, either direct or indirect, given the nature of EL.

In this study epistemic stretchers include *sort of*, *probably*, *could be*, *possible*, *maybe*, and the like. *Could* in the sense of 'personal ability' is not considered a stretcher. Other words can be stance markers as well: *like* is both an epistemic stance marker (of imprecision, in 'she like said that they would') and a discourse marker. Two items are selected for discussion in this section, both among the 20 most frequent elastic expressions: *probably* (ranked 10th) and *sort of* (ranked 11th) as shown in Table 5.1, to demonstrate how stance-taking is manifested through EL.

The expression *I think* is an epistemic stance marker, often occurring in conversation (Biber et al. 2010: 972). It is also called a 'subjective expression' (Stubbs 1986b: 3), and signals hedging (Handford 2010: 120). The verb *think* marks a degree of certainty, less certain than *know* but more certain than *suspect* (Biber et al. 2010: 972). The following examples from the data show how *I think* works as an epistemic stretcher.

> Well, he's obviously done his job pretty good today, I think ...
> I think that it would probably warrant a quarantine infringement for it, personally ...
> ... you've only met, I think, twice you told me ...
> ... (smiling) you should always believe your mother, I think.
> I think there might be tabbies in there ...
> I think it could be steroids.
> I think something here maybe?

Table 5.12 *Epistemic stance markers in three varieties of English (per 10,000 words)*

Epistemic stance markers	American English	British English	Australian English
1 Epistemic-doubt			
probably	9	6	7
maybe	8	2	5.5
perhaps	1	2	1
2 Epistemic-subjective			
I suppose	0.2	0.6	0.5
I guess	1.2	0	1.7
3 Epistemic-imprecision			
sort of	2	2	6.5
kind of	4	6	2.9
Total	**25.4**	**18.6**	**25.1**

I think in all these examples has a common feature: it indicates 'I am not so sure about ...' The implicature enables *I think* to perform pragmatic functions such as mitigation or self-protection. In addition to mitigating, *I think* also performs an emphatic function, as in 'I think at the very least we need to frisk this guy' or 'I think I've done nothing wrong'. This supports the findings in my recent work (Zhang 2014), which is an investigation of the pragmatic functions of *I think* using an integrated approach. Zhang and Sabet (in press) also explore *I think* in terms of its frequency, position and clustering, based on the conception of linguistic elasticity, concluding that *I think* is elastic in terms of its fluidity in form and function.

There are two types of stance: implicit and explicit. Biber et al. (2010: 557) consider both *possible* and *I think* as epistemic stance markers showing levels of certainty or doubt. The difference is that *possible* expresses stance implicitly and *I think* does so explicitly (2010: 976–7), making the position of *I* (the speaker) more prominent. The frequency of epistemic stretchers in American, British, and Australian English is presented in Table 5.12. The data for American and British English are adopted from Biber et al. (2010: 869–70, 982), and the Australian data are based on the Australian officers' utterances in this study.

Table 5.12 shows that overall, equal use exists between American and Australian English; British English speakers appear to use fewer epistemic stance markers. In the use of individual items, Australians are more similar to Americans than to the British. On average, Americans use more group 1 words, while Australians prefer group 2 and group 3 words. Some individual words stand out: *probably* is used most by all three groups, a clear favourite with high scores; *maybe* is favoured by Americans; *sort of* by Australians; the word that for the British came on top was *kind of*, they didn't use *I guess*.

5.5 Epistemic stretchers

Table 5.13 *Frequency of* probably *clusters*

	probably + past event	*probably* + future event
Raw frequency (*n* = 255,851)	44	40
Normalised frequency (per 10,000 words)	1.7	1.6

5.5.1 *Probably* and its clusters

In Table 5.12, *probably* is used mainly by Americans, but the British and Australians are not far behind. It is the 10th most frequent word in this study (see Table 5.1). Ruzaitė (2007: 158) confirms that 'hedging words express probability and are indicators of the speaker's degree of certainty. Such modality words as *maybe* or *perhaps* suggest a lower degree of the speaker's commitment to the truth of the claim and make the claim less categorical'. She finds that words 'are of different degrees of assertiveness'; for example, *maybe* is less assertive than *probably*. According to Ruzaitė, these words function to soften the impact of speech by making it less categorical.

Table 5.13 shows that *probably* co-occurs with past events almost at the same rate as with future events, which means that speakers are equally uncertain of both past and future probability. This does not support the assumption that people are more certain when talking about something that has already happened than about something in the future.

(5.15)

Data: Episode 85, from turn 85:1:21 to 85:1:36, two speakers, over 16 speaking turns.
Context: Officer (male in his 30s) and a passenger (Australian male in his 20s). The officer is questioning the young man about his erratic behaviour.

85:1:21 OFFICER:	Were you in contact with any cocaine/MDMA?
85:1:22 JIM:	Yeah, well, like, there was **probably** like a little bit when we were over in Mexico.
85:1:23 OFFICER:	How long ago was the last time that you took drugs?
85:1:24 JIM:	Oh, **probably** in Mexico.
85:1:25 OFFICER:	In Mexico?
85:1:26 JIM:	Yeah.
85:1:27 OFFICER:	How long was that? About a week ago or ...?
85:1:28 JIM:	No, it was **probably** about two weeks ago.
85:1:29 OFFICER:	**Probably** about two weeks ago?

108   Linguistic realisation of elastic language

(5.15) (cont.)

85:1:30 JIM:	I'm sure.
85:1:31 OFFICER:	Have you had drugs then today?
85:1:32 JIM:	I don't know, man, like.
85:1:33 OFFICER:	(indecipherable)
85:1:34 JIM:	I've been over for nine months, like, **probably** ... I don't know. (shrugs)
85:1:35 OFFICER:	I thought if you were buying drugs over there, you'd be keeping track of where they were.
85:1:36 JIM:	(laughs) We **probably** lost some as well.

Probably is used for past events in excerpt (5.15). Jim has been tested positive for traces of cocaine, and the officer needs to find out if he has any on him. In answering questions, Jim uses five *probably*, either evading or simply reflecting his imprecise memory of past events. *Probably* is used by Jim to elasticise quantity (*probably like a little bit* in turn 85:1:22), place (*probably in Mexico* in 85:1:24), time (*probably about two weeks ago* in 85:1:28), past action (*probably lost some* in turn 85:1:36, here *we* refers to someone who was with Jim at the time). When the officer asks how long ago Jim stayed in Mexico in 85:1:27, using an approximate stretcher ('About a week ago or ...?'); Jim comes back with *probably about two weeks ago*. The unspecified answer appears unsatisfactory, as the officer asks for clarification ('*Probably* about two weeks?' in 85:1:29). To respond to the officer's request, Jim gives a firmer answer: 'I'm sure'. The answer seems fine this time, so the officer moves on to another issue.

In turn 85:1:32, Jim ducks the officer's question ('Have you had drugs then today?'): instead of giving a straight yes or no Jim says 'I don't know, man, like'. *I don't know* is an expression that often co-occurs with EL. Ruzaitė (2007) investigates the ways in which approximators and quantifiers co-occur with multiple means of self-distancing (e.g. a mix of *I think, might, sort of, um,* and *I don't know*). A particularly distinctive feature of excerpt (5.15) is that discourse markers (*well* and *like* in 85:1:22) combine with elastic expressions. There is also co-occurrence of different types of elastic expression, such as *probably about two weeks ago* (epistemic stretcher + approximate stretcher) in 85:1:28. The clusters intensify the degree of uncertainty and provide linguistic evidence for the speaker's lack of commitment to what he says. A typical elastic utterance is 'I've been over for nine months, like, probably ... I don't know. (shrugs)' in 85:1:34. Jim chooses *probably* to make 'nine months' fluid, couples it with *like*, and ends with 'I don't know'. He may be doing this to protect himself from getting into trouble. (It becomes clear in the end that Jim's unusual behaviour was caused by too much drinking on the plane, and he is allowed to go.)

5.5 Epistemic stretchers 109

(5.16)

Data: Episode 19, from turn 19:3:18 to 19:3:23, two speakers, over six speaking turns.
Context: Officer Sean (male in his 20s) and a passenger (Australian male in his 30s). Sean is searching the passenger's bag for possible drug possession.

19:3:18 SEAN:	So we'll empty the bag. We've got to do a thorough search to make sure that you haven't got it.
19:3:19 PASSENGER:	Oh =
19:3:20 SEAN:	=Okay.
19:3:21 PASSENGER:	Oh jeez ... (pause) condoms everywhere.
19:3:22 SEAN:	We're happy with that bag mate, that's fine. (pause) (pats his own chest) We'll also **probably** just do a body pat down, is that alright?
19:3:23 PASSENGER:	If you can do it quickly, yeah.

Probably is used for future events in excerpt (5.16), unlike the ones used for past events in excerpt (5.15). The passenger's bag tests positive for traces of cocaine, but nothing is found. Sean suggests a frisk search in turn 19:3:22: 'We'll also probably just do a body pat down, is that alright?' He may feel that the frisk is somewhat imposing, so he tones down the request: *probably* is a marker indicating friendly attitude. Sean does not have to use it, but it mitigates the impact of the request by making it less categorical. Sean starts the request with a pleasant confirmation ('We are happy with the bag search, and it is fine'). Here *we* is used rather than *I*: *we* represents the institution, and may distance Sean personally from the bag search. He also uses *mate* to create informality. Then he uses the mitigating expression *probably*, coupled with *just* to reduce the imposition of his request. He does not use the common term 'frisk'; the less formal expression 'a body pat down' minimises the impact of the request, together with a gentle 'is that alright?' All these steps aim to persuade the passenger to agree to the frisk. (The strategies worked perfectly and the passenger agreed to the request. He was searched and nothing was found, so he was free to leave.)

5.5.2 *Sort of* and its clusters

Table 5.12 shows that compared with Americans and British, Australians use *sort of* three times more than the other two groups. *Sort of* ranks 11th of the most frequent elastic words in Table 5.1. The frequent occurrence of *sort of* in this study echoes findings in other studies: for example, *sort of* (and *a bit*) is one of the six most frequent words in business communication (Handford 2010: 167).

Table 5.14 *Three frequent* sort of *clusters*

	sort of + noun	*sort of* + verb	*sort of* + adjective
Raw frequency (n = 255,851)	85	37	16
Normalised frequency (per 10,000 words)	3.3	1.4	0.6

Sort of changes the truth condition of the utterance it modifies, and its approximate function is termed 'adjuster' (Austin 1962). The pragmatic force of *sort of* makes it a downtoner, hedge, or modaliser of the speaker's attitude (Channell 1994: 111). Its use shows no precision for the situation being described; 'rather this is just one kind of occasion on which speakers express hesitancy about the aptness of the words they have employed in their utterance' (Kay 1984: 162). *Kind of* implies a reservation (the speaker's sense of inaptness) and apology (I *kind of* have to go, because I have to pick up my daughter' (1984: 164). Kay argues that 'loosely speaking and technically appear to convey that speaker has clearly in mind the defect in his speech about which he is warning, kinda and sorta seem to convey the opposite idea, that the speaker is not prepared to specify the precise nature of the defect pointed to by the hedge' (1984: 167, underlined by me). For example, after 'loosely speaking, he is a Chinese', the speaker tends to go on to specify why *loosely speaking* is used. However, in 'He is sort of Chinese', the speaker usually does not specify what *sort of* means. The use of *sort of* seems to amount to a 'verbal shrug of helplessness' (1984: 167), an implicature that 'Chinese is not the right word' but 'I cannot do any better'.

While Kay says that the *kind of* cluster represents a somewhat defective meaning, Sperber and Wilson (1991) claim that *sort of* signals imprecision, more appropriate than exactness in conversation. Aijmer (2002: 209) finds that *sort of* creates common ground, and the hearer can figure it out even if it is said in approximate fashion. She points out that *sort of* tends to co-occur with *you know* and *I mean*, used between close friends, especially young people who want to present themselves as 'similar'. Using *sort of* can distance the speaker some way from the responsibility implied in their speech. *Sort of* also performs functions such as mitigating, politeness, and informality.

Table 5.14 shows that '*sort of* + noun' is the most favoured cluster, followed by '*sort of* + verb'. '*Sort of* + adjective' is the least used among the three patterns, six times less than '*sort of* + noun'. The stretcher *sort of* modifies some concept or category represented by a noun, and also adjusts the typical understanding of an action represented by a verb. The following samples are cases where *sort of* co-occurs with a verb:

5.5 Epistemic stretchers 111

I've got a feeling next time they, sort of, come through they'll remember to ...
... which pretty much sort of matches up ...
... sort of came over and was looking at this passenger ...
..., and sort of looking at the positions of the customs officers ...
... the younger guy was erm sort of coercing the older guy and ...
That's about the last thing we want to, sort of, import into Australia ...
... so they don't, sort of, breed readily.
... because he might not sort of think that that is a problem ...
... to conceal the food which, sort of, tips me over the edge to want to fine the gentleman ...
... these control briefs which, sort of, feel a little bit padded ...
What was, sort of, happening back then that ...?
... and it can just all, sort of, accumulate and they can lose the plot momentarily ...

These twelve examples illustrate hedged actions: *sort of* + *come through*, *match up*, *come over*, *look at*, *coerce*, *import*, *breed*, *think*, *tip over*, *feel*, *happen*, and *accumulate*. The speaker's attitude in these cases is not totally behind the statements made, implying that there is elasticity between *sort of* an action and a prototypical action; the boundary between the two types overlaps.

Sort of is often uttered with some prominence, indicated in print by a comma at each side. This usage also occurred with other parts of speech: 'This is only a primitive, sort of, exam, so we'll have to look into that further.' The following analysis of excerpts (5.17) and (5.18) demonstrate how the clusters '*sort of* + noun' and '*sort of* + adjective' are used.

(5.17)

Data: Episode 20, from turn 20:2:48 to 20:2:53, two speakers, over six speaking turns.
Context: Officer Rosemaree (female in her 30s) and a passenger (Indian male in his 20s). Rosemaree is examining undeclared raw cotton brought in by the passenger.

20:2:48 ROSEMAREE: (talking to camera) You can see here, (pause) there's all sorts of contamination in the cotton. India has a range of erm different diseases that ... (pause) that Australia doesn't have. And we need to be really careful about what this cotton may be contaminated with.
Australia's got quite a strong cotton industry, and you can see here there's some **sort of** infestation – whether it be plant or what. We don't know what that is. So we can't allow that into Australia at all. (pause) And there's a large amount of it here too.
(talking to passenger) What ... what are you going to do with this one?

112   Linguistic realisation of elastic language

(5.17) (cont.)

20:2:49 PASSENGER:	Ahh, this is er used for God.
20:2:50 ROSEMAREE:	Ah, so ... so your worship =
20:2:51 PASSENGER:	=And er some ... yes and some er ghee is for in this.
20:2:52 ROSEMAREE:	Ghee is put in it?=
20:2:53 PASSENGER:	=And ... yeah.

Sort of occurs often when officers talk to the camera, as shown in excerpt (5.17). This suggests that *sort of* tends to be used for information providing and commentary, as when they brief the TV audience about what is happening.

Officers have found that the passenger has not declared some prohibited food. Rosemaree finds that he has also brought in raw cotton. In turn 20:2:48, she turns to the camera to explain to the audience why she cannot allow the contaminated cotton into Australia. She says 'you can see here there's some sort of infestation – whether it be plant or what'; here, *sort of* is a stance marker. The implicature is that Rosemaree is not sure of the precise nature of the infestation, cannot be more specific, and has no more suitable word for the situation. She indicates that perhaps infestation is not the right word, but it is all she can think of for the time being. Or perhaps infestation is the right word, but she is unsure of the category or degree of infestation. *Sort of* is an indicator of the speaker's lack of knowledge or evidence that would enable her to present more precise information or to be categorical.

In turn 20:2:48, other surrounding linguistic evidence helps *sort of* to make an elastic understanding of infestation. *Some* used before *sort of* is a general stretcher expressing something unspecific. Following *sort of*, Rosemaree says the infestation may relate to plant or something else: 'We don't know what that is.' She does not know for sure if it is an infestation, and if so of what kind. Under the circumstances, she adopts the 'go epistemic' maxim to make her stance known, and adheres to Grice's (1975) Quality Maxim that one should be truthful. She uses the stance marker *kind of* to protect herself from the risk of being inaccurate. (The passenger was eventually fined $220 for bringing undeclared and prohibited items into Australia.)

(5.18)

Data: Episode 12, from turn 12:1:85 to 12:1:89, two speakers, over five speaking turns.
Context: Officer Mark (male in his 40s) and officer Dean (male in his 20s) are discussing a case of possible drug trafficking.

| 12:1:85 MARK: | Was his stomach hard, was it? |
| 12:1:86 DEAN: | Sorry? |

5.6 Padding expressions

> (5.18) (*cont.*)
>
> 12:1:87 MARK: Was his ...=
> 12:1:88 DEAN: =Yeah, (pause) (moving hands over his stomach in 'bloated' fashion) a little bit bloated, **sort of** (pats stomach) protruding but (pause) erm (pause) nothing found on the body. But (pause) he was er really willing to take his shoes off and that sort of thing, so it suggests he probably doesn't have any on his body, so ...
> 12:1:89 MARK: Okay.

In excerpt (5.18), two officers Mark and Dean are discussing the frisking of a passenger. Dean is describing what he felt when he patted the passenger's stomach. He uses *a little bit bloated* first, suggesting that the stomach was somewhat unusual. Then he picks *sort of protruding*, expressing hesitancy about the aptness of the word *protruding*. As a downtoner, *sort of* reduces the degree of a protrusion; Dean uses the stance marker to express elastically the extent the passenger's stomach stuck out, which seems the best he can do under the circumstances. Dean expects Mark to have no trouble understanding the implicature of *sort of protruding* because of their similar and shared backgrounds. He may also believe that Mark does not want to know the exact extent to which the passenger's stomach extended, so *sort of* is good enough to serve the purpose.

In turn 22:1:88, Dean uses a general stretcher *and that sort of thing*, a general mention of the category of related actions exemplified by *to take his shoes off*. As he and Mark share common ground, he does not need to provide a more exhaustive list. The term indicates an in-group membership and institutional bond between the officers. (An internal body scan revealed hidden heroin and the passenger was sentenced to prison.)

Both *probably* and *sort of* are implicit stance markers. The manifestation of elasticity of epistemic stretchers exemplified by *probably* and *sort of* exists in that stretchers make claims less categorical, observing the 'go epistemic' maxim to achieve communicative goals such as mitigating or self-protection.

5.6 Padding expressions

In addition to the four categories of stretcher (approximate, general, scalar, and epistemic) discussed above, some padding expressions are used to accentuate the elastic use of language. They are signposts to signal the use of EL. Expressions such as 'I'm not sure', 'I can't remember', 'I don't know exactly' and 'I can't promise 100 per cent' are used 'as padding round other vague terms, in order, perhaps, to mitigate the very vagueness of the other term,

114   Linguistic realisation of elastic language

vaguely covering up vagueness' (Cotterill 2007: 112). In this study, a padding expression refers to one that may or may not be elastic itself but is an indicator of elasticity in the surrounding text; it may or may not be adjacent to other elastic expressions.

Some discourse markers co-occur with EL and act as precursors or primitive forms of EL, indexical of elasticity of language. For example, *well* (termed a pragmatic marker and discourse particle in Aijmer 2013: 3) is reflexive, acting as a context cue. Discourse markers have a large indexical potential and are polysemous, with discourse functions at textual and interpersonal levels (Aijmer 2002: 277). Tausczik and Pennebaker (2010: 36) find that when people are less than certain about something, they use more filler words (e.g. *I mean, you know*). The following excerpts illustrate the co-occurrence of padding expressions with EL.

You know

It is used together with EL to involve the hearer (Romero Trillo 2002), and highlight the shared knowledge of speaker and hearer (Handford 2010). In some cases, *you know* may be regarded as a vague expression, if it functions as a placeholder for something the speaker does not want to say overtly. For example, 'she is not a popular girl, because she always does odd things, and kind of you know ...', where *you know* is a placeholder for some unpopular traits or things. The speaker expects that the hearer will sense the negative meaning of *you know* and know that the speaker does not want to say more because of the unpleasant nature of the unsaid. This usage is similar to the expression of *ni dongde* in Chinese.

(5.19)

Data: Episode 4, from turn 4:2:29 to 4:2:32, two speakers, over four speaking turns.
Context: Officer Michael (male in his 30s) and officer Larry (male in his 40s) are examining live reptiles illegally posted to Australia.

4:2:29 MICHAEL:	There you go, it's another one.
4:2:30 LARRY:	This one looks in better nick than that last one anyway. (pause) Yeah, that last one looked like (pause) **you know** it was a bit ... bit weaker. And obviously there was evidence of it bruising on its head. (pause) But this one looks pretty good eh?
4:2:31 MICHAEL:	He does, he looks ... (pause) He's very young.
4:2:32 LARRY:	Certainly had some interesting er (pause) confiscations in the ... the way ... the way people conceal these things. It's er (pause) quite amazing.

5.6 Padding expressions   115

Officers spotted reptiles inside two packages sent from Thailand. In turn 4:2:30, Larry (the head vet) is talking to his colleague Michael (manager of the herpetofauna unit), describing the condition of the reptiles. Larry thinks the second one is in better condition than the first. He presents his findings in a qualified way, saying 'Yeah, that last one looked like (pause) you know it was a bit ... bit weaker'. He first uses *yeah* as a co-constructing backchannel and general acknowledger; *looked like* and *a bit ... bit* are elastic expressions indicating he is not absolutely sure, or wants to mitigate the tone of his statement in case Michael disagrees. Larry uses *you know* to invite Michael's contribution, indirectly and gently appealing for his confirmation. Prior to *you know* there is a pause, suggesting that Larry stalls and is searching for a word. In the later part of this turn Larry's tone is somewhat more affirmative, indicated by the use of *obviously* and *evidence*. At the end of his speaking turn, Larry uses *eh*? to again solicit a reply from Michael. Michael agrees with Larry in the next turn.

(5.20)

Data: Episode 23, from turn 23:3:36 to 23:3:39, two speakers, over four speaking turns.
Context: Officer Aruna (female in her 40s) and passenger (New Zealand male in his 30s). Aruna is interviewing the passenger about his past convictions.

23:3:36 ARUNA:	What can you tell me about these offences?
23:3:37 PASSENGER:	Um, **you know**, some of the stuff that I don't even, **you know**, I don't even think about anymore. **You know**, it was when I was younger, I was, I had a bit of a, **you know**, but I'm trying to straighten out my life now and get my – excuse the language – shit together, and if my past makes me not get into this country, then (shrugs) that's the way it is, **you know**. It's all my fault, **you know**, I understand that, I know I've got a past and I, I'm not that person anymore, **you know**.
23:3:38 ARUNA:	Okay. We'll take that on board and I'll discuss that with my um, duty manager, and then we'll make a final decision as to whether you will be um, allowed to enter Australia, okay?
23:3:39 PASSENGER:	Thank you.

Excerpt (5.20) displays quite a few instances of *you know* in the single speaking turn 23:3:37. The implied meaning of *you know* is expected to be understood by the hearer; its use requires shared knowledge between speaker and hearer. *You know* is this passenger's buzzword: he uses it seven times, primarily for emphasis to make sure Aruna listens, understands and agrees with him. *You know* is also used for pausing, especially when positioned at the end of a sentence. As *you know* is used a lot in excerpt (5.20), it runs the risk of some *you know* becoming meaningless. One *you know* differs: in 'I had a bit of a, you know, but I'm trying to straighten out my life now', *you know* acts as a placeholder or ellipsis for something the speaker does not want to say aloud: a run-in with the law or shady history. When something is sensitive or embarrassing, *you know* may be used as a pronominal phrase. The implicature is clear enough for Aruna to get. (The passenger was returned to New Zealand because he did not qualify for a special category visa, as his past convictions added up to more than a 12-month sentence and he had failed to declare this.)

Well

When *well* co-occurs with EL, it serves as an introduction for vagueness in language (Rowland 2007: 94). *Well* is a hedge, advising the hearer that the upcoming utterance will in some way flout one or more of Grice's maxims of cooperation (Brockway 1981). In Sperber and Wilson's (1995 [1986]) relevance-theoretic framework, *well* is a marker of insufficiency, signifying that 'the most immediately accessible context is not the most relevant one for the interpretation of the impending utterance' (Jucker 1993: 435).

Aijmer (2013) finds that *well* is used more frequently in dialogue than monologue, so it is primarily dialogic. This is supported in this study: *well* occurs in dialogue 17.1 times, but only 0.7 per 10,000 words in monologue. Aijmer also finds that the pragmatic function of *well* (sometimes uttered with a drawl) is multifaceted, signalling an insufficient answer, doing self-repair, being transitional according to an agenda, marking ongoing commentary, introducing a new contribution, agreeing, disagreeing, presenting an opinion or evaluation, acting as a boundary signal or a topic changer. The most relevant functions regarding EL are indicating imprecision, doing a word search when starting a new sentence, and hesitating (Stubbe and Holmes 1995), which are the focus of this study.

(5.21)

Data: Episode 5, from turn 5:3:17 to 5:3:20, two speakers, over four speaking turns.
Context: Officer Ross (male in his 40s) and officer Rachael (female in her 30s) are inspecting a package from England.

5:3:17 ROSS: It's a solid part of somebody's (pause) history, and it's a document that's been signed by (pause) you know the King of ... of England back in the ... the 1750s ... **well**

5.6 Padding expressions

(5.21) (cont.)

	1760s, which is just ... (pause) to have some document like that signed by the King, it's a priceless document. So I think probably the best thing (pause) is if we put that in a freezer for ten days ...=
5:3:18 RACHAEL:	=Okay=
5:3:19 ROSS:	=... at negative 18 degrees ...=
5:3:20 RACHAEL:	=Mhm hmm.

A wooden antique which is 200 years old is badly moth-eaten; two officers need to determine what treatment needs to be taken before allowing it into Australia. In excerpt (5.21), Ross (senior entomologist) explains the significance of the item and a possible solution. In turn 5:3:17, he uses *well* in '... it's a document that's been signed by (pause) you know the King of ... of England back in the ... the 1750s ... well 1760s ...', performing self-repair. Initially, Ross utters *1750s*, then changes to *1760s*, using *well* as a precursor to the correction. Both *1750s* and *1760s* are elastic expressions, and *well* acts as word changer to signal the insufficiency of the former date and the self-correction. *Well* 'is closely associated with consideration, deliberation, hesitation', evidence of its reflexive nature (Aijmer 2013: 32). In (5.21), Ross uses *1750s* and *1760s* instead of a precise year of signature. This could be for privacy or because he thinks that a precise year is not important; an elastic expression serves for effectiveness of information.

In turn 5:3:17, *you know* and the preceding (pause) draws attention to the importance of the signature. At the end of 5:3:17, Ross says 'So I think probably the best thing (pause) is if we put that in a freezer for ten days.' He is suggesting an action to treat this item and ensure its safe release, and he makes the suggestion in a mitigated way (*I think*, *probably*, *if*), revealing that he does not want to be seen as dominating, adopting a less authoritative and more collegial manner.

I mean

This is used primarily in dialogues in this study (123 times), yet appears in monologues merely twice. It usually appears in the clause initial or medial position, as something that speakers say before they start or continue an utterance. Speakers tend to pause around *I mean*, suggesting that it is used for stalling and word search. It can also do self-repair by correcting what has been said or adding more information, by introducing a clause that modifies the prior one. This function has the effect of altering a general statement into something more specific, or vice versa. *I mean* can co-occur with EL to reflect the thinking process of the speaker, whose conflicting ideas are yet to be sorted out.

(5.22)

Data: Episode 37, from turn 37:2:21 to 37:2:27, two speakers, over seven speaking turns.
Context: Officer Cemile (female in her 40s) and passenger Robert (American male in his 20s). Cemile is questioning Robert about his financial support.

37:2:21 CEMILE:	Is Michael also going to be supporting you, while you're in Australia?
37:2:22 ROBERT:	Mmh-hm. Yeah, yeah.
37:2:23 CEMILE:	Yeah? So, you're relying on him.
37:2:24 ROBERT:	Well, no, (shrugs) you know, completely. **I mean**, I guess that's kind of like a main ...
37:2:25 CEMILE:	It would be completely if you've only got $150 on you.
37:2:26 ROBERT:	You don't think I can make this last, ah, until I leave? Ask him. I didn't know.
37:2:27 CEMILE:	Not a problem.

Musician Robert entered Australia with a tourist visa, but he should have applied for an entertainment visa because he intends to take part in a band performance. Michael is Robert's friend in Australia. In turn 37:2:24, Robert first uses *well* to bring in his disagreement with Cemile, his 'shrug' seeming in accordance with his sentiment. *You know* introduces *completely* to hedge the disagreement. The first part of this speaking turn: 'Well, no, (shrugs) you know, completely', argues that Robert might not 'completely' rely on Michael's financial support.

In the second part of 37:2:24, Robert further elasticises his argument by saying '**I mean**, I guess that's kind of like a main ...' *I mean* clusters with stretchers *I guess*, *kind of*, *like* to stall for a word search. He wants to find a word to explain what he meant by 'not completely'. *I mean* is in clause initial position, depicting Robert's unsettled thinking process. The stretchers *I guess*, *kind of*, *like*, are all used to modify 'a main ...'; it is possible that Robert wants to say that while Michael is 'a main' supporter, he does not intend to 'completely' rely on Michael. However, Robert does not convince Cemile, who disagrees with him in the next turn. (Robert is allowed to enter Australia, but he fails to get the correct visa on time so is unable to perform with the band.)

5.6 Padding expressions

Er/uh/um/erm/ah/oh

These are discourse fillers (Ruzaitė 2007: 161), 'inserted by speakers to give processing time' (Channell 1994: 197). In Chinese, discourse fillers, such as *aiya* (oh boy!), or *hehe* (a mimetic word for chuckle), tend to be used to avoid being offensive and to ward off mentioning something unpleasant, sensitive or embarrassing. For example, in a popular Chinese TV dating show called *You Are The One*, a man from Africa appears on stage in a bid to date one of the 24 women on the show. He mentions that before he came to China he thought every Chinese person was a Kongfu master like Bruce Lee. When asked if he still thinks that way now he is in China, he says '*Aiya, hehe*' to deflect the question, avoiding saying that he had been naïve. He uses discourse fillers to smartly steer clear of possible offence to the Chinese audience. Discourse fillers, used together with EL, tend to show hesitation or stalling for a word search.

(5.23)

Data: Episode 94, from turn 94:1:14 to 94:1:15, two speakers, over two speaking turns.
Context: Officer Robert (male in his 40s) and passenger (American male in his 20s). Robert is examining the passenger's bag.

94:1:14 ROBERT:	**Ah**, just the sides of the bag here. Just checking it's solid, nothing built into the ribs or anything like that. How long you had the bag?
94:1:15 PASSENGER:	**Oh**, that is my brother's bag. (arms folded standing away from counter) **Um**, that is my brother's bag. **Um**, he's had it for probably a couple years, **um** ... Not really sure what he's done with it, but, **uh** ...

The young college student is noticed when a detector dog reacts to his belongings. Robert starts with the discourse filler *ah* to buy time to find something appropriate to say to the passenger. He then uses the stretchers *just* (twice) and *or anything like that*, to mitigate the negative impact of searching the bag. The implicature is 'I'll merely have a quick and routine look, nothing more', and the general extender *or anything like that* may indicate that he is not expecting to find anything specific. His choice of language shows his friendly and considerate attitude.

In 94:1:15, the passenger responds to Robert's question using five fillers. The first two (*oh* and *um*) indicate that he needs some time to collect his thoughts and confirm that the bag is actually not his. The last three fillers are

120   Linguistic realisation of elastic language

used together with *probably, a couple years, not really sure* to highlight the tentativeness of what he says and his reluctance to make a categorical statement. The passenger appears unsure if the bag is clean and is probably worried that if the bag has been tampered with he will be in trouble. His body language (arms folded, standing away from counter), suggests that he is somewhat defensive and indicates a sense that if anything is dodgy, it will not be because of him. (In the end the passenger was cleared and free to go.)

Generally speaking, discourse fillers are used by speakers to obtain some time to think what or how to say next. When co-occurring with EL, the fillers make the elasticity of an utterance obvious and easy to recognise.

Non-verbal activities

These activities often signal cues to help the understanding of EL. For example, a pause may indicate a search for words, and nervous laughs indicate that the speaker may be trying to evade. Utilising such cues in context helps to make the data analysis of this study rigorous.

(5.24)

Data: Episode 3, from turn 3:1:9 to 3:1:10, two speakers, over two speaking turns.
Context: Officer (male in his 40s) and officer David (male in his late 30s). They are examining a heavy industrial grinding wheel using an X-ray machine.

3:1:9 OFFICER: We can see a disk. (**pause**) It looks like there's some inconsistencies in the middle of the disk.
3:1:10 DAVID: If you change the sensitivity er (**pause**), I mean we're getting quite a lot of (**pause**) evidence that there's probably something (**pause**) inside there that may be organic. Now that may just the make-up of the object that's inside, or it could indicate that erm (**pause**) there is er something that we might be interested, in the way of narcotics, inside it. So we'll open it up and have a look.

The officers are finding something concealed deep inside a grinding wheel, and that something turns out to be almost two kilos of cocaine. The officer in 3:1:9 pauses before saying 'It looks like there's some inconsistencies in the middle of the disk.' This pause indicates that he needs some time to organise his thoughts and words for the next sentence, given that he is not certain about what is inside the wheel. After the pause he chooses EL (*looks like, some*) to express a hedged description.

David pauses four times in 3:1:10. The first pause is preceded with the discourse filler *er*, which enhances the effect of stalling for a word search, and is followed by the discourse marker *I mean*, which introduces the utterance: 'if you change the sensitivity er (pause), I mean we're getting quite a lot of (pause) evidence that there's probably something (pause) inside there that may be organic.' The elasticity here is manifested in *quite a lot of, probably something, may be*. There are three pauses in the sentence, surrounded by elastic expressions. The last pause follows the same pattern: 'that erm (pause) there is er something that we might be interested', with the pause positioned around discourse fillers (*erm* and *er*) and stretchers (*something* and *might*).

The pause pattern in excerpt (5.24) is that the speakers tend to pause around discourse fillers and especially stretchers, to give themselves time to put together something appropriate. Pauses may also indicate hesitation and uncertainty. They suggest that communicating in EL may need time to think things through. A non-verbal pause effectively acts as a signal for surrounding EL, helping the hearer to get ready for processing.

5.7 Linguistic patterns of elastic language as a manifestation of elasticity

The empirical evidence in this study reveals the linguistic manifestation of EL, particularly the stretch work realised by the four categories of stretcher, approximate, general, scalar and epistemic. Some are preceding stretchers ('He is sort of annoyed'), some succeeding stretchers ('He is annoyed, I think'), others middle stretchers ('There are 20 or 30 bags'). The different positions allow stretchers to elasticise in different directions: preceding stretchers work forwards, succeeding stretchers work backwards, and middle stretchers spread sideways.

The process of elasticisation explained in Chapter 3 is shown in the data: with a source input (e.g. *bags*) the speaker stretches the input by adding a stretcher (e.g. *many*) to produce a stretched output (*many bags*). The schema is: source input => stretching => stretched output. The stretched output is not necessarily a simple addition between input and stretcher; its pragmatic meaning is bounded by the context in which it occurs. For example, in *about 100 pounds* in excerpt (5.1) and *about a year* in excerpt (5.2), although the same stretcher *about* is used, its stretching impact on *100 pounds* and *a year* are different due to the different natures of the items it modifies and the contexts in which the two expressions are made.

Elasticity manifests in the interconnection of the four categories of stretcher: they play more than one role and belong to more than one category. For example, quantifiers typically are approximate stretchers, but they can also be used for generalising where precision is impossible (Ruzaitė 2007: 98).

Typically, multal quantifiers (for large quantities) tend to make broad generalisations (*many, much, lots of, a number of*), and paucal ones are used to indicate a lesser degree (2007: 99). The analysis in excerpts (5.3) and (5.4) shows that *some* is used as a general stretcher but can also be an approximate stretcher, as in 'She has bought several goldfish; some have fun tails, some are comet.' Another overlapping case is *many* and *few*, both appearing in these data as approximate and scalar stretchers. The multiple functions of stretchers suggest that EL is not categorical.

EL is stretchable: expressions elasticise from their unmarked position. In *many bags* and *few bags*, *bags* is the base, and *many* and *few* stretch it up and down respectively. The same applies to *very* (strengthening) vs *sort of* (mitigating). In *about 100 pounds*, *about* stretches 100 to an interval around 100. The data demonstrate what is assumed in the elasticity theory proposed in this study: that stretchers can stretch the meaning of expressions vertically and horizontally.

The four categories of stretcher have different focuses and perspectives. Prince et al. (1982) argue that the difference between an approximator (e.g. *a bit*) and a shield (e.g. *I think*) is that the former influences the truth condition of the proposition it modifies but the latter does not. For example, the truth values of 'She is tall' and 'She is a bit tall' are not the same, but the truth values of 'She is tall' and 'I think she is tall' are the same. A shield indicates that the speaker is not fully or personally committed to the truth of a proposition. Approximators are phrasal vagueness; shields are clausal vagueness (Kärkkäinen 2010: 213).

In this study, the truth condition and syntactic structure of EL are not major concerns: what is focused on is the pragmatic meaning and function of stretchers. They are used strategically, enabling interlocutors to negotiate and co-construct a pragmatic meaning from EL. Stretchers typically correspond to four maxims: 'go approximate' as shown in excerpts (5.1) and (5.2); 'go general' as shown in excerpts (5.3) and (5.4); 'go scalar' as shown in excerpts (5.5) and (5.6); and 'go epistemic' as shown in excerpts (5.7) and (5.8). The maxim 'go approximate' mainly works on a vague quantity, 'go general' on a vague quality. The maxim 'go scalar' utilises the degree of claim on continua, and 'go epistemic' primarily focuses on the speaker's stance and attitude.

Investigating beyond EL itself provides a richer picture of EL behaviours. Warren (2007) explores how discourse intonation patterns impact on VL, revealing that some of them enhance vagueness. Similarly, padding expressions (discourse markers/fillers and non-verbal activity) join force with stretchers to highlight the stretch work of EL. In 'So I can do em ... Let's say weekly or something like that from here on out. I don't think it pays to do it any more often than that', Koester (2007: 56) classifies 'let's say' as a hedge. It would be a padding expression in this study as 'let's say' is not elastic, but it leads in to EL, 'padding' it. Padding expressions are primitive forms of EL, indexical of elasticity. Non-verbal signs such as pauses also occur around EL. Ruzaitė (2007: 160) finds that pauses are a recurrent feature of VL utterances, often a sign of reconsidering the VL in question. In this study, pauses as 'fillers' are often indicators of uncertainty and lead in to the use of EL.

Stretchers are a combination of literal meaning, implicature and hidden meaning. *About 100* tends to refer to a literal imprecise meaning, *sort of a frisk search* refers to an implied meaning (implicature: not a standard frisk search), *not exactly have past convictions* is a hedged statement with a hidden meaning (maybe have past convictions in one way or another). The speaker of *sort of a frisk search* intends the hearer to infer the implicature, but the speaker of *not exactly have past convictions* may not want the hearer to realise his hidden meaning. The understanding of EL may also involve the speaker's expectation of and belief about the hearer's expectation. For example, *very* refers to a significant amount (Moxey and Sanford 1993) more than average, *some* is a quantity considered normal, *so many* and *probably not* are to warn the hearer of something not usually expected.

Global elasticity can take the form of various continua made of stretchers from different categories. *A bit – some – often – very – most* is a scale consisting of stretchers from the categories 'approximate', 'general' and 'scalar'. The global elasticity represented by the continuum possesses relational and interactional features, highlighting a holistic component in EL study.

5.8   Summary

This chapter demonstrates the linguistic realisation of elasticity of EL, namely how the concept of elasticity is manifested linguistically in the data. Four categories of stretcher are examined in terms of their clusters and frequency distributions: approximate, general, scalar and epistemic. Table 5.1 lists the top 20 most frequent stretchers in the data, from most to least frequent: *very*, *some*, *anything*, *something*, *lot* (*a lot*, *a lot of*, *lot of*, *lots of*), *quite*, *things*, *a bit*, *much*, *probably*, *sort of*, *could be*, *about*, *possible/possibly*, *maybe*, *stuff*, *a little bit*, *too*, *so*, *or something*. The typical members for 'approximate stretcher' are *about* and *some*; for 'general stretcher' *anything*, *something*, *things*, *stuff*, and *or something*; for 'scalar stretcher' *very*, *quite*, *too*, and *so*; for 'epistemic stretcher' *probably*, *sort of*, *could be*, *possible/possibly*, and *maybe*. The 'general stretcher' category ranks higher than the other three; that is, general stretchers are the favourite among the participants.

The eight stretchers analysed in detail are the top two most frequent words in each of the four categories: 'approximate' (*about*, *some*), 'general' (*anything*, *something*), 'scalar' (*very*, *quite*), and 'epistemic' (*probably*, *sort of*). The most frequent *about* clusters are '*about* + number' and '*about* + a/an +

quantity/period of time'. The clusters are used to suggest that the speaker cannot remember the exact amount, or that precise numbers are not important. The maxim 'go approximate' serves to express numbers/quantity in a non-precise fashion. The most preferred *some* clusters are '*some* + noun/noun phrase', *some sort of* and *some of*. *Some* indicates an unspecified amount, stretching around the moderate area on a scale of quantity. It also refers to an unknown person or unrevealed item. It can express fluid quantity and hedge certainty to minimise the risk of being wrong.

The general stretcher *anything* is used frequently in the form 'there's anything', *anything else*, and *or anything*. Speakers prefer to use the *anything* cluster to describe something unknown at the time of speaking, as it is a protector when discussing a future or unknown event. *Anything* is also used to deliberately avoid providing accurate information. It has a larger set of possibilities than *something*: that is, *anything* is more general than *something*. *Something* appears often in clusters: *or something (like that)*, *something else*, *something like*. *Something* mitigates the abruptness of a blunt question, signalling tentativeness. *We* behaves as a special general stretcher.

A salient feature of scalar stretchers is their relational meaning: the interpretation of one term depends closely upon the neighbouring terms on the same scale. Scalar stretchers have three groups: the lower end of a scale (e.g. *a little*, *hardly*), middle (e.g. *some*, *fairly*) and high end (e.g. *many*, *very*). The items on a continuum are not categorical, in that their respective positions are relational and not exactly located. The most frequent scalar stretcher is *very*, and the top five most frequent *very* clusters are *very good*, *very much*, *very high*, *very hard*, and *very nervous*. *Very* is typically used for emphasis. *Not-very* stretchers perform an opposite function, to de-emphasise. The word *quite* is another favourite scalar stretcher, although its stretching power is less than that of *very*. *Quite* often occurs with adjectives and adverbs: for example, *quite serious* indicates that the seriousness of an offence is more than usual, stretching the degree of seriousness upwards to warrant a written warning but not a fine.

Epistemic stretchers carry the speaker's stance and attitude, particularly the speaker's judgement about the certainty and reliability of the utterance in question. *Probably* appears with past events as much as with future events, indicating that speakers are less than certain about both. This does not support the assumption that people are more certain when talking about something that has already happened than about something yet to happen. *Probably* clusters are used to evade, or simply to reflect the speaker's imprecise recall of a past event. They also intensify the degree of uncertainty and provide linguistic evidence of a speaker's lack of commitment to what is said. *Probably* also indicates a friendly attitude, mitigating the impact of an imposition. The other epistemic stretcher *sort of* tends to be highlighted by a comma at each side, and

5.8 Summary

implies that the speaker is not sure of the precise nature of something, an indicator of the speaker's lack of knowledge. As a downtoner, *sort of* reduces degree: a speaker using *sort of* assumes that the hearer does not want to know exact information, and *sort of* is good enough to serve the purpose. *Sort of* also mitigates and self-protects.

Padding refers to an expression that may or may not be elastic and has more pragmatic than semantic meaning. Padding frequently occurs with EL, acting as co-textual clue to enhance understanding. For example, the speaker in excerpt (5.19) utters *you know* to indirectly and gently appeal to the hearer for attention and confirmation, based on their shared knowledge. *Well* in excerpt (5.21) helps with word-search and self-repair. *I mean* in excerpt (5.22) stalls for time and brings in further EL, depicting the speaker's uncertain thinking process. Discourse fillers such as *er*, *uh*, *um*, *erm*, *ah*, and *oh* indicate that the speaker needs time to decide what to say next or to highlight the tentativeness of what has been said. When co-occurring with EL, fillers make the elasticity of an utterance easier to recognise. Utilising all the cues in context can make data analysis rigorous and convincing. For example, non-verbal activities often offer clues to help understanding. A pause is for word searching, and a nervous laugh may indicate that the speaker is trying to evade. Speakers tend to pause around discourse markers or fillers, and especially elastic stretchers, to gain some time for speech management.

I and *we* are overlapping and interchangeable: *I* may be upgraded to *we* to empower the speaker and obtain cooperation. *We* is not exactly a stretcher, but its stretchability makes it a good example of a quasi-general stretcher or padding expression, given the general nature of *we* shown in the data.

These findings confirm the linguistic manifestation of elasticity of EL, and reveal that speakers observe the four maxims of EL in order to enhance its use: 'go approximate', 'go general', 'go scalar', and 'go epistemic'.

6   Strategies of elastic language

EL consists of words with blurred edges. These are in fact an advantage (Ullmann 1962; Wittgenstein 1953) because 'vagueness is not only an inherent feature of natural language, but also – and crucially – it is an interactional strategy. Speakers are faced with a number of communicative tasks, and they are vague for strategic reasons' (Jucker et al. 2003: 1739). The pragmatic functions of VL have not been widely studied until recently. 'The art of being vague is a neglected concern for the linguist, and yet an important part of the armoury of every speaker and writer' (Sinclair, in Channell 1994, xviii). One of the three principles of elasticity theory is the strategic use of EL. Elasticity of language coincides with being strategic (Glinert 2010: 70), and the nature of being strategic requires elasticity to respond to the needs of different contexts and communicative goals.

This chapter is a qualitative study, providing an in-depth investigation into the use of EL in real-life data. It looks at the contextualised function of EL, in particular why EL is used and the results of using it. This chapter discusses six strategies: just-right elastic, rapport elastic, mitigating elastic, intensifying elastic, self-protection elastic, and evasive elastic; these six categories are not meant to be categorical. 'Elastic' is a metaphor to depict EL's function as being stretchable and flexible to meet the needs of communication. The analysis takes both sides into consideration: when speakers choose EL, they assume that the hearer can infer what is not spoken through their shared knowledge (Carter and McCarthy 2004). Responses from the hearer indicate how well the speaker's elastic communication has worked. While there are occasions when the hearer asks for clarification, most hearers have no problems.

Interpretation of EL involves context: the hearer is guided to look for contextual implications, such as implicature, a contextual deduction (Sperber and Wilson 1995 [1986]). However, inferences about the pragmatic function of EL may be problematic. Cotterill (2007: 104) warns that it is important 'to be cautious in any attempt to interpret a speaker's motivation for producing VL'. 'Even the wider context may not clarify which meaning the speaker/ writer intended' (Biber et al. 2010: 858), because inference is subjective and vulnerable to dispute given its pragmatic ambiguity and functional complexity

(Holmes 1995). In this study, pragmatic functions of EL are analysed with the help of contextual clues and the researcher's best interpretation of a particular use of EL. Ruzaitė (2007: 54) states that 'categories of vague language have very little meaning when decontextualised; they become informative and comprehensible only when used in context'. It is important and necessary to take any categorising of EL functions as 'best guesses', as it may be problematic to claim any category of EL function is more categorical than the empirical evidence can support. Ruzaitė (2007: 167) provides the following example: 'Erm <u>I'm not sure</u> what time yet but erm <u>it's more likely</u> to be <u>sort of</u> just before lunch or just <u>sort of</u> or <u>maybe</u> just after lunch or <u>round</u> four o'clock ...', where many of the co-textual clues point to *round* as 'expressing uncertainty'.

While it is difficult to distinguish the categorical functional categories of EL, it is possible to discuss them based on available empirical evidence. In the following analysis, contextual clues are used to infer the most likely implied messages and functions of EL. Most stretchers in the selected excerpts are among the 20 most frequent EL expressions (Table 5.1), so they are representative of the data.

6.1   Just-right elastic

As Table 2.11 defines, just-right elastic refers to EL expressing uncertainty and tentativeness when certainty is not feasible or precision is not important; under such circumstances the speaker provides an appropriate amount of information. This strategy indicates to the hearer that a literal or precise meaning is either unavailable or unimportant (or the speaker would have provided it). This category, termed 'giving the right amount of information', originated with Channell (1994). EL is considered primarily to adhere to the Maxim of Quantity (Grice 1975), to speak as informatively as, but not more than, is required for the purpose of exchange. Often, speaking vaguely is good enough or even more effective than speaking precisely (Jucker et al. 2003). It is possible that meaning is only vague to the hearer; it could be non-vague to the speaker. Either way, whether involuntarily or voluntarily vague, the information provided by the speaker is the right amount: hence its name, 'just-right elastic'.

Using just-right elastic is in line with the principles of Relevance Theory (Sperber and Wilson 1995 [1986]). Channell (1994) confirms that using non-numerical quantifiers avoids flouting the Maxim of Quantity. When EL is used, neither party is normally bothered to specify precise referents indicated by the extension of the word meaning, because 'to be consistent with the principle of relevance, the expression has to yield additional contextual effects which are worth the processing effort. This process is guided by the principle of relevance, and it exploits the common ground between partners' (Jucker

128   Strategies of elastic language

et al. 2003: 1749). Interlocutors observe the relevance principle when they decide to foreground or background certain information. When there is no need to process precise information, the speaker redirects resources to non-precise information to reduce the hearer's processing efforts.

Approximate stretchers are typically used for just-right elastic. For example, when there is no certainty about something or when the contextual clues suggest that precision is not a priority, the speaker uses approximation and quantifiers. Cotterill (2007: 105–6) sees VL as 'a kind of evidential shorthand, a means by which both lawyers and, particularly, witnesses are able to cover a large amount of evidential ground in only a few turns, presenting the crime narrative in abbreviated terms'. Cotterill emphasises that shorthand is only possible when both parties share knowledge about what is being discussed. This is echoed in Koester's (2007: 48) finding that speakers use VL when they assume some knowledge shared with their hearers, because VL can 'cover a lot of ground, without having to go into too much detail'. EL is used as an appropriate and effective means to communicate at a suitable level in a suitable manner, as illustrated in the following excerpts.

(6.1)

Data: Episode 85, from turn 85:4:9 to 85:4:13, three speakers, over five speaking turns.
Context: Officer Kim (female in her 30s), officer Ryan (Indian male in his 30s), and passenger (Chinese male in his 20s). Kim and Ryan are examining the passenger's bags for undeclared food and other goods.

85:4:9 KIM:	We need to check what's inside your jeans. Do you know what's inside there?
85:4:10 PASSENGER:	Not sure.
85:4:11 KIM:	You're not sure.
85:4:12 RYAN:	It looks like there's some pills over there. What do you reckon? **A bit** of organic stuff over there.
85:4:13 KIM:	Yeah.

Previously an excessive amount of tobacco was found in the passenger's bags. Then the officers discovered three pairs of jeans with the pockets sewn shut and something secured inside. Kim in 95:4:9 asks the passenger to say what is inside, but the passenger does not provide any information. Ryan in 85:4:12 speaks in a hedged manner: 'it looks like there's some pills over there'; *looks like* and *some* are stretchers. Ryan then asks for Kim's opinion, again indicating that Ryan is not sure about what he sees. Ryan continues with 'a bit of organic stuff over here', where *a bit* is an elastic quantifier and *stuff* is a general stretcher.

6.1 Just-right elastic 129

Ryan uses *a bit* for two possible reasons: he does not know the exact amount, or he does not think there is a need to report the precise amount even if he knows it. (The 'stuff' turns out to be a Chinese delicacy – bird's nest; the passenger pays a $220 fine for not declaring it.)

Ryan adopts just-right elastic to deliver a less than certain utterance. He observes the Maxim of Quantity by providing 'not less and not more' information than suits the situation. In the next turn, Kim's agreement with Ryan's veiled evaluation suggests that the officers have no problem with elastic communication, and so EL is used effectively.

(6.2)

Data: Episode 92, from turn 92:1:15 to 92:1:23, two speakers, over nine speaking turns.

Context: Officer Sarah (female in her 20s) and passenger (Australian male in his 20s). A laser is being seized from the passenger.

92:1:15 SARAH:	Okay, what's this one?
92:1:16 PASSENGER:	That's a laser.
92:1:17 SARAH:	Okay. At this point – just because I've found that one – I'm just going to caution you, okay, just get you to listen carefully. You do not have to say or do **anything** unless you wish to do so, but **anything** you do say or do may be used in evidence. Do you understand?
92:1:18 PASSENGER:	Am I in trouble for **something**? I'm just ...
92:1:19 SARAH:	Do you understand that caution?
92:1:20 PASSENGER:	Yeah, yep. Am I getting arrested **or something**?
92:1:21 SARAH:	No, you're not. These ones are prohibited imports into Australia, so we will be seizing that from you. (Passenger visibly upset and swears under his breath)
92:1:22 PASSENGER:	Where's, uh, where's it say? Is it written **somewhere** that you can't bring lasers **or something**? Did I miss that?
92:1:23 SARAH:	It's just question one on your incoming passenger card, **anything** that might be considered a weapon.

The passenger has come back to Australia from Bali with prohibited souvenirs, one of which is a laser, which is not allowed into Australia; for this he receives a caution from Sarah. The passenger is unsure of the precise purpose of a caution, so asks if he is in trouble or being arrested. General stretchers *anything* and *something* (five in total) are distinctive in this excerpt. In 92:1:17, Sarah reads out a caution which is a standard legal warning. In it, *anything* expresses indefinite referent(s), sufficient to serve the institutional objective. It is not feasible to provide an exhaustive list of things people might say or do;

more importantly, there is no need to do so. *Anything* does a good job in this situation. In the next turn, the passenger asks if he is in trouble for *something*, suggesting that he is uncertain about the situation he is in. Both *something* and *anything*, as discussed in Section 5.3, express unspecific information, but *something* covers a relatively smaller range and tends to have a more specific referent. The passenger's use of *something* instead of *anything* indicates that he knows he is in trouble in one way or another, but not exactly what the trouble is. This difference between *something* and *anything* is also applicable to *somewhere* in 92:1:22 and *anything* in 92:1:23.

In 92:1:20, the passenger asks 'Am I getting arrested or something?' The general extender *or something* suggests that the speaker is uncertain about the implication of a caution. He wonders if it means an arrest or something similar. *Or something* suits the situation perfectly, as the passenger is unable to provide a more specific list of items that are similar to an arrest; even if such a list were possible, he might not think that Sarah wants to hear it. He assumes that Sarah has shared knowledge and can infer what the *or something* means, more or less, and that is good enough. General extenders such as *or something*, as Evison et al. (2007: 142) argue, 'capture the fluidity and instability of the diffuse complex, the preconceptual phase where the language user attempts to make meaning from diverse phenomena and experiences, and reaches out to his or her interlocutor in an appeal to equally diffuse and unstable shared experience'. The same explanation applies in 92:1:22: 'Is it written somewhere that you can't bring lasers or something?' where *or something* refers to a category of items similar to a laser. The use of *or something* implies that additional members of the categories 'arrest' and 'laser' are similar but not exact. According to Terraschke and Holmes (2007: 215), *or something* here could be an affective appeal from the passenger to Sarah for sympathy for his situation.

Sarah and the passenger use the strategy of just-right elastic to provide an appropriate level of non-specificity. In the particular context there is no need to be precise, and general meanings serve their goals well. Based on their shared knowledge, EL assures successful exchanges between speaker and hearer. For Sarah as an officer, her institutional objective is maintained, and for the passenger his uncertainties are properly conveyed by the use of EL.

6.2 Rapport elastic

EL is often used for interpersonal functions. Rapport elastic is for solidarity, informality, and friendliness between interactants, often used between friends or strangers. Existing literature mostly focuses on rapport between familiar friends (Channell 1994; Evison et al. 2007; Spencer-Oatey 2000; Terraschke and Holmes 2007), but EL is also used between strangers (officers and passengers) to establish some sort of trust in order to get things done. This finding supports the work of Adolphs et al. (2007: 75–6), where a nurse uses VL to establish an interpersonal relationship with her patient while meeting the intrusive institutional requirements of eliciting sensitive personal information.

This study is based on institutional data. Linell and Bredmar (1996: 368) consider that institutional encounters differ from daily contexts, the former being 'an environment created partially to make it possible to talk professionally about issues which are not naturally talked about in everyday life'. At the same time, they find that professionals, such as midwives, try to create an informal atmosphere that partially imitates an everyday-life type of conversational genre. In Fairclough's (1992: 205) terms, this is the 'conversationalisation' of institutional discourse. In this study there are situations where interactants (mostly officers) deliberately use EL to create an informal, less business-like atmosphere in a bid to achieve certain goals. EL is used to solicit collaboration, establish bonds, and maintain solidarity.

General extenders are typically seen as rapport builders between interlocutors (Cheng and Warren 2001; Crystal and Dave 1979; Terraschke and Holmes 2007). Aijmer (2013) finds that *and*-extenders (conjunctive, e.g. *and something like that*) tend to emphasise social in-group membership and closeness, while *or*-extenders (disjunctive, e.g. *or that sort of thing*) indicate tentativeness. As discussed in excerpt (6.2), *or something* marks a speaker's uncertainty. *Or*-extender is also a marker of social stratification in society (Dines 1980); *and that* is a 'non-standard form' of general extender (Channell 1994: 24).

Like general extenders, placeholders (e.g. 'I am going you-know-where next week') can also 'fulfil social goals, such as to invite collaboration or to establish a bond' (Jucker et al. 2003: 1751). General stretchers such as *stuff* and *that thing* can 'maintain an informal atmosphere in order to establish more camaraderie' between interactants (2003: 1750). Cutting (2000, 2001, 2002) finds that VL is used to assert in-group membership and show solidarity, as well as to exclude outsiders.

Shared knowledge and common ground are the basis of rapport building using VL (Handford 2010; Koester 2007; O'Keeffe 2004). The use of VL is viewed as 'a strong indication of an assumed shared knowledge' (Carter and McCarthy 2006: 202), or implicitly refers to shared knowledge (Koester 2007: 48), 'a kind of implicit communication whereby speakers indicate an assumption of shared experience and hence closeness or common ground' (Overstreet and Yule 1997b: 256). Particularly, VL operates 'at different levels of assumed shared knowledge: some knowledge can be assumed to be shared by all mature and aware human beings; other knowledge is more locally constrained and culture-bound' (Evison et al. 2007: 154). For example, academics in Australia would have little problem understanding 'He has been busy lately with ARC

132   Strategies of elastic language

applications *and things like that*', where ARC stands for the Australian Research Council. The speaker does not provide a complete category membership, probably believing that hearers can figure it out by themselves. Thus, certain vague expressions work among people who have similar backgrounds and VL is a marker of in-group membership based on shared knowledge of the issues in focus (Carter and McCarthy 2006; Cutting 2000; Evison et al. 2007). When a speaker uses vague expressions, the hearer is expected to construct cooperatively the relevant meaning (Jucker et al. 2003), even if the two are strangers.

(6.3)

Data: Episode 34, from turn 34:1:7 to 34:1:11, two speakers, over five speaking turns.
Context: Officer (male in his 50s) and officer Nick (male in his 50s) are discussing a case of a suspicious suitcase bound for Thailand.

34:1:7	NICK:	Do we know what time he checked in?
34:1:8	OFFICER:	That we can have access to, all that information, but I don't know at this stage.
34:1:9	NICK:	I just want to (pause) void his defence that he's checked in and someone's had his bag for two hours.
34:1:10	OFFICER:	Maybe I can confirm weights **and things like that** ... whether that confirms anything for you ...?
34:1:11	NICK:	Yeah.

A passenger has been taken off the plane and arrested for illegally exporting live reptiles. He denies the charge and insists there was nothing wrong with his bags when he checked in. In excerpt (6.3) Nick is talking to another officer about how best to handle the situation. In turn 34:1:7, to make sure that no excuses are left for the passenger, Nick wants to know the time the passenger checked in. His colleague replies that he does not know but can find out. Nick explains the reason he wants to know the time: to void a possible line of defence. His colleague replies, 'Maybe I can confirm weights and things like that ... whether that confirms anything for you ...?' He wonders if it will help to confirm weights and the like at check-in: if they are the same then as now, evidently the bags have not been tampered with. The colleague's tone is collegial and tentative, manifested by his use of elastic expressions such as *maybe* and *anything*.

The colleague uses the general extender *and things like that* to emphasise the social similarity and group membership of himself and Nick. It projects and marks shared knowledge (O'Keeffe 2003) to establish a bond to fulfil the institutional goals. The officer expects Nick to know what *and things like*

6.2 Rapport elastic

that implies. Evison et al. (2007: 139) state that the underpinning significance of Vygotsky's 'social space' is that 'speakers must have expectations about what their co-participants know, and that such expectations are negotiated within social space'; within a socially defined group, general extenders become a tool for creating shortcuts.

Expressions such as *and things like that* are used interactively to construct rapport, appealing to the understanding of the hearer (Terraschke and Holmes 2007: 214). The fact that the officer in 34:1:10 could have said more (instead of using the general extender) suggests that he does not want to provide extensive and detailed information; he may think that precise information is not what Nick wants to hear. Using a general extender is more effectively appeals to Nick's colleginality and support. Finally, the officer gets what he was hoping for: Nick says yes, so the rapport elastic has worked well in this case (as for the smuggler, he is found guilty and sentenced).

(6.4)

Data: Episode 29, from turn 29:3:77 to 29:3:86, two speakers, over 10 speaking turns.
Context: Officer Michael (male in his 40s) and passenger (New Zealander female in her 20s). Michael is questioning the passenger on drug issues.

29:3:77	MICHAEL:	I'm Michael, I'm the supervisor here today.
29:3:78	PASSENGER:	Hi.
29:3:79	MICHAEL:	As the officer's told you, we've got some readings on the ion scan machine. Um, like he would have said, we don't care whatever you use. It's not our concern, we don't worry about that. We only worry about **stuff** that you happen to be carrying today. And with the experience I've had here it would indicate that you've had something within the last few days.
29:3:80	PASSENGER:	Right. Well it's not true. Honestly, it's not true.
29:3:81	MICHAEL:	Yeah? You haven't used anything at all?
29:3:82	PASSENGER:	(shakes her head) No. Definitely no.
29:3:83	MICHAEL:	What sort of **stuff** have you been using? Like cocaine readings came up so you've used cocaine?
29:3:84	PASSENGER:	Yeah, that's it really.
29:3:85	MICHAEL:	Hash, marijuana, **stuff** like that? Smoking=
29:3:86	PASSENGER:	=Oh yes, I smoke a bit of weed. (laughs) But not in the last few days.

The passenger is a young model. In 29:3:79, officer Michael emphasises that they don't care about what drugs the passenger uses: what concerns them is if she is carrying any. He says 'we only worry about stuff that you happen to be carrying today', implicitly asking if she has any drugs on her today. The general stretcher *stuff* helps create a not-so-serious atmosphere here, and so does the padding word *happen*; these strategic moves aim to encourage the passenger to tell the truth. At the end of the turn, Michael uses *within the last few days*, where *few* is an approximate stretcher, indicating a fluid meaning of 'very recent'.

Michael's questions are met with a definitive denial from the passenger. Michael uses *stuff* again in 29:3:83: 'what sort of stuff have you been using?' (a new questioning tactic) to invite collaboration. This time he is asking 'what kind', backed by the evidence of cocaine reading. *Stuff* here indicates that Michael is trying to establish some rapport with the passenger to make his persuasion more acceptable. This strategy seems to work better: in the next turn the passenger admits that she has been using drugs. Michael is encouraged to push further in 29:2:85, asking 'hash, marijuana, stuff like that?' this move is slightly different from the previous uses of *stuff* (general stretcher), as *stuff like that* is a general extender. It is a tactical move to create an impression of informality and encourage the passenger to come clean. In the next turn, the passenger admits 'I smoke a bit of weed', where *a bit* is an approximate stretcher, indicating a small and unspecific quantity. (The passenger is not found to be carrying any drugs, so is let go.)

Excerpt (6.4) shows that Michael uses EL to create a less business-like atmosphere and secure an admission. EL is used to cloak institutional interrogation and invite cooperation from the passenger. This strategy attempts to present a sense of rapport, of 'common ground and familiarity' (Koester 2006: 91): the speaker suggests something like 'trust me, I know your stuff, so tell the truth'. Handford finds that general extenders function strategically to create an impression of convergence; in his data VL appears more in external meetings, where people do not know each other well, than in internal meetings (2010: 163–4). In a way the findings in these data concur with Handford's, suggesting that it is problematic to assume that rapport elastic occurs exclusively among familiar faces; it works among strangers (e.g. officer and passenger) as well as acquaintances.

Other stretchers build interpersonal relationships, like *I guess*, which can be used to sound more modest, as in the following:

We all had our difficulties and challenges, and the fact we all here and um you know, eh, have sort of I guess triumphed, and the greatest sporting um (pause) uh thing um you can possibly compete in our sport. It's very honouring and humbling thing. I, I think, you know, it makes me wanna to keep going. (Trickett 2012)

Libby Trickett is a gold medallist in the 2012 London Olympics, speaking at a press conference after her competition (the 4 × 100 metre relay). There are a number of stretchers (e.g. *sort of*, *I guess*, *I think*) and padding expressions (e.g. *you know*) in her speech, which function to appeal to the audience. For example, *I guess* here shows modesty and cannot be swapped with *I think*.

Rapport elastic performs an interpersonal pragmatic function, by implying a sense of sameness and group identity between speaker and colleagues, or speaker and strangers. The establishment of a bond serves to achieve institutional and other types of objective.

6.3 Mitigating elastic

VL mitigates by its nature (e.g. Aijmer 1997; Jucker et al. 2003; Prince et al. 1982; Trappes-Lomax 2007), and mitigating elastic is a typical strategy in EL. In this study, EL serving politeness is also part of mitigating elastic, because mitigation is often a means of being polite.

Vague expressions for mitigation are called downtoners or detensifiers (Hübler 1983), and diminishers (Biber et al. 2010). They are 'modifiers which are used by a speaker in order to modulate the impact his/her request is likely to have on the hearer' (Blum-Kulka et al. 1989: 284). These expressions usually indicate degree and apply to gradable expressions. In particular, they reduce scalar intensity, soften impact, mark probability (Ruzaitė 2007: 41), or minimise the weight of imposition (Trappes-Lomax 2007: 133). Adolphs et al. (2004: 20) find that lexical items encode vagueness prominently in the whole health professional corpus, and VL may 'serve as a deference strategy by softening the imposition on the caller and leaving room for elaboration or retraction from any particular question or suggestion'. The process of elaboration and retraction is similar to what is termed stretch work in this study, as participants elasticise to achieve communicative goals.

While most EL can mitigate, certain types of stretcher may do it more often than others. For example, quantifiers expressing a small quantity mitigate more frequently than those expressing a large quantity (Ruzaitė 2007: 213). General extenders can also perform downtoning: in 'so, you wanna get a hamburger or something?' *or something* gives the hearer some flexibility and does not impose; it mitigates 'the potential impact that an overtly direct utterance might have' (Quaglio 2009: 142). Typical mitigating expressions include *sort of, could be, possible/possibly, a bit, a little, a little bit, and something like that, slightly,* and *somewhat*.

A most loaded term is 'hedge', used in a diverse way in the literature. Often a hedge is treated as a synonym for VL, making a less intense tone or avoiding full commitment towards a claim (Brown and Levinson 1987; Hyland 1998b; Prince et al. 1982). The interchangeable use of the terms may not accurately reflect the whole dynamics of the notion of VL, because hedging is only one of many functions and VL has much more to offer (Ruzaitė 2007: 37–8). Hedges are a defined category (*sort of, kind of*), as opposed to intensifiers (*very, extremely*) (Bradac et al. 1995; Hyland 1998a, 2000). Stenström (1994) considers hedges to be approximators and Jucker et al. (2003: 1746) state that vague expressions 'introduce vagueness into a proposition or increase the degree of vagueness of an utterance'; downtoners are used when speakers find that an available word does not adequately cover the meaning they have in mind. For example in 'I sort of understand why he does that', *sort of* indicates that the speaker does not totally *understand*, but there is no word which can exactly convey what the speaker wants to say so *sort of* is used to reduce the 'standard' of *understand*.

Mitigating strategies effectively soften a negative impact, and are frequently used when the topic is sensitive or embarrassing. For example, this speaker is saying something unfavourable about another person: 'The fact is, anyone who believes prices always go up is, I think, a fool'.[1] While ANZ chairman David Gonski is warning of the risk of a correction to Australia's booming housing market, it seems that he does not want to be too blunt or offensive, and *I think* functions as a cushion to achieve that effect. Based on intercultural conversations, Terraschke and Holmes (2007: 215) find that it is possible to interpret general extenders as contributing effectively to the softening of a complaint or criticism. Drawing on chaplaincy data from hospitals, Adolphs et al. (2007: 74) find that when a chaplain talks to patients, VL is an important part of his/her sensitive, informal management of the interaction, 'helping to facilitate the patient's conversational involvement, while mitigating the force of directives' to supply personal information. They find that for medical personnel, VL is used as a 'softening device to tone down the alarming nature of possible medical diagnoses', demonstrating once more that EL serves to mitigate in real life.

One of the purposes of mitigating is for politeness and face, and VL is viewed as an effective device for achieving this. 'Politeness is one obvious reason for deviating from superficially clear or rational behaviour' (Stubbs 1986a: 1). Face is defined as 'the public self-image that every member wants to claim for himself' (Brown and Levinson 1978: 66). Positive face refers to people's desire to be appreciated by others, and negative face refers to an individual who does not want to be imposed upon. A 'face-threatening act' occurs in a situation when speech 'runs contrary to the face wants of the addressee and/or the speaker' (Brown and Levinson 1978: 70). 'Vagueness is used as one way of adhering to the politeness rules for a particular culture, and of not threatening face' (Channell 1994: 190). To avoid being blunt and impolite, VL is needed and desirable (Carter and McCarthy 2004). Trappes-Lomax (2007: 135) notes that VL 'attends to the face needs of the speaker'

---

[1] Gonski, http://www.smh.com.au/business, 3 September 2014.

6.3 Mitigating elastic

or serves 'other-protective face-work'. Speakers tend to look after their own as well as hearers' face, and VL can maintain face for both speaker and hearer.

VL appeals to hearer's face by acknowledging respect. Carter (1998) affirms that VL is always highly significant in terms of its pragmatic functions, in particular creating polite and non-threatening interactions. Brown and Levinson (1987) too state that vagueness is a face-preserving technique. In intercultural workplaces, Chefneux (2012) finds that VL serves for politeness and accountability (as in justifying tasks that are not completed).

The types of EL used for mitigation are wide-ranging. For example, *I think* is to 'reinforce the speaker's attempts to save face' (Ruzaitė 2007: 158), and fulfils the function of mitigating a face threat (Aijmer 1997; Handford 2010). *Stuff* and *thing* are used when the speaker does not wish to use a specific name or noun, to avoid being impolite, insulting or pretentious (Channell 1994: 162). *A bit* is 'principally interpersonal, functioning as a pragmatic device rather than as a semantic adjustment', and without it an utterance may be 'more emphatic, the illocutionary force significantly stronger'; *a bit* 'functions as a deference strategy', a marker to indicate that the speaker does not want to make any bold statements or intrude any privacy (Adolphs et al. 2007: 72–3). Quantifiers are also used as 'a politeness strategy to minimize face-threat' (Ruzaitė 2007: 183).

(6.5)

Data: Episode 44, from turn 44:2:2 to 44:2:7, two speakers, over six speaking turns.
Context: Officer Paul (male in his 40s) and passenger (Indian male in his 40s). Paul is questioning the passenger to find out if he intends to work illegally.

44:2:2 PAUL:	Okay. I might say at the start that I have some concerns with all this documentation that you have. It raises, in my mind, the issue that you (pause) **possibly**, you are working here in violation of your visa conditions.
44:2:3 PASSENGER:	No, sir. I am not working.
44:2:4 PAUL:	When we do your bag search ...
44:2:5 PASSENGER:	Yes.
44:2:6 PAUL:	We find out all this information which is not relating to looking after your niece. This is actually getting involved in a business area, isn't it?
44:2:7 PASSENGER:	No, she ... I am not getting involved in any business. I needed to look after the house, the dog, and the daughter.

Passengers who make multiple trips in and out of the country in order to renew their tourist visa may be working in Australia illegally. This passenger had previously been in Australia on a tourist visa for six months, and has now returned for an extended period. The passenger claims that he is here

138   Strategies of elastic language

to look after his niece, but she is a 24-year-old adult. Paul has discovered some documents in the passenger's bags that indicate that the passenger may intend to work illegally.

Paul's job is to find the truth from the passenger. In 44:2:2, Paul starts with a hedged tone: 'I <u>might</u> say at the start that I have <u>some</u> concerns with all this documentation that you have'. He uses *might* and *some* to make his concerns sound somewhat less authoritative to smooth the way for his next move: 'It raises, in my mind, the issue that you ... <u>possibly</u>, you are working here in violation of your visa conditions'. The epistemic stretcher *possibly* functions to reduce the force of Paul's confronting judgement, which will be unpleasant for the passenger to hear. EL, such as *possibly*, 'softens expressions so that they do not appear too direct or unduly authoritative and assertive' (Carter and McCarthy 2006: 202). Paul also pauses before *possibly*, indicating his hesitation and the need for some time to search for the right word to deliver his negative assessment to the passenger.

Mitigating strategy is considered a tension management device (Trappes-Lomax 2007), important 'in managing tensions and minimizing impositions' (Adolphs et al. 2007: 76). Paul's basic assertion (working illegally) is negative in tone, so EL is employed to soften its impact: the use of *possibly* changes the strength of Paul's claim. The purpose of using hedges is to veil the negative evaluation, making the passenger feel less threatened and more willing to admit his true intention. While the passenger may be aware that his welfare is at stake, Paul's request for the passenger to tell the truth has been softened by his use of EL.

In response to Paul's mitigated persuasion, the passenger replies in 44:2:3 with a direct denial. Paul's approach then becomes direct in the following turn 44:2:6. (Paul later is told by the niece that the passenger actually worked on a part-time basis during his previous stay in Australia on a tourist visa; his visa is cancelled and he departs for Malaysia later that day.)

(6.6)

Data: Episode 5, from turn 5:1:165 to 5:1:182, two speakers, over 18 speaking turns.

Context: Officer Satinder (male in his 50s) and officer Greg (male in his 50s) are talking about a New Zealand passenger.

5:1:165 SATINDER: Even though he meets the criteria for the grant of SCV (special category visa for New Zealanders, noted by author), his erm (pause) continuing (pause) behaviour in terms of criminality ... (pause)
5:1:166 GREG: Yes::=
5:1:167 SATINDER: =... and although he's here for a short stay (pause) that sort of ... sort of ...=

6.3 Mitigating elastic 139

(6.6) (cont.)

5:1:168 GREG:	=Yeah.=
5:1:169 SATINDER:	=... you know, **could be** that (pause) we're putting the Australian community at risk.
5:1:170 GREG:	As they're both deeply involved, she's married in New Zealand so they can't really spend (pause) a lot of time together.
5:1:171 SATINDER:	Mhm.
5:1:172 GREG:	So this is a chance for them to get away together, just to spend time (pause) with each other.=
5:1:173 SATINDER:	=So extramarital affair.=
5:1:174 GREG:	=Yeah ... well (pause) we're not the moral ...=
5:1:175 SATINDER:	= Kind of ... no. =
5:1:176 GREG:	=... we're not the moral police er ... yeah ...=
5:1:177 SATINDER:	=No but, that's what it appears to be. Okay.=
5:1:178 GREG:	=Yeah, and that's:: their business, not ours. But then again he did (pause) deliberately ... well I believe he deliberately ...=
5:1:179 SATINDER:	=Deliberately misled.=
5:1:180 GREG:	=... er misled us ...=
5:1:181 SATINDER:	=Yes.=
5:1:182 GREG:	=... in answering 'no' to criminal convictions.

In excerpt (6.6), a New Zealand man travelling with a female friend fails to declare criminal convictions on his passenger card, and officers believe he is hiding a crooked past. In turn 5:1:169, Satinder indicates that the passenger's criminal history might be a risk to Australians, in 'although he's here for a short stay that sort of ... sort of ... you know, could be that we're putting the Australian community at risk'. Satinder uses *could be* coupled with *sort of* (twice), to be polite to his colleague by sounding less imposingly expert (Aijmer 1984: 124). Before *could be*, the padding expression *you know* is used as a launching pad to eliciting Greg's involvement. *Could be* combined with *you know* gives Greg an opportunity to correct or demur. Satinder's move works: in turn 5:1:172 Greg joins in and steers the discussion in a new direction: whether officers should be moral police.

When Satinder points out that the two passengers are having an extramarital affair, Greg in 5:1:174 mentions gently that it is irrelevant: 'Yeah ... well (pause) we're not the moral ...' Greg agrees with Satinder at first, hesitates for a second, then uses the padding word *well* and a pause to gently introduce an indirect disagreement. Satinder replies with the hedge *sort of*, to insist on his opinion implicitly: *sort of* extramarital affair nevertheless. After Greg continues to explain 'we're not the moral police er ... yeah' in 5:1:176, Satinder replies 'No but, that's what it appears to be' in 5:1:177. Satinder agrees with Greg first, then uses *appear to be* to tactically reinforce his differing view. In 5:1:178, Greg reaffirms his view, then seems to want to move the conversation along by mentioning that the passenger misled on purpose. Greg says, 'But then again he did (pause) deliberately ... well I believe he deliberately ...' where *well I believe* emphasises that this is a subjective evaluation and appeals for Satinder's confirmation. Satinder agrees with Greg in this case that the passenger indeed misled them.

Excerpt (6.6) demonstrates that EL functions to maintain the self-esteem and face of the speaker and mitigate a potential breach of protocol by using terms like *could be* and *sort of*. The tactical use of hedges aims to qualify the assertiveness of what is said so that others may express different opinions without strongly opposing the speaker; it provides a degree of freedom (Brown and Levinson 1987). In the non-verbal activity in excerpt (6.6), the officers tend to pause when EL is introduced, as in 5:1:167, 5:1:169, and 5:1:170. They also often talk with latching between utterances, indicating that they are eager to contribute to the discussion. (The case ends with the passenger being allowed to enter Australia, because although he gave a false statement his offenses were all of a relatively minor nature.)

The maxim of 'go general' also serves the function of keeping face. A general term may be used for vanity: if John has obtained a PhD from Harvard or Yale University, he would have no hesitation in saying 'I have a PhD from Harvard/Yale'. However, if the degree came from an on-line 'buy-a-degree' site based in the States, he may say 'I have a PhD from the States'. He is not lying: the university is American, so 'technical' truth is involved here. The strategy of using a general term over a specific name is at play. The speaker is using elasticity to keep face or for vanity.

The data analysis in excerpts (6.5) and (6.6) illustrates that language contains many 'weak expressions' (Drew 1992: 503) that mitigate the impact of utterances, maintain face, and keep conversation moving smoothly (Brown and Levinson 1987), warding off face threats and avoiding embarrassment (Linell and Bredmar 1996: 366; Hamilton and Mineo 1998: 6) and acting as markers of politeness (Metsä-Ketelä 2006: 123). They can tone down or lower the force of a claim – but they can also tone up or increase it, which is discussed in the next section.

6.4 Intensifying elastic

Intensifying elastic increases the strength of a claim, and is exemplified by scalar words such as *very* and *a lot* (Preisler 1986; Zhang 2011). Quantifiers expressing a large quantity, such as *many, much, loads, tons of, a great deal of, a number of*, tend to emphasise (Ruzaitė 2007: 161). They can be used for persuading (Channell 1994), showing authority (Hinkel 2003), and

6.4 Intensifying elastic

strengthening the evaluation of utterances (Koester 2006). Hinkel (2003) finds that VL is used more often for assertiveness than mitigation. The assertive function of EL is, however, overlooked as it is not commonly perceived as an EL function.

(6.7)

Data: Episode 9, from turn 9:2:53 to 9:2:64, two speakers, over 12 speaking turns.
Context: Officer Paul (male in his 40s) and passenger (Thai male in his 40s). Paul is questioning the passenger about suspicious documents he carries.

9:2:53 PAUL:	Okay. So, from what you've told me . . .=
9:2:54 PASSENGER:	=Yeh.=
9:2:55 PAUL:	=. . . I find it **very** hard to believe that you've been on holiday for six months.
9:2:56 PASSENGER:	(pause) Yep.
9:2:57 PAUL:	Now where have you been working in that time?
9:2:58 PASSENGER:	Er:: . . . (pause) some picking fruit.
9:2:59 PAUL:	So you were not (pause) looking for business opportunities, were you? A couple of these notebooks have **a lot of** names and telephone numbers in them, and addresses. (pause) Who . . . who are they . . . wh-who are these people? (pause) Like for example . . .=
9:2:60 PASSENGER:	=Some . . . some fr-friends.
9:2:61 PAUL:	Yeah? Like what does . . . what does this entry refer to?
9:2:62 PASSENGER:	That one, I see the . . . (pause) I see some farm . . . (pause) oranges.
9:2:63 PAUL:	Yes. This is . . . this is a **much** bigger list than just looking at what equipment the farms have, (pause) because you've got accommodation showing here . . .
9:2:64 PASSENGER:	Yeah.

This is the third time the passenger in excerpt (6.7) has come to Australia, and he maintains that his visit is for a holiday which includes looking for business opportunities. The passenger's story does not add up, so Paul warns him that there are severe penalties if he does not tell the truth. In 9:2:55 Paul says, 'I find it very hard to believe that you've been on holiday for six months', where *very* is a scalar stretcher to boost the force of his assertion. By using *very*, Paul makes it abundantly clear that he does not believe what the passenger says. This push is tactically followed by a stern question: 'Now where have you been working in that time?' in 9:2:57. Paul's strategy elicits an admission from the passenger that he did some fruit-picking.

Paul seems to think that the passenger has come for much more disturbing reasons. To get to the bottom of it, in turn 9:2:59 Paul employs *a lot of* (scalar stretcher) to emphasise the large number of names, phone numbers and addresses in the passenger's notebooks, very odd for someone who claims to be a tourist. In responding, the passenger tries to minimise the number of people mentioned, using a general stretcher *some* in 'some ... some fr– friends'. Paul continues to challenge the passenger in 9:2:63 saying 'This is ... this is a much bigger list ...', where *much* is again used to highlight the considerable length of the list.

The boosters (*very, a lot of, much*) in excerpt (6.7) are all used by Paul as authority markers to persuade the passenger to tell the truth. With the help of intensifying elastic, Paul is able to intensify the tone of his challenge and put pressure on the passenger. The pursuit of truthfulness is an institutional goal for him, and EL is one of the tactics used. (The intensifying elastic seems effective. After hours of interviewing, Paul's strategies pay off and the passenger admits he is involved in an international operation organising employment for illegal workers.)

(6.8)

Data: Episode 1, from turn 1:1:49 to 1:1:83, two speakers, over 11 speaking turns.
Context: Officer Jim (male in his 50s–60s) and passenger (Canadian male in his 30s). Jim is persuading the passenger to permit a frisk search.

1:1:49 PASSENGER:	If you ... if you ... if you understood my ...=
1:1:50 JIM:	=We have ...=
1:1:51 PASSENGER:	=if you understood my ...=
1:1:52 JIM:	=Yeah, yeah, but that's only because=
1:1:53 PASSENGER:	=my ... my ground ... I'm **so** sure of myself.
...... (1:1:54 to 1:1:77 are omitted as less relevant)
1:1:78 JIM:	Okay. The ... the only other thing is, yeah ...
1:1:79 PASSENGER:	There could be traces on my shoes.
1:1:80 JIM:	Yeah, which is actually ... (pause) there's ... at this stage=
1:1:81 PASSENGER:	Yes.=
1:1:82 JIM:	=there's no removal of clothing. But if we go to the next stage, if you refuse a frisk=
1:1:83 PASSENGER:	=I'm **so** sure ... I'm **so** sure of myself, sir that ...

The passenger refuses a frisk search; he says that he is acting on principle. He is uncooperative and tries to convince Jim that there is no need to frisk him, arguing that it is not right to do the search as he is clean of drugs. The scalar stretcher *so* is used repeatedly by the passenger for emphasis, once in 1:1:53, twice in 1:1:83. The three uses strengthen the force of the argument that he should not be subjected to a search. Jim on the other hand persuades the passenger to do the search by trying to mitigate its impact: in 1:1:52 the use of *only* indicates a lesser degree of something, and in 1:1:82 Jim mentions there is no need to remove clothing, to decrease the degree of intrusiveness or to imply what will happen if he keeps refusing – full body search. However, the passenger seems adamant. (The emphatic assurance turns out to be a hyped show to hide the fact that the passenger has almost one kilo of cocaine in his groin, for which he is sentenced to seven and a half years in jail.)

Intensifying elastic can be employed in a wide variety of situations, functioning as it is an authoritative and institutional tool used by an official to find out the truth, at the same time as an individual tool to hide truth from authorities. Its intensifying strategy is elastic enough to serve opposing functions, and likely anything between as well.

6.5 Self-protection elastic

VL can serve self-protection by hedging a speaker's statement to safeguard his or her interests or avoid the risk of being blamed or criticised (Channell 1994). Trappes-Lomax (2007) asserts that VL is a means of self-protective avoidance in the process of tension management. Vague expressions serving self-protection are typically called 'shields', used for plausibility, expressing doubt and uncertainty (e.g. *I think*, *probably*, *seem to*) or presenting information attributed to someone else (e.g. *according to what he said*) (Prince et al. 1982).

VL functions to express the extent of the speaker's commitment to what he or she says. One of its main purposes is to reduce the vulnerability of a speaker's speech (Martinovski 2006: 2066). When a speaker can be exact but does not choose to do so, the implicature is that the 'speaker is being defensive' (Channell 1994: 188). Koester (2007: 45) finds that when discussing a sensitive topic, VL such as *thing* is used as 'a kind of shield' to avoid committing the speaker or saying something inappropriate. Hedges like *kind of*, *sort of* and *could* 'lessen the forcefulness of the utterances', distancing the speaker from delicate or 'dangerous' issues (Linell and Bredmar 1996: 372; Ruzaitė 2007: 159). Similarly, *might*, *possibly*, *likely*, *probably*, called 'deresponsibilizing mechanisms' by Brown (1980: 128), indicate that the speaker's commitment to the statement is less than complete (Rowland 2007: 82). Expressions like *to all intents and purposes*, *more or less*, *as far as I can see*, *in a way* weaken 'a speaker's commitment to some aspect of an assertion' (Cruse 2006: 79) and can be used for self-protection.

Another means of self-protection, as we have already seen, is using special general stretchers such as *we* (see Section 5.3.3 for details). The immigration officers tend to use *we* for self-protection, as illustrated in excerpt (5.10). The self-referring *we* aims to 'invoke an institutional over a personal identity' (Drew and Heritage 1992: 30), deployment of a universalistic approach (Peräkylä 1993: 305) or anonymisation (Linell and Bredmar 1996: 369–70). Officers use this when they do not wish to speak from a personal stance but as the official representative of Australian Customs.

144   Strategies of elastic language

(6.9)

Data: Episode 69, from turn 69:2:26 to 69:2:33, two speakers, over eight speaking turns.
Context: Officer Maurice (male in his 40s) and a passenger (male in his 30s, face pixellated). Maurice is questioning the passenger about some medication.

69:2:26 MAURICE:	Alka-Seltzers. All right, we won't worry about those. They're just for indigestion, yes?
69:2:27 PASSENGER:	I've got **a little bit** pain, because I don't know what happened. I get **a little bit** nervous.
69:2:28 MAURICE:	This one here you say is your medication. It is? What is it?
69:2:29 PASSENGER:	Actually it's heavy painkillers.
69:2:30 MAURICE:	A painkiller.
69:2:31 PASSENGER:	For the disc and the meniscus on my knee.
69:2:32 MAURICE:	You take this for the pain or the swelling?
69:2:33 PASSENGER:	Yes, for the pain.

The officers believe that a narcotics courier may have been on the passenger's flight. During the search, the passenger asks to take some painkillers, which arouses the officer's interest, as it is known that smugglers who ingest drugs often take painkillers to ease the resultant discomfort. In turn 69:2:26, Maurice asks if some medication is just for indigestion. The passenger does not answer the question directly; instead he talks about his pain: 'I've got a little bit pain, because I don't know what happened. I get a little bit nervous'. He attributes his pain and nervousness to the unknown and uncertain situation he is in. The repeated use of *a little bit* seems to do the job of self-protection. The passenger may not want to be seen as too much in pain or nervous, as that may cause more suspicion. He uses *a little bit* to lessen the degree of pain and nervousness and avoid unwanted attention. EL shields his statement from being interpreted precisely, taking advantage of the fact that that 'ordinary language leaves room for people to be vague, to avoid precision and the commitment associated with it' (Sinclair, in Channell 1994, xviii). (It turns out that the passenger is carrying heroin internally and is charged with drug smuggling.)

(6.10)

Data: Episode 54, from turn 54:1:131 to 54:1:135, two speakers, over five speaking turns.
Context: Officer Nick (male in his 30s) and passenger (Chinese male in his 30s). Nick is doing a routine baggage search.

54:1:131 NICK:	Would you like something to drink, sir? Can I get you a drink of water?

6.5 Self-protection elastic

(6.10) (*cont.*)

54:1:132 PASSENGER:	Water?
54:1:133 NICK:	Would you like a drink of water?
54:1:134 PASSENGER:	Yeah, please.
54:1:135 NICK:	Sure. (to camera) The passenger is getting quite aggravated for reasons I can't quite understand. He just **seems** to be, **sort of**, going off on strange tangents and it's just weird, **sort of**, behaviour. He **may** have something to hide or **maybe** he's just genuinely upset and **maybe** he's tired. There's lots of factors that could influence people's behaviour. So **maybe** it's something very innocent, **maybe** there's something underneath that. It's hard to say.

Officer Nick is puzzled by the passenger's odd behaviour. In 54:1:135, he makes it clear at the start that he does not understand why the passenger is aggravated. He uses an array of EL to explain his assessment of the situation in a cautious and self-protective way: *sort of, may, maybe*. He comments that the passenger *seems* to be ..., *sort of* going off ..., *sort of* weird ... and explores what may trigger such responses: (1) *may* have something to hide, (2) *maybe* genuinely upset, (3) *maybe* tired. Nick says it's *maybe* very innocent, or *maybe* something underneath. He finishes by saying 'It's hard to say' to indicate his uncertainty and unwillingness to commit to any specific diagnosis.

The word *maybe* in excerpt (6.10) is a typical shield which 'can successfully convey a speaker's lack of full commitment to a proposition under consideration' (Rowland 2007: 87). Nick uses it, together with other elastic expressions, to indicate that he is not sure why the passenger does what he does. As an officer, Nick needs to deal with the passenger's aggravated behaviour and find out why the passenger acts strangely. It seems that VL in this case 'adds a degree of tentativeness' while still performing its institutional duties (Adolphs et al. 2007: 74). Nick may not want to be seen as falsely confident. He adheres to Grice's qualitative maxim: only say something one believes to be true. (It turns out that one of Nick's guesses is correct: the passenger has hidden his criminal convictions and consequently is refused entry into Australia.)

When speakers use EL for self-protection they do not necessarily want the world to know. Channell (1994: 20) confirms that language is purposefully and unabashedly vague; at the same time Trappes-Lomax (2007: 123) argues that 'disguising a vague intent may be, in itself, a self-protective device', which he calls 'abashedly vague' or 'vaguely vague'. In fact, EL can be both unabashedly and abashedly fluid depending on context, and speakers may or may not want to let hearers know their true intent in using EL.

6.6 Evasive elastic

VL is called equivocation (Eisenberg 1998), where the speaker, or both the speaker and the listener, do not speak overtly but use veiled language (Channell 1994). EL is used to withhold information and deflect questions, a type of strategy called evasive elastic, in which the speaker adopts a competitive approach and shows little cooperation. Evasive use of language often occurs in adversarial discourse, as when an officer and passenger are in an investigator–defender relationship. In the process of defending themselves, passengers characteristically employ evasive behaviours, especially if they are in a dire situation and fear their freedom is at stake. Evasive elastic is adopted by passengers as a tool for conflict management, to reduce the danger faced.

Two useful notions to consider are positive and negative communication goals. The former refers to things the speaker wants to achieve in communication, the latter to things the speaker want to avoid (Trappes-Lomax 2007: 118). Evasive elastic aligns with negative goals. Cruse (2006: 171) talks about the different strengths of implicature with the following example: 'A: Who was driving? B: Some old woman' (compare 'an old lady'), where B's reply carries a number of weakish implicatures involving sexist and ageist prejudices that he could probably deny if challenged'. In other words, B is manipulating evasive elastic to avoid being caught. Janney (2002: 462) does not think that people talking vaguely is 'loose talk' (Sperber and Wilson 1985/86, 1995 [1986]), as they can be very careful and calculating in using VL, carefully constructing a story that will convince the hearer. This raises the issue of appropriate stretching of EL (e.g. mitigation, politeness) and inappropriate or overstretching (e.g. evasion; see Section 9.5 for more discussion).

A distinctive feature of evasive elastic is to make use of hidden meanings of language when the speaker does not want the hearer to know his/her true intent. EL is a means to avoid having to be totally truthful. The strategy consists of a continuum: at best hiding or withholding information; at worst deliberately deceiving. The scale represents the degree of evasiveness: the amount by which EL is exploited to serve inappropriate purposes.

Conflict arises when one wishes to tell neither the truth nor a lie. In this situation, VL can be used intentionally to manage the conflict (Bavelas, Black, Chovil and Mullett 1990: 54–63). Tension can also be created when interlocutors have conflicting communicative goals. Trappes-Lomax's (2007: 120–2) model of 'approach–avoidance' conflict describes a situation in which a single goal has both positive and negative qualities. The area of 'avoidance' is occupied when the negative motivation (what is feared by the speaker) totally outweighs the positive (what is wished for); otherwise the area of 'approach' is occupied. Tension occurs when the motivation sits somewhere between negative and positive. In such an 'approach–avoidance' situation, VL may be employed to manage the conflict: so customs officers and most passengers are highly motivated to 'approach', but some passengers opt for 'avoidance' or 'approach–avoidance'.

Evasiveness in communication is more widespread than we might expect. Based on British courtroom data, Cotterill (2007: 107) finds that the inconsistency of witnesses in court suggests they are 'being evasive' and are 'at best unreliable and at worst deceptive' when they use VL to answer questions. Similarly, in Chinese the general word *guowai* (overseas, abroad) can be used quite loosely. For example, if someone has heard of some research finding but does not know it for sure, s/he may speak evasively by using the general expression *guowai yanjiu biaoming* ... (overseas research shows ...) to avoid clarifying the exact source of the assertion.

Lawyers also are 'on occasion responsible for producing unclear, ambiguous and vague questions which are often mirrored in the responses produced by witnesses. There is also the potential element of deliberate obfuscation on the part of the lawyer' (Cotterill 2007: 103). She lists six reasons witnesses produce vague responses, not all of which are intentional, but adds that in forensic contexts, such as courtrooms and police interviews, 'the possibility of deliberate deception is relatively high compared to most other settings' (2007: 104).

Some seemingly evasive cases may not necessarily be intentional. O'Keeffe (2003: 9) argues that 'without access to the speakers for personal reflection' they are innocent (providing 'sincere responses') until proven guilty of deception. Cotterill (2007: 112–13) also points out that for vulnerable people such as children, the disabled and non-native speakers, 'vagueness may be a necessary linguistic resource which forms a part of their linguistic repertoire, and does not necessarily indicate a deliberate avoidance of detail'. As there are non-native speakers in this study, careful attention has been taken in the data analysis, and both contextual and linguistic evidence are used for clues to any possible evasion. The information about each interviewed passenger's guilt or innocence helps to determine if answers are evasive/deceptive.

While EL is typically used to carry out evasive elastic, other types of expression can perform the same strategy. For example, someone may prefer to say that he or she comes from North America rather than Canada, because he or she thinks that the United States is better than Canada. Someone is unlikely to be a CEO if he or she introduces himself/herself or is introduced as a senior manager. These general terms are used in an evasive way. On the discursive level, evading can be developed over sequential moves (Janney 2002: 461), as is shown in the following excerpt (6.11) from the O. J. Simpson case:

148   Strategies of elastic language

(6.11)

P: I'm asking you about what you did ...
S: **I feel** responsible for **every** injury she had.
. . . . . .
P: Now, when you were waiting, you called Kato Kaelin on the telephone, did you not?
S: I don't know. I was trying to call **everybody**.
P: Well, you tried reaching Mr Kaelin, right?
S: Yes. I tried calling **everybody**. I called **everybody**.

(quoted from Janney 2002: 464)
(P, Daniel Petrocelli, plaintiffs' attorney; S, Simpson)

Excerpt (6.11) shows that Simpson manipulates specific and general expressions to deflect the questions. When the attorney asks a specific question, Simpson evades it by using general terms: *I feel, every, everybody*. Technically these are not vague terms, but in context they become unspecific and Simpson himself is removed from the context. Employing evasive elastic, Simpson minimises his own part in the tragedy. For example, when asked what he did to his wife, Simpson does not answer directly, but uses *I feel* (not *I did*): 'I feel responsible for every injury she had.' His reply is too general to answer the question of what he did or did not do, merely indicating a moral responsibility and avoiding saying what he physically did. Similarly, when asked if he made a phone call to Kato Kaelin, Simpson evades by saying he called *everybody*, to avoid giving a straightforward answer. Simpson's answers are evasive and inadequate when a specific question is put to him. The sequence that emerges is *specific question > general answer*: an example of evasiveness at sequential level where no particular word is vague but the whole utterance is unspecific. Excerpts (6.12) and (6.13) below illustrate evasive strategies at work.

(6.12)

Data: Episode 18, from turn 18:1:75 to 18:1:89, two speakers, over 15 speaking turns.
Context: Officer John (male in his 40s) and passenger (Malaysian male in his 40s). John is finding out if the passenger is a genuine tourist.

18:1:75 JOHN: So this is packing for ... for five nights?
18:1:76 PASSENGER: I ... I just ...=
18:1:77 JOHN: =And you're going to Phillip Island and Sovereign Hill?
18:1:78 PASSENGER: Er Sovereign Hill mhm.
18:1:79 JOHN: And you're going to fly to Syd-...=
18:1:80 PASSENGER: =**Maybe** ...=

6.6 Evasive elastic

(6.12) (cont.)

18:1:81 JOHN:	=... to Queensland and the Gold Coast?
18:1:82 PASSENGER:	Yeah, **maybe**. **Maybe** ... **maybe** I ... I never ... I never ...=
18:1:83 JOHN:	=And you've got $2,000 ... (pause)
18:1:84 PASSENGER:	(nods) Mhm.
18:1:85 JOHN:	... at the most, (pause) to do all that.
18:1:86 PASSENGER:	But I ... **I don't know** how much the air ticket, er from ... from Melbourne to Queensland. **I don't know** how much the air ticket.
18:1:87 JOHN:	Oh ... it all seems very rehearsed to me. Very rehearsed.
18:1:88 PASSENGER:	But I'm telling the truth.
18:1:89 JOHN:	You don't ... you don't seem like a normal tourist to me.

At Melbourne airport, John is risk-assessing a passenger who claims to be a tourist. John believes that the passenger is not telling the truth about why he is here. The passenger does not seem to be prepared for his holiday in terms of packing and finance. To begin, John asks if the packing is for five nights, and the passenger ducks the question. In 18:1:79 John asks if he plans to fly to Sydney; the passenger says *maybe*. John asks if he is going to Queensland and the Gold Coast. The passenger answers: 'Yeah, maybe. Maybe ... maybe I ... I never ... I never ...' in 18:1:82. These *maybe*s suggest that the passenger is trying to hide the fact that he does not have much idea where he is going. John expresses doubts about visiting all these places with at most $2,000, and the passenger responds with 'I don't know', suggesting that he has not done much homework for his 'tour'. In 18:1:87, John expresses his suspicion of the true intention of the passenger; the passenger asserts that he is telling the truth, but John disagrees.

John's communicative/institutional goal is to find the truth about the passenger; in contrast the passenger's goal is to hide his true intention. To accomplish this, the passenger resorts to 'avoidance' (e.g. *maybe* and 'I don't know'). Facing the risk of being refused entry if he is not a genuine tourist, the passenger uses evasive elastic to avoid being exposed. (John's suspicion turns out to be true: the passenger is not a genuine tourist and is here in search of work, so is refused entry.)

(6.13)

Data: Episode 65, from turn 65:3:9 to 65:3:32, three speakers, over 24 speaking turns.
Context: Officer Kathleen (female in her 20s), officer Leigh (male in his 30s) and passenger Michael (Australian male in his 20s). Kathleen is questioning the cash amount brought in by Michael.

65:3:9 KATHLEEN:	You've been in Singapore for the last three years?
65:3:10 MICHAEL:	Yes.

(6.13) (cont.)

65:3:11	KATHLEEN:	Okay, that's fine. Anything else?
65:3:12	MICHAEL:	Oh, yeah, I did notice this. Sorry, I've got **lots of** yen in my pocket; is that okay?
65:3:13	KATHLEEN:	How much?
65:3:14	MICHAEL:	Like **a bit** over three million.
65:3:15	KATHLEEN:	Okay, so you have cash?
65:3:16	MICHAEL:	I do have cash, in my pocket ...
65:3:17	KATHLEEN:	Right.
65:3:18	MICHAEL:	... but in yen.
65:3:19	KATHLEEN:	That's all right, it's still ... it's equivalent, you know yourself, you just read it?
65:3:20	MICHAEL:	Yes, but I just didn't understand it, so I think it's more than that, so **maybe** that one would be a yes.
65:3:21	KATHLEEN:	All right, so **approximately** ... three ...?
65:3:22	MICHAEL:	Three million.
65:3:23	KATHLEEN:	Three million yen. All right, Hendo, can you find out the conversion of three million yen? He thinks that he's over ten grand, so ...
65:3:24	KATHLEEN:	All right, have you got your airline ticket there as well?
65:3:25	MICHAEL:	Yes.
65:3:26	LEIGH:	38,000.
65:3:27	KATHLEEN:	What?
65:3:28	LEIGH:	Does that sound right? Is it 78 ... the exchange rate 78.88?
65:3:29	MICHAEL:	Yes.
65:3:30	LEIGH:	38,000.
65:3:31	MICHAEL:	(shrugs) (indecipherable) Three years of savings.
65:3:32	KATHLEEN:	You said it was **just over** 10,000? (Michael looks down – dejected)

Michael has spent three years teaching English overseas and brought back more than $10,000 cash. People are required to declare cash of more than $10,000; failure to do so runs the risk of being fined, losing the money or even going to jail. Michael didn't declare his cash on the entry card. In 65:3:12, he mentions that he has *lots of* yen, where *lots of* is a stretcher indicating that the amount is more than most people carry. Kathleen asks for a specific amount and Michael answers 'Like *a bit* over three million', employing the approximate stretcher *a bit*. When asked about the cash declaration card, Michael in 63:2:20 uses the epistemic stretcher *maybe* to make a veiled admission that he made a mistake by ticking 'no' on the card. In 65:3:21, Kathleen confirms with Michael the amount of the cash using *approximately three* (million), suggesting that her expression is interchangeable with Michael's previous description of *like a bit over three million* in turn

65:3:14. It appears that at this stage Kathleen does not mind working with an approximation; a precise number is not important yet.

As the questioning progresses, it turns out that Michael has almost four times the limit of $10,000. At this point, Kathleen confronts Michael for not being straight about the cash amount, because there is a huge gap between $10,000 and $38,000. (In the end he is given a warning but is allowed to keep all his hard-earned cash.)

There are degrees of acceptance of evasiveness. There is a clear mismatch between Kathleen's expectation and $38,000. Understandably Kathleen is not happy about the unacceptable evasiveness. This is shown by Michael's body language as well: he looks down and appears dejected in turn 65:3:32.

The findings in this study show that evasiveness may be motivated by fear, misunderstanding, or even deception. EL can evade, implying a speaker's competitive attitude, and is most commonly found in adversarial discourse.

6.7 Strategic functions of elastic language as a manifestation of elasticity

As demonstrated in this chapter, of the six EL strategies, just-right elastic, rapport elastic and mitigation elastic tend to be cooperative, intensifying elastic and self-protection elastic may go either way, and evasive elastic is typical of a lack of cooperation. Existing literature tends to discuss these pragmatic functions in isolation, but this section looks at them collectively.

The six functions have different prototypical focuses, but are also interconnected. My other work (Zhang 2014) looks exclusively at the pragmatic functions of *I think*, and concludes that the five functions of *I think* are not always discrete but overlap, manifesting the elasticity of *I think*. The overlapping features also occur in this study: the interconnection of EL strategies involves two phenomena: the intertwining between stretchers and their pragmatic functions, and multifunctional EL.

6.7.1 Intertwining between stretchers and their functions

The findings indicate several correlation tendencies between the four categories of stretcher and six EL strategies, shown in Table 6.1.

Table 6.1 shows that six out of six strategy categories have no one-to-one match with types of stretcher, and four out of six can be realised by all four types of stretcher; thus, the relationship between stretchers and strategies is dynamic. While there is no systematic correlation between stretchers and strategies, there are some typical correlations. For example, *very* in the data is

Table 6.1 *Stretchers and strategies of EL*

EL strategies	Typical stretchers used
Just-right elastic	all four types of stretcher
Rapport elastic	all four types of stretcher
Mitigating elastic	general stretcher, epistemic stretcher, approximate stretcher (small-amount quantifiers)
Intensifying elastic	intensifier, approximate stretcher (big-amount quantifiers)
Self-protection elastic	all four types of stretcher
Evasive elastic	all four types of stretcher

used primarily for intensifying elastic. When participants need to mitigate, they tend to go for general stretchers, epistemic stretchers, and approximate stretchers (small-amount quantifiers). Ruzaitė (2007: 161–2) observes 'an evident correlation between the type of a quantifier and its functions'. For example, the emphasising function tends to be realised by multal (big-amount) quantifiers (e.g. *many, much, loads*), usually quantifying generic lexemes (e.g. *many people*). The mitigating function, on the other hand, often involves paucal (small-amount) quantifiers (e.g. *a little, a bit*), such as *some stuff*. The data in this study show that the function of quantifiers may change depending on the preceding modifiers: *quite a few* is emphatic, whereas *just a few* is mainly used as a mitigator; *not many problems* is mitigating, but *many problems* is emphatic.

6.7.2 Multifunctional elastic language

Word meaning can be drawn from the functions it serves. In this study, at a local level a stretcher may be multifunctional, while at the same time a strategic function may be carried out by more than one stretcher. At the global level, functions are interconnected and overlapping; an assumption that functions are discrete and clear-cut is not supported. Each of the six strategies can be realised by different stretchers and there is no fixed relationship between the two sets, as shown in Table 6.2.

Table 6.2 shows that no strategy is always realised by one stretcher exclusively, and one stretcher can perform more than one pragmatic function. Rowland (2007: 93) finds that *about* is used as a device of 'propositional attitude', 'in particular, to serve shield-like ends'. Rowland argues that *about* is used more as a 'shield' than a 'rounder' in the sense of Prince et al. (1982). In this study, *about* is often used as just-right elastic, as shown in excerpt (5.1), in that the speaker appears to think that there is no need to provide a precise number.

6.7 Strategic functions of elastic language 153

Table 6.2 *Realisation of EL strategies*

VL strategies	Stretchers
Just-right elastic	e.g. *a bit* in (6.1), *anything, something, or something, somewhere* in (6.2)
Rapport elastic	e.g. *things like that* in (6.3), *stuff* in (6.4)
Mitigating elastic	e.g. *possibly* in (6.5), *could be* in (6.6)
Intensifying elastic	e.g. *very, a lot of, much* in (6.7), *so* in (6.8)
Self-protection elastic	e.g. *a little bit* in (6.9), *seem, sort of, may, maybe* in (6.10)
Evasive elastic	e.g. *maybe* in (6.12), *lots of, a bit, maybe, approximately* in (6.13)

Table 6.2 lists *a bit* serving as just-right elastic in excerpt (6.1), but evasive elastic in excerpt (6.13); *a little bit* acts as self-protection elastic in excerpt (6.9). The epidemic stretcher *maybe* serves self-protection in excerpt (6.10), but evasive elastic in excerpt (6.12). In addition, *a lot of* performs as intensifying elastic in excerpt (6.7), and *lots of* acts as evasive elastic in excerpt (6.13). The two functions (intensifying and evasive) realised by *a lot of/lots of* are opposing in nature, indicating that the roles a stretcher may play are multiple, depending on context. This is in line with the work of Holmes (1990), where VL such as *I think* and tag questions can act as hedges as well as boosters.

While one stretcher can realise more than one function in different situations, stretchers can also perform more than one function in the same situation: that is, one stretcher can be multifunctional simultaneously. For example, *maybe, I don't know* in excerpt (6.12) and *lots of, a bit, maybe* in excerpt (6.13) realise evasive elastic, where passengers use EL to hide their true intentions. Meanwhile, these items can also be viewed as self-protection elastic, because the reason the passengers evade is to shield them from being exposed and punished.[2] There is no categorical one-to-one relationship between stretchers and strategies, particularly as one stretcher can realise more than one function in different situations as well as in the same situation. The functions are complementary, and co-exist. These phenomena are manifestations of elasticity, which is non-linear in nature. Most stretchers are highly multifunctional.

Officers use EL to mitigate while pushing to fulfil their institutional duties (see excerpt 6.5). These things may seem contradictory, but in fact the mitigating strategy is a device by which to carry out their duties. This kind of phenomenon is also apparent in Adolphs et al., who note that the term *or anything* 'leaves room for a patient to add their own description of the situation' (2004: 19). VL is seen as performing two apparently conflicting

---

[2] However, self-protection and evasive strategies are not the same, as participants can do self-protection without being evasive, or can be evasive but not for the purpose of self-protection.

154   Strategies of elastic language

needs: to act as a marker of politeness and minimise imposition on a patient; and to elicit a fuller description of the patient's symptoms as a necessary requirement to make a diagnosis (2004: 64). The first is a means by which to achieve the second; the two in fact complement each other. The implication is that linguistic categories do not have to be all-or-none. A common practice has been to put a 'problematic case' in a 'not classifiable' category, working on an assumption that categories are clear-cut, so anything that does not fit is ignored. However, there is an alternative view of linguistic categories: they are elastic and multi-faceted. As Ruzaitė notes, 'I do not attempt to specify these functions categorically or precisely. It is a difficult and challenging task to determine what function a quantifier performs in a specific utterance without knowing the real intentions of the speaker. Besides, vague language categories usually perform more than one function in the same utterance' (2007: 53).

This does not mean that EL functions cannot be categorised. As Ruzaitė states, with the help of various clues (context, broader context, situational cues, knowledge of the research), linguistic categorising can be accomplished, but the categories remain interconnected as they have different focuses and overlapping boundaries.

6.8   Summary

This chapter discusses the strategic functions of EL, one of the three principles of elasticity theory. The data show six categories of EL at work: just-right elastic, rapport elastic, mitigating elastic, intensifying elastic, self-protection elastic, and evasive elastic, where 'elastic' is a metaphor depicting EL as stretchable and flexible to meet the needs of communication. The six elastics are analysed in relation to 12 excerpts and relevant contextual clues. It is problematic to treat the categories as categorical, for they are interconnected and overlapping.

The analysis of excerpts (6.1), *a bit*, and (6.2), *anything, something, or something, somewhere*, show that just-right elastic expresses uncertainty and tentativeness when certainty is not feasible or when precision is not important. EL, used under duress or voluntarily to provide the right amount of information, is 'just-right' elastic. Approximate stretchers are typically picked for just-right elastic terms, as approximation is often good enough in the context.

Rapport elastic is illustrated in excerpt (6.3), *things like that*, and excerpt (6.4), *stuff*, as a strategy for solidarity, informality, and friendliness between interactants. It is applied between friends as well as strangers. General extenders, such as *things like that*, typically realise rapport elastic. They mark group membership based on shared knowledge at different levels (e.g. specialised subjects, local and regional knowledge, and common knowledge). Rapport

6.8 Summary

elastic makes an appeal for closeness and intimacy by establishing sameness and group identity between speaker and colleagues/strangers.

Mitigating elastic involves downtoning and politeness, typically realised by softeners and exemplified by *sort of*, *possible*, *a bit*, *a little*, *and something like that*. Data in excerpt (6.5), *possibly*, and excerpt (6.6), *could be*, reveal that softeners often occur in discourse that is negative, sensitive, or embarrassing in nature. Speakers tended to use the mitigating strategy to maintain face and convey politeness. EL is able to ward off face threats and tone down or lower the force of a negative utterance.

Intensifying elastic has an effect opposite to mitigating elastic in that it increases the strength of a claim. This move is typically realised by the use of scalar words such as *very* and *a lot*, called boosters or intensifiers. Data analysis in excerpt (6.7), *very*, *a lot of*, *much*, and excerpt (6.8), *so*, shows that speakers use intensifying strategies to persuade the hearer to tell the truth. When they hear an intensified tone of speech, the hearer sometimes is compelled to do what is requested by the speaker. At the same time, an emphatic tone may be used as a red herring. The intensifying strategy is versatile: for example, it may represent an authoritative and institutional marker for officers to find out the truth, or a trick by passengers to hide the truth from the authorities.

Self-protection elastic hedges a speaker's statements to safeguard his or her interests. The linguistic realisation of this strategy can be in any type of stretcher, but most typical is the shield: for example, *I think*, *probably*, and *seem to*. The data in excerpt (6.9), *a little bit*, and excerpt (6.10), *seems*, *sort of*, *may*, *maybe*, reveal that EL can reduce the vulnerability of a speaker and prevent the saying of something inappropriate. EL is used to shield a speaker from being understood precisely, and so may convey a sense that the speaker lacks full commitment. Speakers sometimes are not keen to let others know their intention, to protect themselves.

Evasive elastic indicates an attitude of uncooperativeness, used to withhold information and deflect questions. Data in excerpt (6.12), *maybe*, and excerpt (6.13), *lots of*, *maybe*, *a bit*, show that EL is used to serve negative communication goals (things speakers want to avoid). Speakers are reluctant to tell the whole truth, or may even be deceptive by overstretching EL. When evasive moves occur, the hearer tends either to accept them when they don't interfere with communication, or to reject them if they became obstructive.

Elasticity manifests at local and global levels. At a local level, each function has its own individual focus, but none has categorical boundaries: hence local elasticity. The six functions are different strategies which are interconnected and overlapping: hence global elasticity. Despite some correlation tendencies between the four categories of stretcher and six EL strategies, no systematic correlation can be established. One stretcher may perform more than one function, and one function may be realised by more than one type of stretcher. Stretchers can perform more than one function in one situation as well: they are simultaneously multifunctional. The non-linear, fluid behaviour of EL demonstrates the manifestation of its elasticity. The implication is that linguistic categories do not have to be all-or-none; they can be elastic and multi-faceted.

7 Elastic language, power and gender

While EL is a linguistic phenomenon, social functions affect its use (Cutting 1998) and 'the elasticity of VL is culturally and socially specified and adapted, because the interpretation of VL is socially and culturally co-constructed' (Zhang 2011: 579). The use of EL interacts with social factors such as power status and gender. The intersection of the social impact and the manipulation of EL are shown in the ways interlocutors negotiate their linguistic moves. Social factors play an important part in communication (e.g. Scollon and Scollon 1995); for instance, both children and adults opt to make indirect requests to people with high power status (Blum-Kulka et al. 1989). The impact of social factors on the use of EL is another manifestation of the elasticity of language.

This chapter discusses the influence of power status and gender on EL by considering the frequency distribution of stretchers and providing relevant excerpt analysis combining quantitative and qualitative approaches. This is because overall distribution does not always tell the whole story, and excerpt analysis can offer details of how EL is actually used.

Frequency is determined based on the four types of stretcher: scalar (boosters: *very, quite, too, so*), epistemic (hedges: *probably, possibly, could be, maybe*), approximate (*about*) and general (*something*). Ten stretchers are selected for close study, based on two criteria: firstly, they are among the 20 most frequent, so are representative; and secondly, their pragmatic functions are relatively clear, and minimally problematic in categorisation. Boosters and hedges, which serve opposing pragmatic functions (Du Bois 1987; Quirk et al. 1985), are often markers of a speaker's stance and attitude. The former indicates assertiveness by emphasising and strengthening, and the latter indicates tentativeness by weakening and mitigating. When more boosters are used by a group, say, of customs officials, that group may be deliberately opting for an assertive attitude. If another group, say passengers, seems to prefer hedges, then they are taking a less assertive stance, as hedges are indexical of less authority and non-committal (Rowland 2007: 89–90). A group that uses few hedges will appear more authoritative or committed to what they say.

In addition to boosters and hedges, *about* and *something* are chosen for analysis. The first is a typical example of an approximate stretcher, and the second of a general stretcher. For example, we may say 'Sorry, I'm in the middle of *something*' when we want to tell the salesman on the phone that we have to go; *something* is unspecific but appropriate and effective. The analysis reveals how different groups use these two key words in making approximations or general utterances. The analysis of four boosters, four hedges, and *about* and *something*, is adequate to show variations in the social factor patterns in question.

7.1 Power

Power refers to the ability to influence others and to minimise risks to one's interests: that is, the ability to sanction others without having one's own interests challenged. Hutchby and Wooffitt (1998: 170) define power as the 'structurally provided ability to constrain the actions of others'. The officers in this study represent authority and have institutional power over passengers; professionally or personally they have little to lose. That cannot be said of the passengers, who are expected to do what officers request and have everything to lose if found guilty of something. There is a power asymmetry, with the officers having more power than the passengers. Officers and passengers are strangers and out-groups, although among the officers there are acquaintances and in-groups with the same institutional goals. The management of power is a balancing act, and is not necessarily static: while the officers appear to have more power than the passengers, this can be adjusted or reclaimed in some situations.

As there is a power imbalance, there is also speech asymmetry, demonstrated first in the fact that the officers ask questions and the passengers are expected to answer. Such a one-directional situation can be considered an 'asymmetrical speech event' (Shuy 2014: 10). Two concepts, discursive imbalance and power imbalance, are manifested in this. Discursive imbalance occurs when 'one speaker always has a dominant role in controlling the discourse'; and power imbalance refers to 'encounters between people of unequal status' (e.g. manager–subordinate, customer–supplier) (Koester 2007: 53). In the exchanges between officers and passengers, both discursive imbalance and power imbalance exist, both in favour of the officers. For instance, the officers speak much more than the passengers: of the quarter of a million words in the corpus, four-fifths are spoken by officers and only one-fifth by passengers.

VL is 'tightly related to the situations where power relationships manifest themselves' (Ruzaitė 2007: 48), and it reflects the more powerful position of the speaker (Koester 2007: 50). Rowland (2007: 94) observes that the power relationships between participants are part of context. In his school classroom data, 'the child is obliged to conform to the expectations and demands of the teacher/interviewer. VL is one way he or she can redress the power imbalance while observing the social norms that constrain their actions and responses', and is one of the devices speakers can use to tailor their contributions (Channell 1994).

Cotterill (2007: 103–4) finds a power asymmetry in the courtroom where the defendant is expected to be responsive and cooperative. Examples provided by Channell (1994: 190) suggest that when students (with lower power status) talk to tutors, they tend to show deference by using VL (e.g. *sort of*). Carter (2013: 41) notes that occupying the relatively powerless role of a suspect 'makes disagreeing with an officer, avoiding answering questions, and other interactionally disapproved acts ... more difficult'. In the institutional data of this study, the passenger is expected to be truthful and cooperative. In such contexts, while a general power asymmetry may be assumed, the specific and eventually established power positions need to be observed from actual evidence; it is problematic to automatically assume any fixed, default position for passenger and officer (similar positions include student and tutor, suspect and policeman). The power balance is dynamic; one party may opt out of their expected position, and power plays are manifested in the use of EL.

The Australian Customs officers tend to initiate conversation with a passenger, often from a dominant position. Their professional duty is to elicit potentially lethal and freedom-threatening disclosures from passengers suspected of some wrongdoing, and often they are met with resistance or even hostility from someone facing the possibility of being fined or imprisoned. The conflict between the parties necessarily produces tension. To manage the tension and determine the truth, the officers use EL to gain the cooperation of the passenger. This is often effective enough to accomplish their institutional goal. Officers do not necessarily want to appear authoritarian; they seek some sort of cooperation 'while pursuing the necessarily intrusive institutional requirements of eliciting personal and sensitive responses' (Adolphs et al. 2007: 75).

A booster is an indicator of power (Bradac and Street 1989/90). Table 7.1 and Figure 7.1 show that the difference between officers' and passengers' use of boosters is not statistically significant[1] (χ^2 [d.f. 1, n = 255,851] = 2.203, p = 0.13774244). Both groups use a similar proportion of boosters, but the difference for each of the four examples (*very, quite, too, so*) is statistically significant (χ^2 [d.f. 4, n = 255,851] = 63.793, p < 0.001): officers and passengers prefer to use different scalar stretchers. Officers use more *very*, and three times more *quite*, than passengers; and passengers use twice as much *too* and *so* as the officers.

---

[1] In this study, statistical testing of the validity of differences is carried out by the chi-square test, with the significance level set at 5%. Raw frequency is used in the calculation, which is designed to take into account the uneven size of the data sets being compared.

160   Elastic language, power and gender

Table 7.1 *Frequency of stretchers used by officers and passengers*

Category	Item	Officers (n = 201,444) Raw frequency	Officers Relative frequency (10,000 words)	Passengers (n = 54,407) Raw frequency	Passengers Relative frequency (10,000 words)
Scalar	very	553	27.5	121	22.2
(booster)	quite	224	11.1	18	3.3
	too	77	3.8	43	7.9
	so	72	3.6	42	7.7
	Total	**926**	**46**	**224**	**41.1**
Epistemic	could be	151	7.5	11	2
(hedges)	probably	143	7.1	35	6.4
	maybe	73	3.6	68	12.5
	possibly	67	3.3	3	0.6
	Total	**434**	**21.5**	**117**	**21.5**
Approximate	about	111	5.5	49	9
General	something	341	16.9	109	20

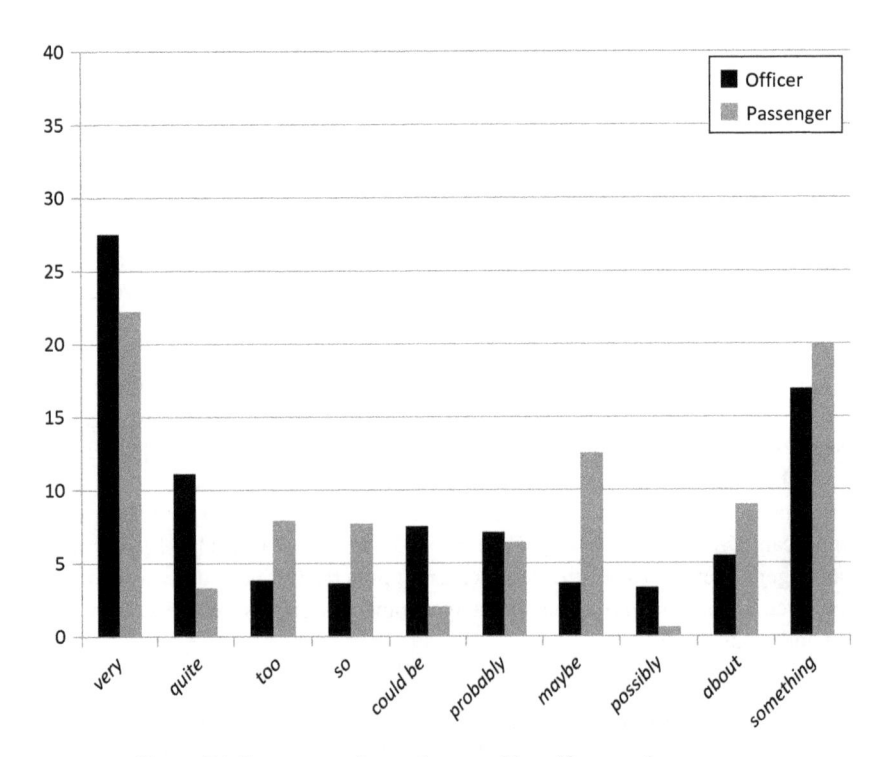

Figure 7.1 Frequency of stretchers used by officers and passengers

7.1 Power

In terms of the total frequency of the four hedges (*could be*, *probably*, *maybe*, *possibly*), the officers and passengers are completely the same: 21.5 per 10,000 words for both groups, as statistically confirmed (χ^2 [d.f. 1, n = 255,851] = 0, p = 1). The officers and passengers hedge at the same rate; neither group is more or less soft-toned. However, again the groups prefer different forms: the officers use twice as many *could be* (7.5 per 10,000 words) and *probably* (7.1) than *maybe* (3.6) and *possibly* (3.3). For passengers, the frequency distribution is more diversified, with the most frequent use *maybe* (12.5), then *probably* (6.4); *could be* comes third (2.0) and the least favourite is, as for the officers, *possibly* (0.6). The difference between the most and the least favourites is 21 times. Discrepancy in the frequency of individual stretchers used by the passenger group is greater than in the officer group. Table 7.1 shows that officers use four times more *could be* and six times more *possibly* than the passengers, but three times less *maybe*; they also use slightly less *probably*. Officers prefer *could be*, *possibly* and *probably*; passengers prefer *maybe*. The frequency difference between the two groups in using the four hedges is statistically significant (χ^2 [d.f. 4, n = 255,851] = 93.818, $p < 0.001$).

Passengers use 40% more *about* than officers, a statistically significant difference (χ^2 [d.f. 1, n = 255,851] = 8.377, p = 0.00379999) indicating that passengers opt for more approximation and less specificity than officers. They also use 15% more *something*, but this difference is not statistically significant (χ^2 [d.f. 1, n = 255,851] = 2.354, p = 0.124962). The two groups do not differ substantially in using the typical general term *something*, indicating that neither group is more general than the other.

Of the total relative frequency of hedges and boosters, officers and passengers are not very different. They are equally assertive or unassertive. They are also similar in using the general term *something*. This is somewhat unexpected, as most would assume that passengers would use more hedges and fewer boosters, given the authoritative position of the officers. It turns out that both sides of the power equation favour similar usage of boosters and hedges (and *something*): the officers use EL to carry out their institutional duties at the same rate as the passengers use it for non-institutional goals.

If we consider that hedges primarily represent uncertainty and an uncommitted attitude, then that attitude is seemingly shared by both officers and passengers. If we consider that hedges are linked primarily to speakers with low power status, then the assumption that officers hold greater power, and passengers less, runs into problems. The empirical evidence shows no clear correlation between EL and power status. The argument applies to the explanation of the booster results as well.

The finding that officers and passengers use similar frequencies of hedges and boosters supports in principle Ruzaitė's (2007: 203) conclusion that a speaker's role does not have much influence on the use of approximators and

162 Elastic language, power and gender

quantifiers. In her classroom study teachers and students used VL to a similar degree and for similar purposes, with only minor differences. Cheng and Warren (2001) also find that VL is not conditional on the status of different speaker groups, in their case of native speakers of English vs Cantonese non-native speakers of English. The speaker's role (officer vs passenger) in this study seems irrelevant as far as the frequency of stretchers is concerned; however, it would be dangerous to claim that the speaker's role does not matter in all discourses. Lehrer (1975) shows that different levels of precision or appropriateness depend on the speaker's role, giving the example of expert wine tasters who might need to describe wine more precisely than an ordinary wine drinker. The speaker's role functions differently in diverse situations, and may be relevant in some and irrelevant in others.

The similarities occur in a general level in this study, but the specific form of EL does vary between speaker groups, with passengers and officers differing significantly in their use of individual stretchers, illustrated in excerpts (7.1), (7.2) and (7.3) below.

(7.1)

Data: Episode 21, from turn 21:2:21 to 21:2:58, two speakers, over 22 speaking turns.
Context: Officer Greg (male in his 40s) and passenger (Saudi Arabian male in his 50s). Greg is asking about undeclared food brought in by the passenger.

21:2:21 GREG:	Why did you tick 'no'?
21:2:22 PASSENGER:	I didn't know what it means for food. I mean, I . . .
21:2:23 GREG:	Okay, I asked you, do you understand the questions, you said yes. (passenger looks at card and winces) It says, 'do you have any food'?
21:2:24 PASSENGER:	Any food, yes.
21:2:25 GREG:	Include dry, fresh, preserved, cooked or uncooked. Any food. You said no.
21:2:26 PASSENGER:	Only, errrrr, in, in, in cooking. (subtitle on screen: 'Only for cooking') Some people meant cooking, I put in the luggage.
21:2:27 GREG:	It says . . .
21:2:28 PASSENGER:	But **maybe** I, I, I'm **maybe** confused. Sorry. I'm **maybe** confused.
21:2:29 GREG:	You must tell me if you don't understand before I open the bag.
21:2:30 PASSENGER:	Mm-hmm.
21:2:31 GREG:	Not after I open the bag and then I find food, then suddenly you don't understand the card. (shakes head and waves arms)
21:2:32 PASSENGER:	Ah, I see, I see. (looks down and shakes head)

7.1 Power

(7.1) (cont.)

21:2:33 GREG:	(still waving arms) I find that **very** hard to believe.
21:2:34 PASSENGER:	(shuts eyes, still head downwards, nodding) Yes, I, I ...
...... (21:2:35 to 21:2:50 are omitted as less relevant)	
21:2:51 GREG:	This is homemade honey?
21:2:52 PASSENGER:	This, er, honey.
21:2:53 GREG:	Homemade?
21:2:54 PASSENGER:	I take it from, er, market. I didn't know.
21:2:55 GREG:	Yes, well, you must declare bee products. It's **a little bit** clouded. It's not **so** clear honey and it **could** have a risk. You must declare honey products. You must declare bee products. Sticky everywhere.
21:2:56 PASSENGER:	No, **maybe** I think for cooking. Because this is only in (pause) this one.
21:2:57 GREG:	Yes, but (shows card) look what the card says. (speaking slowly) Are you carrying any FOOD. Includes DRIED, it would include fresh, it would include COOKED, UNCOOKED AND PRESERVED. Where can you ... where does it say there (pause) only cooked food?
21:2:58 PASSENGER:	(pause) No, I don't know because sometimes I only ... no, no, I don't know.

In excerpt (7.1), the passenger has ticked 'no' in the declaration card, and in turn 21:2:22 says it was because he was unclear about the definition of 'food'. The padding expression *I mean* is used as a discourse device to buy him time to search for the right word. Greg is putting pressure on the passenger in 21:2:25 by emphasising that *food* means all sorts. In turn 21:2:26 the passenger explains that food to him is cooked only, and that was why he didn't declare. What is interesting is that the passenger says 'Some people meant cooking': he could have asked the passenger sitting next to him or one of the cabin crew, and he seems misled by the unspecified *some people*. The general stretcher could also be a red herring: *some people* may be non-existent. The speaker uses *some* here to minimise his responsibility in not ticking 'yes'. In 21:2:28, the passenger again says that he *maybe* is confused. The three repeated instances of *maybe* suggest that the passenger wants Greg to believe that he ticked 'no' by mistake. However, Greg does not seem convinced, as he says 'I find that very hard to believe' in 21:2:33.

In turn 21:2:54, the passenger indicates that the honey is not homemade; he also adds, 'I didn't know' to make his answer murky. In 21:2:55, Greg uses *well* to introduce a stern warning: 'you must declare bee products', stressing his authority (Aijmer 2013). In this single turn, Greg uses *must* three times, clearly showing that he is adamant about what the passenger should do. In describing the honey, Greg says it is *a little bit* clouded and not *so* clear, and therefore *could be* a risk. The stretchers are for the purposes of giving the right amount of information (*a little bit*), emphasising (*so*) and making a cautious judgement (*could be*). In 21:2:56, the passenger uses *maybe* and *I think* to again bring up that he thought 'food' means cooked only, but in a much weaker tone. Greg responds in a stern tone, he speaks slowly and emphasises a number of words to challenge the passenger's 'cooked food' theory. After this, in 21:2: 58, the passenger apparently becomes incoherent, repeating 'I don't know' and suggesting retreat.

The passenger appears to be in a weak position, and does not show much attempt to redress his power status. When Greg tells him that he must do this and that, the passenger responds submissively. Greg uses *must* repeatedly; conversely, the passenger uses *maybe* repeatedly, which is in line with the findings in Table 7.1 that passengers tend to use *maybe* much more than officers. Greg believes that the passenger is not being truthful, so his tone is firm and forceful. The reaction from the passenger is generally accepting. When Greg asks 'Do you understand that?' the passenger nods and answers 'I understand, yes'. It is possible that the passenger is playing powerless as a strategy, because people tend to show more compassion towards the less powerful. A powerful person may underestimate the power of a person displaying weakness. (In the end a penalty fine of $220 is handed down for failing to declare food).

The passenger at times struggles somewhat in expressing his thoughts in English, as in turns 21:2:22/26/54/58. This may be another reason for him not to argue back; perhaps his limited English is a barrier. English is his second language; it would require great effort for an L2 speaker to challenge an L1 officer. The impact of language competence on the use of EL is discussed in the next chapter.

In addition to speech, body language shows power imbalance. Greg continues to wave his arms but the passenger tends to look down, a clear indication that he does not wish to argue. This case is about undeclared food, and although the passenger is found guilty, he does not get a severe punishment. Perhaps he is not keen to fight back and assert his power as there is really not much at stake – unlike the next case, where a passenger has much to lose.

(7.2)

Data: Episode 17, from turn 17:1:1 to 17:1:70, two speakers, over 29 speaking turns.
Context: Officer Jim (male in his 50s) and passenger (American male in his 20s). Jim is asking about the passenger's travel movements and other issues.

(7.2) (cont.)

(Officer Jim looking through passenger's luggage)

17:1:1 JIM:	So how long are you going to stay here this time?
17:1:2 PASSENGER:	**Probably about** two weeks, until I get er::: (pause) everything figured out.

...... (17:1:3 to 17:1:9 are omitted as less relevant)

(Jim looking through passenger's wallet)

17:1:10 JIM:	(holds bankcard up) You've got $600 on that. (pause) You've **probably** got **at most** (pause) $200 there. It's going to cost you ... if you haven't paid for your hotel accommodation for two weeks ...=
17:1:11 PASSENGER:	= So that's still **eight or nine** hundred U-... U.S.=
17:1:12 JIM:	=$70 though ... just say ... let's say 70.
17:1:13 PASSENGER:	That's **eight or nine** hundred dollars U.S. which will be **about 11 to 12** hundred dollars Australian.
17:1:14 JIM:	You're going to be short of money. You're going to be ...=
17:1:15 PASSENGER:	=Well if I am, my parents are a phone call away. And they helped me out when I was in Bangkok, because I needed the money and I didn't have any money.

...... (17:1:16 to 17:1:26 are omitted as less relevant)

17:1:27 JIM:	Have you ever used any dope?
17:1:28 PASSENGER:	No, not really.
17:1:29 JIM:	No, not really. What does 'no, not really' mean?
17:1:30 PASSENGER:	Well it depends on what you mean by dope.
17:1:31 JIM:	Dope **could be** smoke, it **could be** smack, it **could be** coke ...=
17:1:32 PASSENGER:	=Well definitely not smack, definitely not coke, but yeah I do smoke **some** weed from time to time.=
17:1:33 JIM:	= Yeah. (pause) When was the last time you smoked weed?
17:1:34 PASSENGER:	**Maybe** three days ago.

...... (17:1:35 to 17:1:50 are omitted as less relevant)

17:1:51 JIM:	What's ... what's wrong? You don't seem real happy.
17:1:52 PASSENGER:	Well, I mean (indicates laptop) you have me look at pornography on my computer, (pause) okay?
17:1:53 JIM:	(indicates laptop) Par for the course here. You have to look at that sort of thing. We get people come through here, on their computer they have images of children; they have images of **all sorts of things** they shouldn't have.

...... (17:1:54 to 17:1:60 are omitted as less relevant)

| 17:1:61 JIM: | Looking at your travel movements, (pause) where you've been, what you're doing. You've been backwards and forwards here and there, out of Australia and **all that sort of thing**. |

166   Elastic language, power and gender

(7.2) (cont.)

17:1:62	PASSENGER:	And it's wrong to do that because I'm young and this is a time of my life and ...?=
17:1:63	JIM:	=But ... no, no, no, it's ... no:::: no, no, no.=
17:1:64	PASSENGER:	=What's the problem?!
17:1:65	JIM:	No because often you find people who **may::be** committing a criminal act.
17:1:66	PASSENGER:	Mhm.
17:1:67	JIM:	In other words moving drugs across a border ...=
17:1:68	PASSENGER:	= You know what, you're just not listening to **anything** I say.=
17:1:69	JIM:	= I do listen.=
17:1:70	PASSENGER:	=And you're continuing on your little rampant path. (more agitated tone) I'm a **pretty** straight up kid.

During the questioning, officer Jim discovers that the passenger might not have enough money to fund his stay. In turn 17:1:2, the passenger says that he is *probably* here for *about* two weeks, using two stretchers to indicate approximations of the length of his stay. In 17:1:10, Jim says 'You've probably got at most $200', also using two stretchers to indicate approximation. Both the passenger and Jim use *probably* here; throughout the customs exchanges both parties use similar rates of this stretcher. *At most* is a 'partial' approximator (Channell 1994); it has a relatively precise upper limit, in this case $200. In 17:1:11/13, the passenger continues to use approximate stretchers, *eight or nine* and *about 11 to 12*, all suggesting that the exact amount is not to hand or not important. For example, Jim could have counted the cash in the wallet, but he didn't, probably because he didn't think it was needed. When Jim says that the passenger is going to be short of money to pay for his stay, the passenger in 17:1:15 uses *well* (padding expression for introducing a disagreement) to bring in the argument that his parents may help him out.

Jim's institutional duty is to stop illegal drugs crossing the border, so in 17:1:27, he starts to check if the passenger takes dope. The passenger's answer is a hedged denial, somewhat evasive: 'No, not really.' Jim asserts his institutional power to request clarification in 17:1:29, as the hedge is obviously not a satisfactory response; a definite answer is needed. The passenger is not fazed by the request; he requests Jim to define 'dope', as without a clear definition he is not able to oblige. In turn 17: 1:30, Jim defines *dope* as 'could be smoke, it could be smack, it could be coke', three *could be* in a row to indicate multiple possibilities. *Could be* is used much more by officers than by passengers, as shown in Table 7.1 above, indicating that the term is more suitable for performing institutional duties. This agrees with Koester's (2010) argument that directives by their nature generate imposition and therefore act like face threats; mitigating hedges, such as *could be*, are required. The findings in these data support Koester's view that where the officers make requests a lot, *could be* is needed more as well.

In 17:1:32 the passenger denies emphatically that he takes smack or coke, and uses *well* to begin the explanation that he only smokes some weed from time to time. The hedge *some* indicates a small amount, *from time to time* indicates low frequency. The passenger uses mitigating elastic to lessen the severity of smoking weed. In 17:1:34, he uses *maybe* to indicate he is unsure when he last smoked weed: this term is used by passengers three times more than by officers, as shown in Table 7.1.

By now the examination has been going on for close to two hours. In 17:1:51, Jim shows empathy towards the passenger, asking if he is unhappy about anything: 'You don't <u>seem</u> real happy' is a hedged, polite way of asking. In next turn the passenger uses 'Well, I mean' to bring in his complaint, and finishes with *okay* in a raised tone to challenge the officer for an explanation. *Well* in this case is not the typical index of politeness, but 'a sign of power and aggressiveness' (Aijmer 2013: 64): The passenger is reclaiming power. In 17:1:53, Jim explains that all the checks are necessary to stop illegal activities. '<u>We</u> get people come through here' re-emphasises his institutional power, as *we* is a predictor of higher status and *I* of lower status (Tausczik and Pennebaker 2010: 33). As in this excerpt and across these data, officers frequently use *we*; passengers use only *I*.

The general extender *all sorts of things* is used by Jim in 17:1:53 and again in 17:1:61: *all that sort of thing*; this is efficient because an exhaustive list is not possible. In 17:1:62/64, the passenger puts heated questions to Jim. Jim tries to defend his actions by saying there is nothing wrong in young people wanting to see the world, but his job is to keep criminals at bay. In turn 17:1:65, Jim uses *maybe* with a lengthened tone, implying his intention to soften his statement that people commit criminal acts and mitigate the impact to the passenger's face. Having heard Jim's veiled statement, the passenger calms down somewhat in 17:1:66. However, on hearing Jim's next unveiled utterance, 'In other words moving drugs across a border ...', the passenger is unhappy again. He accuses Jim of not listening to *anything* he says, using the general stretcher to refer a wide range of statements. In 17:1:70, the passenger continues to strengthen his power position, using *your little rampant path* to weaken the importance of Jim's institutional pursuit. The passenger declares that 'I'm a <u>pretty</u> straight up kid', which is an intensifying elastic using the scalar stretcher *pretty* to increase the strength of his claim. (In the end the passenger is cleared and free to go.)

The power shifts in this exchange are quite dramatic. Power is claimed by one party at one moment and reclaimed by the other at the next. The power struggle is not fixed; it is dynamic throughout the interaction. When participants talk, there is much noticeable latching, indicating that this is a heated exchange. Jim is concerned that a passenger with erratic travel movements and few funds may not be telling the truth, so continues his investigation. The passenger is annoyed about being searched and questioned for such a long time, and feels he is not being listened to. This leads to confronting encounters where EL serves to emphasise or mitigate, working flexibly and serving both parties, in providing them with power over the other in subtle ways (Tannen 1990). It is useful in this institutional context as it reduces the appearance of being patronising and so reduces possible resentment: for example, in 17:1:65 Jim uses EL to assert in a hedged manner. It is also used to readjust the power balance in a forceful, direct way and maintain the speaker's stance: the passenger in turn 17:1:70 uses EL for exactly that.

Excerpt (7.2) shows that while an officer may have some institutional power over a passenger by default, this does not mean that the passenger will opt to take the lower position every time. The balance of power is fluid and adjustable depending on circumstances, and EL is a useful way of asserting or relinquishing power status.

(7.3)

Data: Episode 22, from turn 22:4:10 to 22:4:29, two speakers, over 15 speaking turns.
Context: Officer Nick (male in his 30s) and another officer (female in her 20s) are checking suspicious goods imported from China.

22:4:10 NICK: Obviously, there's **something** there that we **might** have to have a look at, so, um=
22:4:11 OFFICER: =It looks **very** organic in this housing. (pointing at image)
22:4:12 NICK: Yeah. It **may** just turn out to be **some sort of** filter; **maybe** granulated **or something**, but (pause) on that image, it **really** looks suspicious. If it was going to a person and they're importing a pump, that would look a bit suspicious, but it **seems** to be going to a company, and at this stage, just looking at it, it looks – it's a tool company, so it **seems** legitimate enough.
...... (22:4:13 to 22:4:17 are omitted as less relevant)
22:4:18 OFFICER: I'll grab **some** tools and we'll open this up.
22:4:19 NICK: Yeah, good idea. I can't see **anything** obvious here that ... (peering into package) that's **seems** to be tampered with, so (pause) we'll have to pull it apart. Luckily, we've got **some** screws there that we can, **some** bolts we can undo, so we'll **probably** be able to have a look in here without doing **too much** damage, just in case it's a legitimate, uh, importation. It's coming off **quite** easily (undoing bolts

7.1 Power 169

(7.3) (cont.)		
		with spanner) so that **might** suggest it's been opened before. If there's **anything** in it, it should be under here. (removing interior part from pump)
22:4:20	OFFICER:	(peering into pump) That's carbon paper.
22:4:21	NICK:	**I don't think** there should be carbon paper in there. That's what put the X-ray off, **I suppose**.
22:4:22	OFFICER:	There's definitely **something** inside. It's **very** heavy. Well, look at that. (peering in) It's **very** heavy. (peering in) Well, look at that. What does it say?
22:4:23	NICK:	That's Tylenol cold tablets, (peering in) and **some** other tablets as well=
22:4:24	OFFICER:	=It's actually capsules, yeah, and tablets in there.
22:4:25	NICK:	I didn't see them.
22:4:26	OFFICER:	Two different types. And this one's marked with contact NT. (handling a capsule)
22:4:27	NICK:	These flu tablets contain ephedrine and they can use that in the manufacture of, er, **things** like speed, amphetamines **and stuff like that**. So, obviously, they're **very** difficult to get in Australia in such quantities, so they've **probably** worked out that they can import them in like this and then make their drugs. That's a **pretty** big find, yeah. There's got to be **thousands** in there. What we'll do at this stage is we'll take an itemiser test and ... uh ... we'll just see what that comes up with, because even though it says it's Tylenol, we don't know what it actually is. It **could be anything**.
		(Officer takes swab to machine. Machine shows drugs detected)
22:4:28	OFFICER:	Ephedrine.
22:4:29	NICK:	Oh, good.

According to Lakoff (1990), there are macropolitics and micropolitics. The former refers to group communication strategies in various institutional discourses; the latter involves interpersonal communication. Professionals tend to create their own language, and EL is often used to mystify people outside the profession: 'knowledge of special knowledge is power, normally reserved for the professionals' (1990: 2). The discussion in excerpt (7.3) between two colleagues is somewhat technical, involving housing images on X-ray and itemiser tests which detect minute samples of a wide variety of illicit substances. The officers discuss whether the flu tablets contain ephedrine, which is used in the manufacture of things like speed and amphetamines. EL in this excerpt shows a different kind of power: the power reserved for professionals.

In excerpt (7.3), Nick and his colleague are looking at an X-ray screen, where a suspicious image appears. In turn 22:4:10, Nick starts the discussion by pointing to something that might need to be looked at. The two stretchers (*something* and *might*) make his tone tentative. The female officer responds with the scalar stretcher *very* to emphasise that the thing is organic in nature. Agreeing with her, Nick speculates that the thing 'may just turn out to be some sort of filter; maybe granulated or something'. This sentence consists of the epistemic stretchers *may*, *maybe* and *sort of*, and general stretchers *some* and *or something*. *Some sort of* indicates that the thing may not be a filter, but it looks like one. Given the unclear situation, an elastic description is perhaps the only option for Nick. While he is not sure what exactly the thing inside the container is, he is sure that whatever it turns out to be in the end, it looks suspicious now; he uses *really* (emphatic stretcher) to strengthen the tone in 22:4:12. He also uses *seem* twice to hedge the statement for self-protection in case things are not what they appear to be: the pumps look legitimate enough, but they could be deceptive.

In turn 22:4:18, the officer says *some tools* to indicate that the tools would not be many: here *some* functions as a quantifier of a small amount. The same meaning applies to the other two instances of *some* Nick uses in his next turn, as well as in turn 22:4: 23. In 22:4:19, Nick uses the general stretcher *anything* twice to refer to an unspecific and unlikely item. He also use *seems*, *probably* and *might* to show tentative judgement of the situation. On the other hand he chooses scalar stretchers *too much* (damage) and *quite* (easily) to emphasise the degree of damage and ease of dismantling. In 22:4:21, Nick uses *I suppose* (epistemic stretcher) at the end of the sentence to act as a softener and reduce the assertiveness of his statement.

In 22:4:22, the officer says, 'There's definitely something inside. It's very heavy'. Her tone is certain, indicated by the use of *definitely* and *very*. However, the general stretcher *something* still appears, so while she is sure that there is a thing there, she is not sure what the thing is. In 22:4:27, Nick explains some technical issues. He says that ephedrine in flu tablets can make drugs such as speed and amphetamines, and a general stretcher *things* and general extender *and stuff like that* are used to avoid listing every illegal drug that might contain ephedrine. EL is relevant and effective here, achieving optimal cognitive effect with the least processing effort (Sperber and Wilson 1995 [1986]). *Very*, *pretty* (scalar stretcher) and *thousands* (quantifier) serve the same function of strengthening a high degree of some kind. Both *probably* and *could be* refer to possibility, the former somewhat more specific in degree than the latter: 'It could be anything' is virtually a blanket statement. (In the end the officers' efforts pay off: 7.2 kilograms of pseudoephedrine are found inside the pumps.)

Power is not just about power plays; there are other types of power relation, and excerpt (7.3) shows that EL can be reserved for in-group power among

7.1 Power

colleagues. For example, the use of general extenders often requires understanding and knowledge of the expectations shared by a particular group in order to work effectively (Evison et al. 2007). EL is also seen as a social leveller in Carter (1998), as it 'puts the speakers on an immediately casual and equal footing with their interlocutors'. EL functions as such a leveller for the two officers in excerpt (7.3).

It has been claimed that higher-status individuals tend to speak more often and more freely than lower-status people (Tausczik and Pennebaker 2010: 33), and this is confirmed by the evidence in this study. The officers with a higher (institutional) status, speak four times more than passengers do. Their institutional duties often require officers to make requests of some kind to passengers, as illustrated in excerpts (7.1) and (7.2). Of the three excerpts in this section, excerpt (7.1) demonstrates an imbalance of power between officer and passenger, where the passenger is by and large submissive. Excerpt (7.2) represents another officer–passenger exchange, but the difference is that this time the passenger opts to reclaim his power position. Excerpt (7.3) is an officer–officer conversation revealing the power of in-group knowledge. Higher-status and power positions do not necessarily correlate, and power relations are versatile and multifaceted. Some passengers do manage to use EL for 'asserting power' (Channell 1994: 194). While there may be a power disparity between two sides in interactions, there is also a constant (re)adjustment of the power balance/status to suit the moment-to-moment situation. Any participant may gain power over others and vice versa, a dynamic process helped by EL.

Power status and social distance go hand in hand, and are closely linked with the use of language. The degree of social relationship affects VL use (Cutting 1998). In this study, the power relation coincides largely with social distance. Officers and passengers, taking opposing power positions, are also opposed in social distance: they are strangers. As part of the complex array of social 'accelerators' or 'brakes', both sets of speaker routinely use language to increase and decrease social distance in interaction (Brown and Levinson 1978: 98, 287). For example, in excerpts (7.2) and (7.3), speakers show a friendly and polite attitude or assert their authority depending upon the need of the situation. In particular, although officer and passenger are not likely to become good friends, the officer might rely on reciprocity (see Section 9.2 for details) to create common ground and obtain needed information from a passenger. In excerpt (7.2), a few times Jim's strategy is to use rapport and mitigating elastics to reduce his social distance from the passenger, in a bid to get the truth. Another common factor linked with EL use is age. Murphy (2010) finds that women in their 70s and 80s use very few hedges. Women in their 20s and 40s use similar rates of hedges for saving face, but favour different types of hedge: for example, the 20s group prefers to use more *like*

172 Elastic language, power and gender

Table 7.2 *Different interactional styles between men and women*

Men	Women
informative (content task-, outcome- and referentially oriented)	affective (interpersonally, process- and effectively oriented)
competitive (aggressive interruptions, confrontational)	facilitative (more polite, greater sensitive to maintaining face, supportive feedback, conciliatory)
direct	indirect
autonomous	collaborative
dominating talking time (in public)	minor contribution (in public)

(Adapted from Holmes 1985, 1995, 2000, 2006)

(adverb), while the 40s group uses more *you know* and *I think*. The more senior the participants become, the fewer hedges they tend to use. While this study does not study the effects of social distance and age on EL, these hold very interesting implications for the use of EL.

7.2   Gender

The concept of gender concerns 'any differences between women and men being socially or culturally *learned, mediated* or *constructed*' (Sunderland 2004: 14). Sunderland stresses that those differences are not absolutes; rather they are 'tendencies' and 'variations'. Linell and Bredmar (1996: 376) note that 'features of indirectness have sometimes been considered as a gender-based indicator of female conversation'; more such findings are listed in Table 7.2.

Table 7.2 displays different interactional styles. Men talk primarily for information exchange and are more competitive, direct, autonomous and dominating in speaking. Women talk with more affection, are more facilitative, indirect and collaborative, and not as dominating as men in speaking.

A common view is that women talk more than men, but studies do not bear this out. For example, in conversations among college students in the US and Mexico, both men and women spoke about 16,000 words per day, showing no difference in talking rates (Mehl, Vazire, Ramírez-Esparza, Slatcher and Pennebaker 2007). There is also a conventional perception that VL is women's language, and that women use more vague expressions than men (Channell 1994: 192–3). Carter (1980: 232) claims that women's language has a 'high degree of unspecificity', and Tauszik and Pennebaker (2010: 36) state that 'women use more social words and references to others, and men use more complex language'. Women use words that reflect social concerns; men refer to more concrete objects and impersonal topics (Newman, Groom, Handelman and Pennebaker 2008). However, the 'subjective impression' that women use more VL may arise from the stereotypical view that VL is a device for the less

7.2 Gender

powerful, and women are perceived as such (Smith 1985). The claim that women are vaguer than men is not substantiated. This study offers some new understandings of how gender influences the use of EL.

Works on gendered talk in relation to VL use shed some light on relevant issues (e.g. Bradac et al. 1995; Holmes 1990, 2006). Holmes (1990) finds a significant difference in the use of boosters (e.g. *extremely*) between male and female. Women are found to use more intensifiers, bringing more interactiveness in communication (Wright and Hosman 1983). The use of intensifiers may signify the speaker's power over others: Bradac et al. (1995: 113) find that females use more intensifiers (e.g. *very, absolutely*) particularly in women–women discourse, but more hedges in women–men discourse; hence, women are more assertive in same-sex interactions but less assertive in mixed-sex interactions.

Some studies of EL find gender is of little relevance. Based on a study of the use of *I think*, Aijmer (1997: 23) finds no evidence that the deliberative or tentative use of *I think* is sex-specific. Her data show that the overall frequency of *I think* is higher among male speakers, but there is little gender difference between its two contrastive functions. Another example is some real-life discussion on the issue. In a Chinese TV dating show entitled *You Are the One* (screened 1 April 2012, 10 p.m. on Channel 56 in China), there was a discussion among the female contestants. A (a writer): 'Women tend to turn a round table meeting into a fashion discussion, and men do the opposite.' B: 'I disagree with you, you can only speak for yourself.' C (an English lecturer): 'No gendered talk in the workplace!' While this is anecdotal evidence, it displays different views among women. Holmes (2006: 5) states that people have their expectations about appropriately gendered ways of talking. As for a compliment, such as *nice jacket*, Holmes points out that the expression conveys an admiring or a patronising stance, depending on who says it to whom, and when. It also indicates, according to Holmes, femininity in communities, where compliments on appearance are more strongly associated with women than with men.

Table 7.3 and Figure 7.2 summarise the findings of this study on the impact of gender on the use of EL, showing that men (male officers and passengers) and women (female officers and passengers) use similar total rates of boosters: the difference is not statistically significant (χ^2 [d.f. 1, $n = 255{,}851$] = 1.847, $p = 0.17413272$). Similarly, the two groups show no significant difference in terms of individual use of the four booster words (χ^2 [d.f. 4, $n = 255{,}851$] = 5.334, $p = 0.2547109$). Men use a bit more of *very* and *too*, and women use a bit more of *quite* and *so*, but the differences are not statistically supported. Neither men nor women emphasise to a different degree. The span in frequency for men using boosters is 23.1 (27.5–4.4), for women 19.5 (24–4.5); so women use the four boosters somewhat more evenly than men do.

Table 7.3 *Frequency of stretchers used by male and female speakers*

		Men (*n* = 171,619)		Women (*n* = 84,232)	
Category	Item	Raw frequency	Relative frequency (10,000 words)	Raw frequency	Relative frequency (10,000 words)
Scalar	*very*	472	27.5	202	24
(booster)	*quite*	157	9.1	85	10.1
	too	88	5.1	32	3.8
	so	76	4.4	38	4.5
	Total	**793**	**46.1**	**357**	**42.4**
Epistemic	*probably*	146	8.5	32	3.8
(hedges)	*could be*	118	6.9	44	5.2
	maybe	98	5.7	43	5.1
	possibly	46	2.7	24	2.8
	Total	**408**	**23.8**	**143**	**16.9**
Approximate	*about*	121	7.1	39	4.6
General	*something*	301	17.5	149	17.7

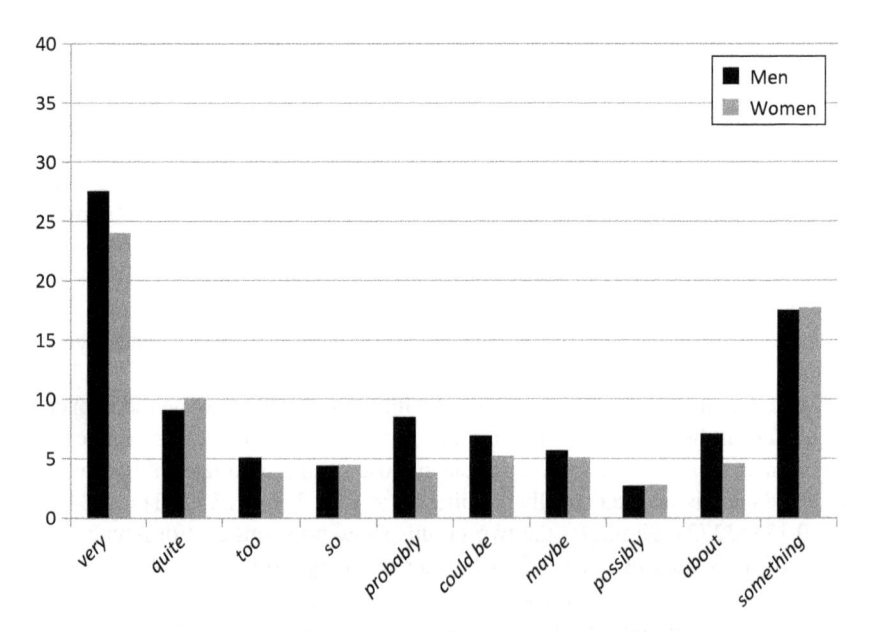

Figure 7.2 Frequency of stretchers used by male and female speakers

7.2 Gender

As shown in Table 7.3 and Figure 7.2, hedges differ in use. Against a common assumption that women use more hedges, men actually use 29% more than women, a statistically significant amount (χ^2 [d.f. 1, n = 255,851] = 12.146, $p < 0.001$): the empirical evidence illustrates that women do not use more hedges than men. The frequency difference in using the four individual hedges is also statistically significant (χ^2 [d.f. 4, n = 255,851] = 20.899, $p < 0.001$). While gender does not seem to impact on the use of boosters, it does make a difference in the use of hedges, and men actually use more. If hedges link to tentativeness, then male speakers in this study are more tentative and vague, which does not support the assumption that EL is women's language

In the case of hedges, men prefer *probably* most and *possibly* least: the ranking is 8.5 words (per 10,000) for *probably*, 6.9 for *could be*, 5.7 for *maybe* and 2.7 for *possibly*. Women prefer *could be* and *maybe* almost equally (5.2 and 5.1), then 3.8 for *probably* and 2.8 for *possibly*. Women and men show some similarity in using the least favourite word *possibly*, they also use *maybe* with similar frequencies (as well as *so* and *something*, as shown in Figure 7.2). However, the two groups differ in the use of *could be*, men using this 25% more than women. The greatest discrepancy occurs in the use of *probably*: men use this 55% more than women. The difference span in frequency for men is 5.8 (8.5–2.7), for women 2.4 (5.2–2.8); so women use the four hedges more evenly than men.

The data show that the two gender groups use similar rates of *possibly* and *maybe*, although differences occur with *probably* and *could be*. This differs from the result shown in Table 7.1 for officers and passengers: the officers use more *could be* and *possibly*, but more than three times less *maybe* than passengers, and both use *probably* at similar rates. The favourite word for officers is *could be*; for the passengers *maybe*. The favourite word for men is *probably*, for women *could be* and *maybe*. Men and women differ most in the frequency of *probably*, which occurs with similar frequency between officers and passengers. Officers and passengers differ greatly in the frequency of *maybe* and *possibly*, but this discrepancy disappears when considering gender. These suggest that power and gender do not necessarily have the same effect on the use of EL.

In terms of *about*, women use approximately 35% less than men, a statistically significant difference (χ^2 [d.f. 1, n = 255,851] = 5.296, p = 0.02137446). Men and women use very similar rates of *something*, and the difference is statistically insignificant (χ^2 [d.f. 1, n = 255,851] = 0.007, p = 0.93332199). This pattern is in line with the rates between officers and passengers, where passengers use more *about*; here men use more *about*. The fact that the men use more approximations again contradicts the common assumption that women tend to be uncertain. Both power and gender factors have an impact on the use of *about*, but a lesser impact on the use of *something*, indicating that *something* is less sensitive to social influences.

176   Elastic language, power and gender

Some of the features in Table 7.2 are not verified in this study: for example, the women in this study do not use more hedges; the men do. Contrary to the assumption that male speech is more direct (Okamoto 2002), this study shows that men and women use similar amounts of booster and men use more hedges, so men tend to be more indirect than direct, based on these data. This finding counters the assumption that females are less assertive and show greater deference than males.

(7.4)

Data: Episode 58, from turn 58:3:1 to 58:1:23, three speakers, over 23 speaking turns.
Context: Officer Cynthia (female in her 50s), another officer (male in his late 30s), and passenger (Asian female in her 40s). The officers are asking about the passenger's nervous behaviour and other matters.

58:3:1 PASSENGER:	(indecipherable) **something** wrong?
58:3:2 OFFICER:	Ah, that **could be** (indecipherable). Are you taking drugs?
58:3:3 CYNTHIA:	When you got off the plane and you saw us all standing there, you got **very**, **very** shocked. Why are you **so** shocked to see us?
58:3:4 PASSENGER:	Well, the airplane go round, round circle, make me, my, the, my blood go up. I'm **very** high already.
58:3:5 CYNTHIA:	Do you want a glass of water?
58:3:6 PASSENGER:	No.
58:3:7 CYNTHIA:	You sure?
58:3:8 PASSENGER:	Yes.
58:3:9 OFFICER:	(to Cynthia) So why is, why does she carry this?
58:3:10 CYNTHIA:	She said in case she gets asked. (to passenger) So where did you get $14,000 to buy a ring?
58:3:11 PASSENGER:	Do you know how ... I work how long – 16 year on the ... in Canada. I work 16 hour there, seven day a week.
58:3:12 CYNTHIA:	Okay.
58:3:13 PASSENGER:	I have **something** wrong?
58:3:14 CYNTHIA:	We're **just** having a look.
58:3:15 PASSENGER:	Oh, my gosh.
58:3:16 OFFICER:	(to Cynthia) What do you think is going on?
58:3:17 CYNTHIA:	I don't know – **something's** going on.
58:3:18 OFFICER:	Do you think it's internal?
58:3:19 CYNTHIA:	I don't know, I don't know. She's been to Vietnam, gone through Macau, gone through Hong Kong. She's met a friend in Macau; the friend's still in Macau. Yeah, it's just **a little**, **very** odd. (to passenger) Have you had any contact with drugs while you were in Macau or Vietnam?

7.2 Gender

(7.4) (cont.)	
58:3:20 PASSENGER:	NO, I DON'T KNOW NOTHING. I am, oh, clear person that do a **lot of things** in my past. I'm **just** not terrible person. I'm **just** a visitor; I do **a lot of things**.
58:3:21 CYNTHIA:	That's all right; we didn't say you were a terrible person.
58:3:22 PASSENGER:	(smooths hair from face)
58:3:23 CYNTHIA:	We're **just** checking.

In turn 58:3:1, the female passenger uses *something* in her question, indicating that she is unsure about what is going on. The general stretcher is suitable here to convey her tentative tone. The male officer in the next turn answers 'Ah, that could be' when he discovers suspicious documents. The epistemic stretcher *could be* is a marker of possibility. The female officer Cynthia uses boosters *very* and *so* in 58:3:3 when she describes the high degree of nervousness of the passenger. The passenger explains that the airplane moved in circles and made her blood pressure shoot up *very high*. In this set of exchanges, both females (Cynthia and the passenger) use boosters to emphasise and strengthen their statements in the women-to-women situation. This is in line with the finding in Bradac et al. (1995) that females use more intensifiers, particularly in women–women discourse.

A $14,000 ring arouses suspicion. In 58:3:9 the officer asks why the passenger carries a receipt for the ring, and the answer is in case she gets asked. The passenger states that she worked a long time for it. In 58:3:13 the passenger again asks if something is wrong. Cynthia uses the hedge *just* to calm her, saying that it's merely a quick look and there is no need to worry. When her colleague asks what she thinks is going on in 58:3:16, Cynthia admits that she is not sure, but thinks something is. Again *something* is used to indicate an unspecific situation. This shows the effectiveness of EL such as *something*, which is undoubtedly an integral part of communication.

When her colleague asks if there is a need to do an internal search of the passenger, Cynthia indicates that she is not sure, but she does think that the travel movements of the passenger are 'just a little, very odd' in 58:3:19. The booster *very* seems to increase the degree of oddness, but the speaker also uses the hedge *a bit* to mitigate the emphatic tone. The combination of hedge and booster makes Cynthia's utterance interesting, as if she wants to be assertive and tentative at the same time, which may reflect her puzzled and indecisive state of mind. This mixed use is a manifestation of the elasticity of EL: there is fluidity between boosting and hedging; language use is not categorical and fixed.

When confronted with the question of drug use, in 58:3:20 the passenger is adamant that she does not take drugs. She repeatedly employs boosters *a lot of* and *just* to assert that she is clean. The passenger's English appears somewhat limited: 'I do a lot of things' may mean that she works hard, so is not a bad person. To calm the passenger Cynthia mitigates by saying 'We're just checking' in 58:3:23, where *just* acts as a hedge. The word *just* in this excerpt performs two opposing functions: booster or hedge. (It turns out that the passenger is telling the truth, and is free to leave.)

This excerpt primarily consists of same-sex and occasionally men–women interactions. All three speakers use boosters, hedges and other type of EL to communicate effectively. EL is used as a tool for confrontation or mitigation, whichever is suitable at the moment in question.

(7.5)

Data: Episode 29, from turn 29:3:57 to 29:3:73, three speakers, over 17 speaking turns.
Context: Officer John (male in his 40s), officer Michael (male in his 40s) and passenger (New Zealand female in her 20s). The officers are questioning the passenger's high cocaine readings.

29:3:57 MICHAEL:	(to John) She's **probably** lying because the readings are **quite** high. I reckon she **might** have had **some** on the plane or before she got on the plane. She **could** still have **some** (indecipherable) **stuff** so . . .
29:3:58 JOHN:	All right. Just with that **little** swab that I done earlier, okay, it's come back with cocaine high readings. (to passenger) Have you been using?
29:3:59 PASSENGER:	Well, I have tried it, yes.
29:3:60 JOHN:	Yeah? How long ago?
29:3:61 PASSENGER:	In London. I don't know, **like** three months ago **or something**.
29:3:62 JOHN:	Nnnn . . . no.
29:3:63 PASSENGER:	Why?
29:3:64 JOHN:	Coke high means you've either just had it on the plane or you've got **some** with you. Have you got **anything** on your body or=
29:3:65 PASSENGER:	=No, look.
29:3:66 JOHN:	**Something** you may have missed?
29:3:67 PASSENGER:	It'll be on the card.
29:3:68 JOHN:	It'll be on the card? You chopped it up with the card?
29:3:69 PASSENGER:	Yeah.
29:3:70 JOHN:	How long ago?
29:3:71 PASSENGER:	I don't know, **two months** ago when I tried it.
29:3:72 JOHN:	It couldn't have been that long ago. That would have wiped off **a fair bit** by now. Do you want me to blow the machine up?
29:3:73 PASSENGER:	Actually that's been in my handbag **quite** long.

Michael and John are talking to a young New Zealand model, on a brief stop in Australia before she goes home to New Zealand. The officers want to find out if

7.2 Gender

she is carrying drugs. In 29:3:57 Michael talks to his colleague John, using *quite* to emphasise that the cocaine reading is high and therefore the passenger is probably lying. In 'I reckon she <u>might</u> have had <u>some</u> on the plane or before she got on the plane. She <u>could</u> still have <u>some</u> (indecipherable) <u>stuff</u> so ...' Michael suggests a couple of scenarios using the hedges *might* and *could*, plus a quantifier *some* and a general term *stuff*. In the next turn, John uses the hedge *little* to indicate that the swab was a quick one. Both male officers use a number of hedges to convey tentativeness and possibility, in line with the general finding of this study that men use significantly more hedges than women.

In 29:3:61 the passenger admits that she used drugs '<u>like</u> three months ago <u>or something</u>', where *like* is an approximator and *or something* is a general extender to strengthen the effect of approximation. The approximation seems accepted by the hearers, because the speaker may not be able to provide an exact time, and more importantly the precise time may not be needed in this situation. In 29:3:64 John pushes for an admission from the passenger: he thinks that she may have used drugs less than three months ago. John uses *some* and *anything*, two general terms to indicate his suspicion. The word *something* in 29:3:66 serves a similar function. John's persistent pursuit pays off: in 29:3:71 the passenger admits that she used drugs *two months* ago. This seemingly exact time could be an approximation as well, like *about two months*, as exact numbers can be used as approximations (Channell 1994). Note that the passenger now changes her line from *three months* to *two months*.

The admission still does not satisfy John. He insists that the high cocaine reading means the drug trace has to be more recent than two months. In 29:3:72, he uses the booster *a fair bit* to strengthen his argument. In answering John's question, the passenger offers another explanation: that the drug has been in her handbag for *quite* long, and this may have caused the high reading. She uses the booster to emphasise her claim. (In the end the passenger was cleared after a frisk search, and free to go.)

In excerpt (7.5), both men and the woman use boosters and hedges to argue their respective cases. It seems that the passenger is less than open about how recently she used drugs, and officers are quite persistent in carrying out their institutional duties. Regardless of gender, EL seems to have served each person's communicative goals effectively.

(7.6)

Data: Episode 31, from turn 31:1:7 to 17:1:18, two speakers, over 12 speaking turns.
Context: Officer (male in his 20s) and passenger Isaac (American male in his 20s). The officer is asking about possible drug use.

31:1:7 OFFICER: So you say the last time you used marijuana was **about** three days ago, is that right?

180   Elastic language, power and gender

(7.6) (cont.)

31:1:8 ISAAC:	Yep.
31:1:9 OFFICER:	You wouldn't have any remnants **or anything** in your pockets today?
31:1:10 ISAAC:	No, definitely no. I made sure of that.
31:1:11 OFFICER:	Yeah.
31:1:12 ISAAC:	Absolutely not. I don't even know the last time I had it inside of a backpack, **you know**, it's been <u>a while</u>.
31:1:13 OFFICER:	So (pause) are you the only person who uses this?
31:1:14 ISAAC:	Yeah.
31:1:15 OFFICER:	So there's no possible chance that you would have (pause) accidently left **something** in here?
31:1:16 ISAAC:	(sighs) I sure hope not.
31:1:17 OFFICER:	Yeah, me too.
31:1:18 ISAAC:	I **really**, **really** hope not.

Excerpt (7.6) is a male-to-male interaction, where the officer is trying to find out if the passenger Isaac is carrying drugs. In 31:1:7 the officer confirms the last time Isaac used marijuana was *about three days ago*. The *about* indicates an approximation; it seems that neither party minds communicating without a precise time. Men, as shown in Table 7.3, use more *about* than women, suggesting that they prefer the use of approximation more.

In 31:1:9 the officer chooses a polite form of questioning: 'You wouldn't have any remnants or anything in your pockets today?' *Wouldn't* and *or anything* (general extender) are used to mitigate the negative imposition of the question. The question is met with a direct denial. In 31:1:12 Isaac says he cannot even remember when he used last, because 'you know, it's been <u>a while</u>'. The discourse marker *you know* is one of the padding expressions discussed in Section 5.6; Isaac may use it to seek understanding and agreement from the officer. The quantifier *a while* emphasises that it's been a long time.

In 31:1:15 the officer asks, 'So there's no <u>possible</u> chance that you would have (pause) accidently left <u>something</u> in here?' He uses *possible* to sound more polite; he does not mention the word *drug*, instead using *something* to imply drugs. The double-hedge aims to construct the elastic question and make it less confrontational. The terms *would* and *accidently* help to establish a friendly, non-authoritative tone. Isaac answers in his next turn that he sure hopes not, and the officer agrees. On hearing what the officer says, Isaac makes his own stance stronger in 31:1:18. He uses a booster (*really*) repeatedly to show an assertive stance in 'I <u>really</u>, <u>really</u> hope not'. The denials of the passenger in previous turns (31:1:10 and

31:1:12) are very strong, stressed in *definitely no* and *absolutely not*; however, after the polite and softened questioning from the officer, the passenger appears to be reciprocally softening his tone as well in 31:1:16, using the stance marker *I hope*. The issue of reciprocity in EL is discussed further in Section 9.2.

The officer tends to hedge frequently, more than Isaac, who is emphatic and assertive, especially in the first part of the exchange. The officer may use EL as a strategy of self-protection, preferring to be tentative to avoid wrongly accusing Isaac. (In the end a frisk search fails to find anything, so Isaac is free to go.)

There are some gender variations demonstrated in this study, especially in the use of hedges and *about* approximation. There are also similarities between the gender groups, as in the fairly even use of boosters and *something*. Gender variance is not a matter of all-or-none, but a matter of different linguistic behaviours in response to different situations. There is no static or fixed stereotype for either men or women in the use of EL. This is in line with Holmes' (2006: 1) argument: 'people's interactional styles at work are anything but uniform, and that stylistic diversity and sensitivity to context are features of the ways in which both women and men interact at work, may help to counter negative stereotypes and undermine the prejudice that affects women in particular in many workplaces'.

7.3 Summary

This chapter discusses social factors of power and gender in the use of EL. A summary of the findings is shown in Table 7.4.

Table 7.4 reveals that the statistically verified differences existing between officer and passenger include individual use of boosters, individual use of hedges, and *about* approximations (passengers use more). Differences between men and women include both overall and individual use of hedges and *about* approximations, and men used more hedges and *about*.

Table 7.4 *Differences between men and women statistically verified*

Category/Item	Type	Officer vs passenger	Men vs women
Booster	overall	no	no
	individual	yes	no
Hedge	overall	no	yes (men more)
	individual	yes	yes
about		yes (pass more)	yes (men more)
something		no	no

The two social factors differ only in two categories: the individual use of boosters (revealed in the power factor, but not in gender); and the overall use of hedges (no discrepancy for power, but there is in gender). There is no difference between power and gender factors for the overall use of boosters, the individual use of hedges, or the use of *about* and *something*. The pattern suggests that the impact of power and gender factors is more similar than different.

In this study the concept of power is defined as the speaker's ability to sanction others as well as the speaker's own interests not being challenged. While passengers are expected to be cooperative, this does not require that the officer have power over the passenger. The impact of the power factor does not occur at the general level (the general frequencies of booster and hedge are the same between officers and passengers), but differ in individual preferences for various boosters and hedges. For example, while both parties use similar rates of *probably*, passengers use twice as much *too* and *so*, and officers use much more *quite* (three times), *could be* (four times) and *possibly* (six times), and three times less *maybe*. Passengers use approximately 40% more *about* than officers, indicating that they opt for approximation. Both sides use *something* at a similar rate.

Power imbalance does exist between officers and passengers: for example, the officers (as institutional representatives) tend to initiate conversations with passengers, and often are in a dominant position to ask questions. However, this does not mean that they want to appear authoritarian. The similarities in the total number of hedges and boosters used by officers and passengers indicate both groups are equally assertive or tentative. They are also similar in using *something*, meaning that neither group is more general or specific than the other.

The results are somewhat unexpected: a common expectation would be that passengers will use more hedges and fewer boosters than officers, given the authoritative position of the officers. The officers use EL to carry out their institutional duties but at the same rate that the passengers use EL for non-institutional goals. If hedges represent uncertainty and an uncommitted attitude, then that attitude is equally shared by officers and passengers. If hedges are linked with speakers with lower power status, then the assumption that the officer has higher power runs into problems. The empirical evidence shows fluidity between EL and power status; no one-to-one match is presented. The same argument applies to the explanation of the booster results, as there is no evidence that passengers are less emphatic than officers. Each takes turns in having power over the other: one party claims power in one situation, the other party readjusts it in another situation, so that the power relation is elastic rather static.

The other social factor is gender. The common perception is that men talk primarily for information exchange and are more competitive and direct.

7.3 Summary

Women are more affective, indirect and collaborative. The data in this study show that men (male officers and passengers) and women (female officers and passengers) actually use similar rates of booster, both as a group (total instances) and individually (different types): that is, men and women use emphasis in similar degrees and manners.

There is a gender difference in the use of hedges, however, in that men actually use more. This result again goes against the common assumption that women use more hedges. If hedges link to tentativeness, then male speakers in the data are less certain, which does not support the claim that EL is women's language. Men in the data prefer *probably* most and *possibly* least, and women prefer *could be* and *maybe* almost equally, and *possibly* least. Women and men show some similarity in terms of their least favourite word, *possibly*. They use *maybe*, *so* and *something* at similar rates. However, the two groups differ in the use of *could be*, and most noticeably in the use of *probably*.

While men and women differ mostly in the frequency of *probably*, the term occurs with similar frequencies between officers and passengers. Officers and passengers differ greatly in the frequency of *maybe* and *possibly*, but this discrepancy is not apparent between men and women. Men and women use boosters with little difference and hedges differently, but there is no difference in the overall frequency of either boosters or hedges between officers and passengers. Women use less *about* than men, but the two gender groups use very similar rates of *something*. The fact that the men use more approximators again contradicts the claim that women are less assertive. Both power and gender factors have an impact on the use of *about*, but not on *something*, and this similarity indicates that *something* is used regardless of social influences.

Power and gender factors do have certain impacts on the use of EL, but not necessarily in the same way. The findings do not support some of the features listed in Table 7.2. For example, men use more hedges in these data, showing that they may be more indirect than women. The officers tend to hedge frequently and appear less confrontational, perhaps as a strategy of self-protection. Passengers, on the other hand, are often more emphatic and assertive as well, in a bid to reclaim power to verify their innocence and improve their disadvantaged situation. The similarities as well as differences in relation to the impact of power and gender on EL use suggest that impact is a matter of degree, matched by appropriate linguistic choices of EL in responding to different situations. Social impacts are not fixed, manifesting the elasticity of EL.

8   Elastic language and speech factors

This chapter discusses the impact of speech factors on EL. Speech factors include speech events, speech genre, and speech competence. Speech event refers to utterances that happen in particular circumstances, such as a given place and time. The speech events this chapter looks at are drug vs non-drug cases, and how the severity of a situation may influence the use of EL. Speech genre refers to types of situated utterance with recognisable speech features, such as greetings, interviews, and conference speeches. The two speech genres discussed are monologue and dialogue, with reference to how EL is used in these opposing genres. Speech competence particularly refers to speaker's linguistic ability, as a first language speaker (L1) or second language speaker (L2). This chapter investigates links between language competence (L1 vs L2) and the use of EL.

The analysis in this chapter again mixes quantitative and qualitative approaches to provide the fullest possible picture of the impact of speech factors on EL. Quantitative data take the form of the frequency of ten stretchers, the same ones investigated in the previous chapters; the analysis depicts tendencies in the use of EL in relation to speech events, genre, and competence. Qualitative data take the form of excerpts from the data, which offer specific uses of EL to provide detailed information of situated EL.

8.1   Speech event: drug vs non-drug cases

EL is influenced by speech events and situations (Biber et al. 2010; Ruzaitė 2007). Biber et al. (2010) claim that VL is found more in conversations or other informal discourse. In particular, for instance, general extenders (*and something like that*) are more frequently used in conversations between counsellors and students than in academic lectures, more frequently in informal interviews and less frequently in family dinner table conversation (Ediger 1995a). In problem-solving and enquiry-based speech events in situations like a maths classroom, VL is also needed because the conditions require something different from a straight 1+1=2 speech event (Rowland 2007).

8.1 Speech event: drug vs non-drug cases

Table 8.1 *Frequency of stretchers used in drug and non-drug cases*

Category	Item	Drug cases ($n = 58{,}962$) Raw frequency	Relative frequency (10,000 words)	Non-drug cases ($n = 196{,}889$) Raw frequency	Relative frequency (10,000 words)
Scalar	*very*	150	25.4	524	26.6
(booster)	*quite*	87	14.8	155	7.9
	too	36	6.1	84	4.3
	so	17	2.9	97	4.9
	Total	**290**	**49.2**	**860**	**43.7**
Epistemic	*could be*	59	10	103	5.2
(hedges)	*probably*	54	9.2	124	6.3
	maybe	32	5.4	109	5.5
	possibly	26	4.4	44	2.2
	Total	**171**	**29**	**380**	**19.2**
Approximate	*about*	36	6.1	124	6.3
General	*something*	204	34.6	246	12.5

This section investigates two types of speech event, drug and non-drug cases, which weigh differently in terms of level of severity. In a drug case the accused may face a frightening, bleak situation and have more to lose than people accused of non-drug crimes. Someone guilty of a drug offence will surely go to jail, but someone carrying undeclared food is more likely to receive a fine; this affects how EL is utilised by the two groups. Drug cases here involve passengers suspected of drug use and trafficking. Non-drug cases include passengers suspected of work permit breaches, carrying false passports, importing forbidden items, failing to declare a criminal history, illegal migration, being a non-genuine tourist, and the like.

As might be expected, hedges are used one-third more in drug cases than in others, as shown in Table 8.1. The difference is statistically significant (χ^2 [d.f. 1, $n = 255{,}851$] = 19.873, $p < 0.001$). Drug trafficking carries severe penalties, and in their defence the accused use linguistic 'weapons' including hedging. The drug-case group also use about 10% more boosters than the other group, but this difference is not statistically confirmed (χ^2 [d.f. 1, $n = 255{,}851$] = 3.073, $p = 0.07960245$). The drug-case group tend to hedge more, but both groups strengthen their claims to similar degrees through the use of boosters. While there is no significant difference between the two groups in the overall use of boosters, there is a statistically verified difference in the use of four individual types (χ^2 [d.f. 4, $n = 255{,}851$] = 30.501, $p < 0.001$). As shown in Table 8.1 and Figure 8.1, both groups use similar rates of *very*, but the drug-case group use about twice as much *quite* and 30% more *too*. The non-drug group use about 40%

186   Elastic language and speech factors

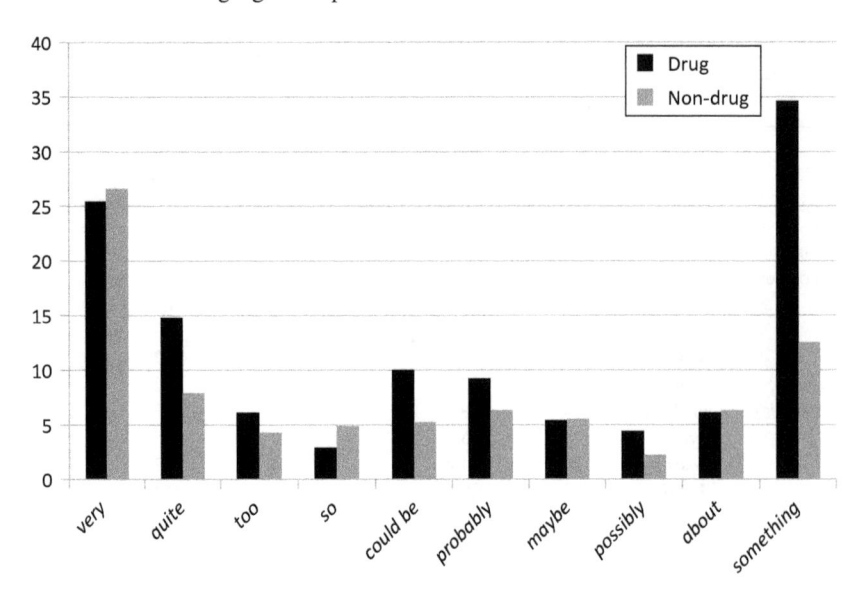

Figure 8.1 Frequency of stretchers used in drug and non-drug cases

more *so*. In emphasising a point, the drug-case group prefer *quite* and *too*, but *so* is the favourite of the non-drug group. As with boosters, there is a significant difference in the use of the four types of hedge (χ^2 [d.f. 4, n = 255,851] = 29.573, $p < 0.001$). Apart from similar rates in the use of *maybe*, the drug-case group use the other three hedges (*could be*, *probably* and *possibly*) more than the non-drug group. This is in line with the overall frequency of the drug-case group using hedges more than the non-drug-case group.

The two groups show little difference in their use of the approximator *about* (χ^2 [d.f. 1, n = 255,851] = 0.027, p = 0.86948178), but there is a significant difference (χ^2 [d.f. 1, n = 255,851] = 126.269, $p < 0.001$) for the general term *something*, which the drug-case group use almost three times more than the other group. This indicates that in drug cases the maxim 'go general' is strongly adhered to. A specific use is demonstrated in excerpt (8.3) below.

(8.1)

Data: Episode 32, from turn 32:1:1 to 32:4:35, two speakers, over eight speaking turns.
Context: Officer (female in her 30s) and passenger (American female in her 20s). The officer is questioning the passenger about her trip.

32:4:1 OFFICER: Why aren't you staying longer than four days?
32:4:2 PASSENGER: Well, once I get married I want to come here and that's
                    why I came, to, like, check it out, **and stuff**.

8.1 Speech event: drug vs non-drug cases

(8.1) (cont.)

32:4:3	OFFICER:	You haven't set a date when you're going to get married?
32:4:4	PASSENGER:	**Maybe like** the end of the year, **or so**.
......	(32:4:5 to 32:4:31 are omitted as less relevant)	
		(The officer now wants to know why the passenger is not travelling with her boyfriend, who has paid for her ticket.)
32:4:32	OFFICER:	He doesn't have a passport? Or ...?
32:4:33	PASSENGER:	He, ah, he does, but **I guess** he's got to, like, renew it <u>**or something like that**</u>.
32:4:34	OFFICER:	Is he a US citizen?
32:4:35	PASSENGER:	I don't know exactly, because **something**, like, going on with his papers, but I don't, I don't, I don't know.

In excerpt (8.1), the American passenger has just arrived via Panama, and is suspected of carrying drugs because of her unusual travel movements. She claims that she has come to see if Sydney is the place to spend her upcoming honeymoon, but the officer feels that she may not be here as a tourist. In 32:4:2, the passenger answers the officer's question: having come from the other side of the world, why does she stay for no more than four days? She starts with the padding word *well*, which acts as a discourse management device, the purpose of which is to gather her thoughts before answering. She uses the general extender *and stuff* at the end to express that she has come here to check Sydney for its suitability as a honeymoon destination, and other similar things. The officer does not seem to need to know the specific list indicated by *and stuff*, appearing satisfied with the elastic usage. More importantly, *and stuff* has a second function: to create a less serious, more casual atmosphere, which may reduce adversity between the parties.

When asked when she is getting married, '<u>Maybe like</u> the end of the year, <u>or so</u>' is used in reply (turn 32:4:4). The time 'the end of the year' is already an elastic expression, but as if that is not elastic enough, the passenger adds three more elastic modifiers: *maybe*, *like*, and *or so*. There seems no need to pile up stretchers to the point of redundancy unless the speaker herself does not have the slightest clue when the wedding will be.

The officer wants to know why the passenger's boyfriend is not here, and wonders if it is because he has no passport or for some other reason. The passenger's answer in 32:4:33 is not straightforward: she hesitates, saying he does have a passport but '<u>I guess</u> he's got to, like, renew it <u>or something like that</u>'. *I guess* is an epistemic stretcher, most likely a strategy of self-protection or even evasion here. The general extender *or something like that* refers to things similar to 'passport renewal', indicating tentativeness and also useful for self-protection. When asked if her boyfriend is a US citizen, the passenger continues her evasiveness in turn 32:4:35 by saying she is not sure, but *something* (unspecified) is going on with his papers. She repeats 'I don't know' to deflect the questions. (In the end it turns out that the passenger carried cocaine; she was sentenced to six years and three months imprisonment.)

The data in Table 8.1 above show that speakers use more hedges in drug cases than in others. Excerpt (8.1) is a drug-case situation, and the hedges are used mainly by the passenger to answer questions evasively for self-protection.

(8.2)

Data: Episode 54, from turn 54:3:22 to 54:3:28, three speakers, over seven speaking turns.
Context: Officers Andrea (female in her 30s) and Heather (female in her 40s), and passenger (Swiss female in her 30s). The officers are questioning the passenger about undeclared fresh fruit.

54:3:22 PASSENGER:	Why can't I just go over there again, put that in the garbage bag, come back and then ...?
54:3:23 ANDREA:	You can't do that, ma'am. Once you've cleared out there and you've cleared the Customs barrier line and you come into the Quarantine, that's it, ma'am. There's no going back that way.
54:3:24 PASSENGER:	I **really** didn't understand that airplane food is ... It's **really** a misunderstanding. Sorry and I was tired to fill that out.
54:3:25 ANDREA:	We understand that, ma'am. It clearly states any food at all, ma'am, and like I said earlier if you're not sure the next time you travel through, you're best to always just mark 'yes'.
54:3:26 PASSENGER:	It's my first time here. I didn't know **really**. Because I'm **really** over-stressed, **you know**.
54:3:27 HEATHER:	The reason that the airline gives you the food is to eat the food on the aircraft.
54:3:28 PASSENGER:	Yeah, it's **too much** for me.

Excerpt (8.2) differs from (8.1) in that it is not a drug case and boosters are prominent, although there is no significant difference in the use of boosters between drug cases and non-drug cases, as shown in Table 8.1. The passenger didn't declare fresh fruit, and requests the officer to let it pass without penalty. Officer Andrea insists that there are only two options: pay the fine of $220 or go to court to resolve the case. The passenger is not happy; she frequently uses

8.1 Speech event: drug vs non-drug cases

boosters to emphasise why she didn't declare the food. In 54:3:24 she uses *really* twice to stress that she thought that airplane food was okay to bring into Australia, and it is all a misunderstanding rather than a deliberate act. In response Andrea strengthens her counter-argument that there is no confusion in the form: any food (including airplane food) needs to be declared.

In turn 54:3:26, the passenger changes her argument, trying to persuade the officer to be lenient. This is her first visit to Australia so she did not know better. Again she uses *really* twice to highlight that she didn't know that airplane food was not allowed into Australia, and to emphasise that she is over-stressed from travelling. She completes her turn with a padding expression, *you know*, to elicit the officer's sympathy. The officers are unmoved. Heather points out that airplane food is to be consumed on the aircraft only. The passenger explains that she could not finish all the food given to her, so brought it with her. The booster *too much* emphasises that the serving was significantly more than she could take. (During the prolonged negotiation, the officers stick to their guns and the passenger eventually gives in and decides to pay the fine.)

(8.3)

Data: Episode 35, from turn 35:1:30 to 35:1:43, three speakers, over 14 speaking turns.
Context: Officer Cintia (female in her 20s), supervisor (female in her 30s) and passenger (German male in his 30s). The officers are questioning the passenger about suspected drug trafficking.

35:1:30 CINTIA:	(talking to the camera) Normally it would look like this with nothing in it and you would see a dark shading which appears to be in the shape of a rectangle, so there's definitely **something** there – an anomaly in the x-ray. At this stage we don't know what it is.
35:1:31 SUPERVISOR:	Hi sir, how are you? I'm the supervisor today. Okay, we've x-rayed your bag today and we've found an anomaly in there.
35:1:32 PASSENGER:	An anomaly?
35:1:33 SUPERVISOR:	Yeah.
35:1:34 PASSENGER:	Yeah?
35:1:35 SUPERVISOR:	It doesn't look like what it should when it goes through x-ray. I've got an empty bag (indecipherable). Okay?
35:1:36 PASSENGER:	(Nods)
35:1:37 SUPERVISOR:	At this point in time **I suspect** that it **may** be concealing narcotics in the base, okay, so I'm going to caution you.
35:1:38 PASSENGER:	Yeah.

(8.3) (cont.)

35:1:39 SUPERVISOR:	You do not have to say or do **anything**, because **anything** you do say or do **may** be used as evidence. Do you understand that?
35:1:40 PASSENGER:	Yes.
35:1:41 SUPERVISOR:	Yeah? Can you repeat to me what you think that means?
35:1:42 PASSENGER:	<u>**I think**</u> this means that if I say **something** you can use it in court, but I have the right to say nothing.
35:1:43 SUPERVISOR:	Exactly right.

In excerpt (8.3), the passenger claims to have come to Sydney for a holiday via Dubai, but he applied for his visa in Kenya, and that causes some concern. A frisk search shows nothing concealed on his body, but an x-ray of his bag tells a different story.

Table 8.1 shows that in drug cases, the general stretcher *something* is used significantly more than in other cases. In turn 35:1:30, Cintia comments that there is definitely *something* in the bag, referring to an unspecified thing. The use of the general term may indicate her uncertainty. The supervisor then tells the passenger that there is an anomaly in the bag, and in 35:1:37, she provides a reason for cautioning the passenger, using *I suspect* and *may* to protect herself in case it turns out to be a false alarm. The standard caution in 35:1:39 consists of two *anything* and a *may* to describe possibility. At the supervisor's request, the passenger interprets the meaning of the caution in 35:1:42: 'I think this means that if I say something you can use it in court, but I have the right to say nothing.' The epistemic stretcher *I think* indicates that the speaker may want to mitigate the certainty of his interpretation, and the general stretcher *something* refers to some unspecified utterance. (In the end the bag is found to contain heroin and the passenger is sentenced to eight years in prison.)

Drug cases tend to be more stressful than other contexts, and the findings show that the situational factor does impact on the use of EL. While all those suspected of illegal activities behave similarly in using boosters, speakers in drug cases use more hedges and *something* than others: these two types of EL are useful for mitigation or evasion in stressful situations. This also demonstrates that the factor of the speech event (drug case vs non-drug case) can influence in some ways the use of EL, including its frequency (macro level) and type (micro level).

Channell (1994) states that VL is interpreted differently depending on context and discourse types; it has also been shown that VL frequency and form vary in different types of discourse, such as academic, business, conversation or public (Cheng 2007). Together with the existing literature, this study

8.2 Speech genre: monologue vs dialogue

demonstrates empirically a pattern for using EL: that is there is a correlation between the degree of hedging and the severity of a situation: the greater the severity, the more hedging; the two are positively related. There is no matching empirical evidence to show a positive correlation between severity and the degree of boosting, however.

8.2 Speech genre: monologue vs dialogue

Speech genre is a style of expression in speech. Whether the factor of speech genre has impact on the use of EL, particularly in terms of frequency and types of EL, can be considered by looking at monologues and dialogues.

As shown in Table 8.2, there are differences between monologue and dialogue. Overall, dialogues use every category of EL more than monologues, except *something*. This indicates that the nature of EL is more relational and interactive than detached and narrative.

Monologues use few boosters; the overall frequency in dialogues is more than twice as many (χ^2 [d.f. 1, $n = 341{,}121$] $= 103.793$, $p < 0.001$) as in monologues. Dialogues also use about 30% more hedges than monologues (χ^2 [d.f. 1, $n = 341{,}121$] $= 14.224$, $p < 0.001$). The difference in use of the four individual boosters is statistically significant (χ^2 [d.f. 4, $n = 341{,}121$] $= 120.654$, $p < 0.001$), meaning that they are employed differently in monologues and dialogues. The only item that does not seem to be influenced by these two speech

Table 8.2 *Frequency of stretchers used in monologue and dialogue*

Category	Item	Monologue ($n = 85{,}270$) Raw frequency	Monologue Relative frequency (10,000 words)	Dialogue ($n = 255{,}851$) Raw frequency	Dialogue Relative frequency (10,000 words)
Scalar	very	110	12.9	674	26.3
(booster)	quite	10	1.2	242	9.5
	too	19	2.2	120	4.7
	so	31	3.6	114	4.5
	Total	**170**	**19.9**	**1150**	**45**
Epistemic	could be	116	13.6	162	6.3
(hedges)	probably	3	0.4	178	7
	maybe	5	0.6	141	5.5
	possibly	3	0.4	70	2.7
	Total	**127**	**15**	**551**	**21.5**
Approximate	about	4	0.5	160	6.3
General	something	150	17.6	450	17.6

Note: No chi-square test was run for individual types of hedge and *about* because some of their 'expected frequencies' are below five and the result would not be meaningful.

genres is *something*, which is distributed evenly and with no significant difference (χ^2 [d.f. 1, n = 341,121] = 0, p = 1). This suggests that general terms such as *something* may be equally popular in monologue and dialogue.

This finding does not support some of the existing literature. For example, based on workplace data between North American and UK office co-workers Koester (2007) classifies three types of speech genre: collaborative, in which interactants participate equally, exemplified by board meetings and seminar discussions; unidirectional (monologue, often information-based), in which interactants participate unequally, exemplified by lectures or briefings; and non-transactional 'off-task' chatting, exemplified by small-talk or office gossip. She finds that VL (*things, stuff, like, sort of, or something*) occur least in non-transactional (corridor chats), moderately in collaborative situations where interactants are on an 'equal footing, at least discursively' (2007: 53), and most in unidirectional speech (boss giving orders and using VL to refer to information vaguely and implicitly). Koester thus calls VL 'interpersonal markers' (2007: 74): 'the results for unidirectional genres seem to indicate that discourse which is information-focused and 'unequal' tends to contain more VL' (2007: 54).

This study finds most EL in collaborative dialogues. Two possible reasons for the discrepancy are that Koester's study and this study are based on different discourses, and that they do not look at exactly the same types of lexical items. Koester examines three types of VL (vague nouns, vague category markers and vague approximators), while this study investigates different expressions, shown in Table 8.2 (above).

As shown in Figure 8.2, EL is used in dialogues more than monologues except in two cases: *could be* appears in monologue about 50% more than in dialogue, and *something* is at the same rate in each genre. *So* occurs in monologue a little less than in dialogue, *very* and *too* about 50% less often. The remaining items (*quite, probably, maybe, possibly, about*) are favoured in dialogue but are almost non-existent in monologue. For example, *probably* occurs approximately 18 times more in dialogue than in monologue. It is not used much by narrators, suggesting that *probably* prefers an interactive to a non-interactive setting.

Cheng (2007: 165) investigates four different spoken corpora: academic, business, conversational and public. She finds that spoken genre differences, for example *very*, occur in academic and public speech less than in business communication and conversations; *about* occurs in an academic context more than in the other three genres. Based on the forms of VL and their frequencies, she claims that everyday conversations employ different forms of VL than public discourse, and on average use VL more frequently than public speeches. Cheng (2007: 178) finds that genre is more of a determining factor than whether the speakers are L1 or L2.

8.2 Speech genre: monologue vs dialogue

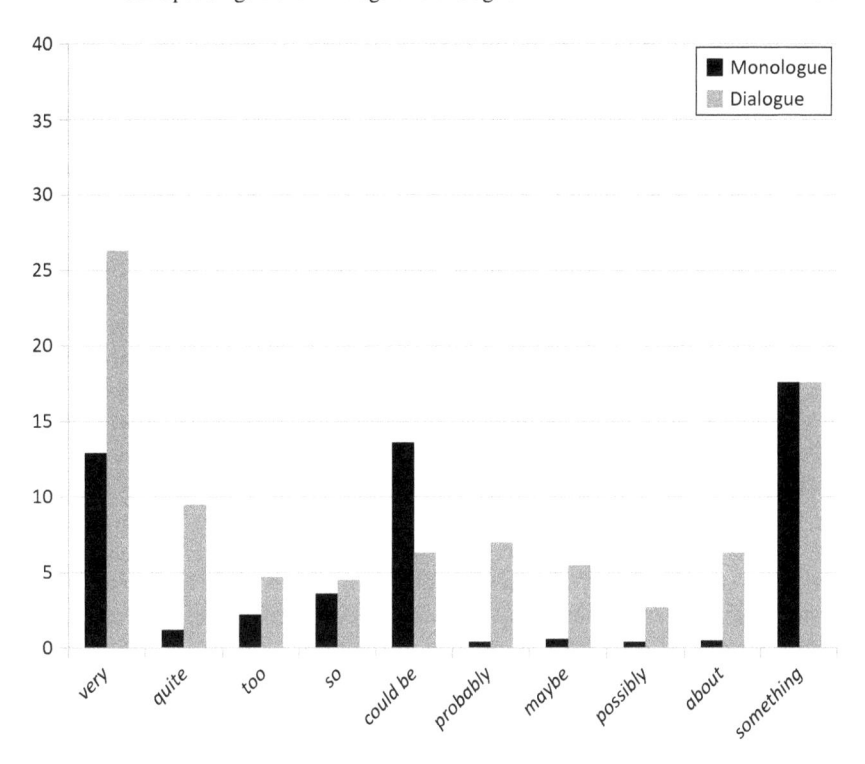

Figure 8.2 Frequency of stretchers used in monologue and dialogue

I think is most frequent in business communication (Handford 2010: 125). O'Keeffe (2006) finds that VL is used similarly in academic discourses and political interviews. In academic discourse, *and so on*, *something like this*, *(and) stuff like that*, and *(or) something like that* are the four most frequent terms; professors are formal and prefer *and so on and so forth*, while students are less formal and prefer *(or) something like that* and *(and) stuff/things like that* (Simpson 2004). Overstreet and Yule (1997b) find that general extenders occur more frequently in a corpus of informal spoken interactions than in more formal contexts. *Things* and *stuff* are more typical in everyday conversation than in meetings (Handford 2010: 163). *Et cetera* and *and everything else* are much more common in external meetings, *that sort of thing* in internal meetings, *and this that and the other* is used more in business English (overwhelmingly among peer groups of British males) than in everyday conversational English (2010: 164–6). In this study, the occurrence of general extenders is insufficient to either support or challenge these findings.

Type of text may also play a role in the use of VL. Carter and McCarthy (1997: 19) state that 'vague expressions are more extensive in all language use than is commonly thought and they are especially prevalent in spoken discourse'. Different written genres also influence the use of VL. For example, emergency procedure writing and literary writing differ in terms of vagueness (Cook 2007: 35). The former strives to be precise, and 'vagueness is a sign of failure'. Literary works are 'systematically imprecise, making vagueness a source of strength' (2007: 28). In literary works, although there may be a reality which the speaker is trying to convey, their success is not to be measured against a preceding reality or winning outcome (Widdowson 1984). On the other hand, as it is about the behaviour and impact of organisations in the real world, an emergency procedure text is measured against reality (Cook 2007: 35). Literary texts have non-linguistic information to convey and no manifestation of extra-linguistic reality, they are therefore vaguer than emergency instructions.

VL appears to be used less in institutional discourse (McCarthy, O'Keeffe and Walsh 2005; O'Keeffe 2006); nevertheless, Koester (2007: 54) points out that 'VL is a pervasive feature not just of casual conversation, but of much work-related talk as well'. Cotterill (2007: 104) notes that 'the stakes are clearly much higher in court, where rights to group membership are to a large degree abandoned, "shared" knowledge about events is disputed and very many "unpleasant things" have to be explored in great detail'. In such discourse, the possibility of using VL is increased. The courtroom situation is similar to the institutional situation in this study, where stakes are also high; the examination of the institutional discourse demonstrates how interlocutors behave in different contextual domains and social spaces (Vygotsky 1978).

(8.4)

Data: Episode 107, from turn 107:2:16 to 107:2:72, three speakers, over 25 speaking turns.
Context: Officer Deb (female in her 40s), officer Ann (female in her 40s) and passenger (New Zealand female in her 50s). The officers are questioning the intoxicated passenger about her erratic behaviour.

107:2:16 DEB:	Alright, what did you get up to last night?
107:2:17 PASSENGER:	I wish.
107:2:18 DEB:	Yeah?
107:2:19 PASSENGER:	I slept with my boyfriend, that's it, told him to f*** off and **and the rest**, had a fight.
107:2:20 DEB:	Had a fight? Had **a few** drinks?
107:2:21 PASSENGER:	Had a sleep.
107:2:22 DEB:	Had **a few** drinks?
107:2:23 PASSENGER:	More than that.

8.2 Speech genre: monologue vs dialogue

(8.4) (cont.)

107:2:24 DEB:	Yeah?
107:2:25 PASSENGER:	Had a kiss, had a cuddle.
107:2:26 DEB:	Yeah?
107:2:27 PASSENGER:	And **the rest**. (laughs)
107:2:28 DEB:	Alright, **too much** detail.
107:2:29 PASSENGER:	Ahahaha, well you asked!
107:2:30 DEB:	So when did you have your last drink?
107:2:31 PASSENGER:	Last year.
107:2:32 DEB:	Last year? Yeah? Was it last night? Or last year?
107:2:33 PASSENGER:	Stop nosing. What are ya?
107:2:34 DEB:	It's my job.
107:2:35 PASSENGER:	Stop it.
......	(107:2:36 to 107:2:56 are omitted as less relevant)
107:2:57 ANN:	(talking to camera) You just don't know if that kind of behaviour is because she's had **a little bit too much** to drink on the plane or it's because she **perhaps** has **something** to hide, or she's nervous, or ... people react differently, so yeah, we're just going to have **a bit** of a further look, see what she has got in her bags.
......	(107:2:58 to 107:2:68 are omitted as less relevant)
107:2:69 PASSENGER:	I can't wait. I want a beer.
107:2:70 DEB:	You want a beer, you just told me you haven't drunk for a year.
107:2:71 PASSENGER:	I was bullshitting like you do. You don't tell me the truth, I'm not telling you the truth.
107:2:72 DEB:	Ah ... I always tell the truth.

In excerpt (8.4), the passenger appears to be intoxicated. A swab test to check if she has been in contact with any illegal substances proves negative. Deb asks what the passenger did last night in 107:2:16, and the passenger uses a general extender *and the rest* to communicate vaguely what she did. In 107.2.20, Deb uses the quantifier *a few* to ask if the passenger had some drinks last night, and it is repeated in 107:2:22. This is because there is no need, or it is impossible, to determine a precise number in the circumstances.

The passenger continues to describe what happened last night in 107:2:27: she says that she and her boyfriend kissed and cuddled *and the rest*, which is again a general extender to indicate an elastic category consisting of things such as kissing and cuddling. When the passenger says *and the rest*, she laughs as well, indicating that she feels it's better left unsaid or that she is joking. Deb in 107:2:28 comments that there is *too much* detail, where *too* is a booster to increase the degree of the quantifier *much*. In 107:2:29, the passenger shows some attitude: 'Well you asked!' This attitude continues on in the following turns. When Deb asks when the passenger last drank, the passenger says *last year*, which is an unusual answer. In 107:2:33, the passenger says that she is annoyed that Deb is nosy, but Deb says that questioning the passenger is part of her job.

Later, in turn 107:2:57, officer Ann speculates about why the passenger behaves erratically. She uses a series of elastic expressions: booster + quantifier *too much* for the amount of drink, and the hedge *a little bit* to tone down the booster effect. This combination may seem contradictory, but if the hedge is meant to mitigate the negative tone of *too much* rather than to modify the amount of drink, then it makes sense. In 'she <u>perhaps</u> has <u>something</u> to hide', the epistemic stretcher *perhaps* and general stretcher *something* suit the description of possibility. In order to check out all these possibilities, Ann says 'we're just going to have <u>a bit</u> of a further look. See what she has got in her bags'. The quantifier *a bit* mitigates the imposition of a bag search.

An interesting phenomenon in excerpt (8.4) is reciprocity. In 107:2:71, the passenger reveals that she is messing about because she feels that the officer does not tell the truth, which the officer denies. This uncovers a behaviour that occurs in dialogues and not in monologues: reciprocal interactions, which require an interactive context such as dialogue; a monologue is unlikely to trigger it (see Section 9.2 for details).

(8.5)

Data: Episode 1, a narrator's talk at the beginning of extract 3.
Context: Officer Annie (female in her 30s) and passengers (Chinese male in his 20s and female in her 40s). The officer is questioning the passengers about undeclared food and other prohibited items.

NARRATOR: At Sydney Airport quarantine officers are flat out processing the morning flights, looking out for any items that **could be** a risk to Australia's environment and primary industries. Officer Annie has detected **some** suspicious material on a baggage x-ray of two Chinese passengers.

This piece of narration (a monologue) in excerpt (8.5) provides some background for the exchanges between officer and passengers that follow. The expression *could be* is used to indicate a possibility. As shown in Table 8.2, *could be* is the only item which occurs twice as much in monologue as in dialogue. It seems that the narrator prefers to employ *could be* to describe possibility. The other stretcher used is *some*, a general expression to indicate a

8.2 Speech genre: monologue vs dialogue

small and unspecified amount of suspicious material found in a bag. (In the end the passengers are fined for carrying undeclared food and traditional medicine.)

(8.6)

Data: Episode 3, a narrator's talk at the beginning of extract 1.
Context: Officer David (male in his 30s) and another officer (male in his 40s) are examining a parcel for suspected drug trafficking.

NARRATOR: Customs officers believe that they **may** have uncovered a **very** professional narcotic concealment. A parcel they selected for examination has had a positive dog reaction and a suspicious x-ray, leading the officers to think that there **may** be **something** in there.

Excerpt (8.6) is a monologue by a narrator providing background information for the exchanges in episode 3, extract 1. In the first sentence, the narrator uses *may* to hedge the absolute certainty of the event, at the same time using *very* to emphasise the highly professional manner of the concealment. Towards the end of the utterance the narrator again uses *may* and the general stretcher *something* to express tentativeness for the time being. The narrator informs viewers that there is enough information to believe that *something* is going on, but we need to wait and see the examination unfold, because that *something* is concealed deep inside a grinding wheel. (Two kilos of cocaine are found and a Sydney man is sentenced to nine years in jail.)

Monologue and dialogue have different interactional modes and requirements, and these have an impact on the use of EL. This finding is in line with some of the existing literature. For example, Adolphs et al. (2007) examine a one million word healthcare corpus with two speech genres, phone-ins and face-to-face consultations, and suggest that mode of interaction may contribute to a higher level of VL use in phone-in data. This is because VL (e.g. *or anything*) 'might serve as a deference strategy to reduce the imposition on the patient', and phone-in interactions 'are fulfilling a particular institutional objective in the elicitation of symptoms, as well as the more interpersonal politeness functions' (2007: 68). VL can also 'casualise the symptom reports so as to downgrade their seriousness' (Adolphs et al. 2004: 20).

Quaglio examines two different data sets, natural conversations and television dialogues in the sitcom *Friends*. The higher frequency of VL in conversation than in televised media is attributed to the 'shared context and the nature of the interlocutors' (2009: 147). Quaglio asserts that the conversation interactants share more specific contexts, and for television interactions the real interlocutors are the millions of people in the audience who must at least minimally share the context in which exchanges take place. Evison et al. (2007: 146) find that conversations involving close friends and family members use the greatest number of general extenders, phone-ins (Liveline in this case) use the second highest, and academic (university classes) data contain the fewest general extenders. The necessary degree of shared knowledge varies in these three types of data: the conversations and phone-in data are predominantly of general issues, because participants come from every walk of life with sociopolitical 'commonage'. The academic data consist of more 'local' academic and disciplinary topics which require specific knowledge by the participants.

Koester (2007: 58) states that 'genre is a key factor influencing the frequency of VL (and many other interactive features of discourse)', and this is confirmed by the empirical evidence in this study, which suggests that EL can be influenced by speech genre, and this is an important consideration in the study of EL. In particular, this study confirms that EL is preferred more in dialogues than in monologues.

8.3 Language competence: L1 vs L2

Passengers in this study are a mix of L1 and L2, and some speak little English. Language competence may be determined by examining the patterns of EL use in these two groups.

Table 8.3 shows that between L1 and L2 speakers there was no significant overall frequency difference in using boosters (χ^2 [d.f. 1, n = 255,851] = 2.689, p = 0.10104321) and hedges (χ^2 [d.f. 1, n = 255,851] = 3.733, p = 0.0533475), suggesting that L1 and L2 speakers are similar in their use of EL, emphasising and hedging at similar rates. The invariance, however, disappears when considering individual types of stretcher, where there is significant difference for both boosters (χ^2 [d.f. 4, n = 255,851] = 26.259, p < 0.001) and hedges (χ^2 [d.f. 4, n = 255,851] = 42.097, p < 0.001). This means that L1 and L2 speakers prefer different types of EL, a tendency that continues with the use of *something* (χ^2 [d.f. 1, n = 255,851] = 7.705, p = 0.00550681), but not with the use of *about* (χ^2 [d.f. 1, n = 255,851] = 3.329, p = 0.06806825). In general, L1 speakers use more EL than L2, but the difference is not statistically significant. This suggests a positive correlation between the frequency of EL and the level of language competence: the higher the level, the more EL use.

This study takes the position of my collaborative work (Zhang and Sabet, in press): when some discrepancy in frequency occurs between L1 and L2 speakers, it does not mean that L2 speakers over-use or under-use some expressions. Rather, when L2 speakers use certain expressions (e.g. *I think*) more or less than L1 speakers, it may simply mean that L1 and L2 speakers

8.3 Language competence: L1 vs L2

Table 8.3 *Frequency of stretchers used by L1 and L2 English speakers*

		L1 (n = 228,451)		L2 (n = 27,400)	
Category	Item	Raw frequency	Relative frequency (10,000 words)	Raw frequency	Relative frequency (10,000 words)
Scalar	very	604	26.4	70	25.5
(booster)	quite	239	10.5	3[a]	1.1
	too	105	4.6	15	5.5
	so	96	4.2	18	6.6
	Total	**1044**	**45.7**	**106**	**38.7**
Epistemic	could be	157	6.9	5	1.8
(hedges)	probably	170	7.4	8	2.9
	maybe	110	4.8	31	11.3
	possibly	69	3	1[a]	0.4
	Total	**506**	**22.1**	**45**	**16.4**
Approximate	about	150	6.6	10	3.6
General	something	420	18.4	30	10.9

[a]While these two observed frequencies are below five, their expected frequencies are above five, making the chi-square test meaningful.

have different preferences, not that L1 speakers set the standard and L2 speakers miss the mark. Particularly if the difference in word frequency between L1 and L2 speakers does not cause any communicative misunderstanding, then labelling L2 speakers as under-users or over-users is unwarranted. This is in line with other work on lingua franca speakers such as that of Metsä-Ketelä (2006: 141), which also argues that lingua franca speakers tend to come up with new meanings for old words: they may deviate from standard or native use of the expression, but their unorthodox use does not necessarily result in communication breakdown.

Figure 8.3 demonstrates that L1 speakers use much more *quite, could be, probably, possibly, about* and *something* than L2 speakers. L1 speakers use somewhat more *very* than L2, which supports the outcomes of Cheng (2007) that L1 speakers use more *very* than L2. L2 speakers use two boosters more than L1: *too* and *so*. Hinkel (2003) investigates the use of hedges and boosters by L1 and L2 speakers in their essays (written data), and finds that L2 speakers stress more than L1 speakers, realised through the use of emphatics (e.g. *a lot*). In this study L2 speakers use particularly more *maybe* than L1, preferring it to express tentativeness. This is not necessarily a sign of over-use, but perhaps a simple preference for the term to express tentativeness.

It may be that the use of EL requires some advanced knowledge of English, so the lesser language competence of L2 speakers prevents them from using EL as confidently as L1 speakers. For example, L1 speakers employ the four

200   Elastic language and speech factors

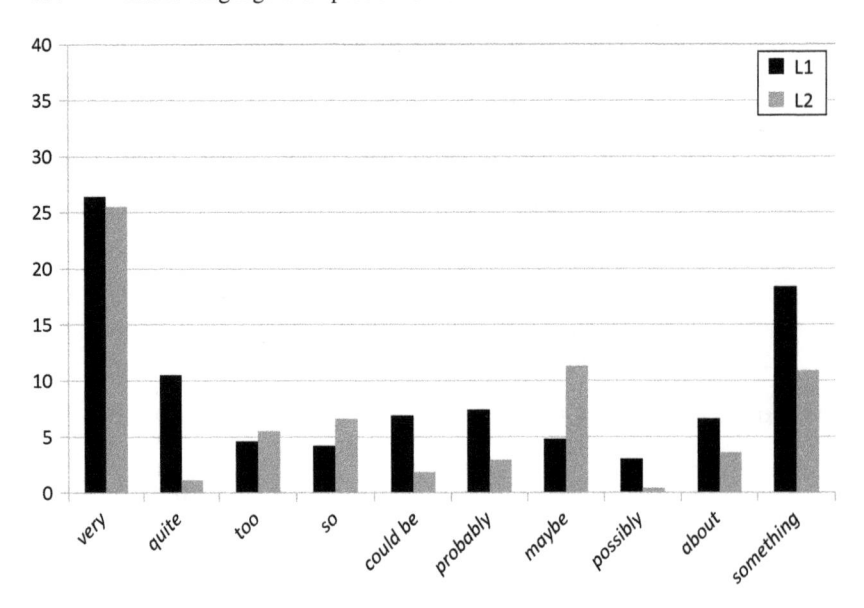

Figure 8.3 Frequency of stretchers used by L1 and L2 English speakers

hedges more evenly than L2 speakers: 6.9, 7.4, 4.8, 3 vs 1.8, 2.9, 11.3, 0.4. L2 speakers use *maybe* much more than the other three words, perhaps a sign that they lack the linguistic ability to work with a wide array of phrases confidently, tending to stick to what they know. L2 speakers sound more informal than L1, as illustrated by the nature of the three words (*maybe, too, so*) that they use more frequently than L1. Cheng (2007: 165) shows that L2 speakers use more *about* than L1 speakers (32.9 vs 30.9 per 10,000 words), but L1 speakers use more *something* (13.8 vs 9.2). Cheng's results are not exactly repeated in this study, where L1 speakers use both *about* (6.6 vs 3.6) and *something* (18.4 vs 10.9) more than L2 speakers.

(8.7)

Data: Episode 5, from turn 5:2:14 to 5:2:41, three speakers, over 28 speaking turns.
Context: Officer 1 (male in his 30s), officer 2 (male in his 30s), and passenger (Chinese female, pixellated). The officers are questioning the passenger about her suspicious quantity of undeclared jewellery.

5:2:14 OFFICER 1:   See it's not ... it's not **one or two** things (pause), you've got the whole bench. (pause) Like for me ... for me ... if you ... if you have a look at that for me, it **looks like** you're coming here to sell it. That's ... that doesn't

8.3 Language competence: L1 vs L2

(8.7) (cont.)

		look like personal use. (longer pause) Do ... do you understand what I'm saying?
5:2:15	PASSENGER:	Yeah, I know.
5:2:16	OFFICER 1:	My problem here at the moment, that you're telling me (pause) that this is all for personal use.
5:2:17	PASSENGER:	(pause) Yeah. (pause) I ... because I ... I ... (pause)
5:2:18	OFFICER 1:	Because look, (pause) if you have a look there, there's **about** 20 bangles.
5:2:19	PASSENGER:	All this, those for friends.
5:2:20	OFFICER 1:	So y-y-(pause) you're saying that you got them for presents, for friends?
5:2:21	PASSENGER:	Yes.
5:2:22	OFFICER 1:	Is there anything else anywhere else? (looking through the passenger's purse)
5:2:23	OFFICER 1:	Can you tell me whose credit ... who:: is ...=
5:2:24	PASSENGER:	=Husband's.
5:2:25	OFFICER 1:	Your husband?
5:2:26	PASSENGER:	Yes.=
5:2:27	OFFICER 1:	=Why are you carrying your husband's credit card?
5:2:28	PASSENGER:	Because he's my husband.
5:2:29	OFFICER 1:	Listen to what I'm going to tell you. (pause) You don't have to say or do anything, (pause) but anything you do say or do may be used in evidence. (pause) Do you understand that?
5:2:30	OFFICER 2:	Ah where's this person?
5:2:31	PASSENGER:	It's my husband.
5:2:32	OFFICER 2:	Ah it's your hubby. (pause) Is that him?
5:2:33	PASSENGER:	Yes.
5:2:34	OFFICER 2:	Was he travelling with you here?
5:2:35	PASSENGER:	Yes.
5:2:36	OFFICER 2:	Okay. (pause) Where is he now – outside?
5:2:37	PASSENGER:	**Maybe**.
5:2:38	OFFICER 2:	Was he carrying any jewellery with him?
5:2:39	PASSENGER:	(pause) **Mmm**:::
5:2:40	OFFICER 2:	We're bringing him in now, (pause) so if you can tell us now if he's carrying your jewellery before we:: bring him in (pause) that'd be **very** helpful.
5:2:41	PASSENGER:	(pause) Yeah, **a little bit** that's all.

The officer finds that the passenger's bag is full of undeclared jewellery, perhaps for commercial use. However, the woman insists that her jewellery is for personal use. In 5:2:14 the officer explains why he thinks this is not so. He uses elastic expression *not one or two things*, meaning that this is not a small amount of jewellery. He uses *looks like* twice to express a hedged evaluation in case he is wrong. At the end of this speaking turn he asks if the passenger understands what he is saying, aware he is talking to an L2 speaker and making sure that she understands what is being said. In 5:2:17 the passenger does not finish her sentence, so no reason is given why such a large amount of jewellery is for personal use. In his next turn, the officer continues to push for an explanation; he asks why the passenger brings *about 20 bangles*, an approximation. The officer could have given a precise number, but the approximator *about* seems a good enough, even a more efficient, choice: there is no need for the officer to count the bangles one by one. The passenger then claims that the jewellery is for her friends.

In 5:2:27 the officer asks why the passenger carries her husband's credit card. It appears that the passenger does not find anything odd about a wife carrying her husband's credit card. This could be some cultural difference: perhaps in Chinese culture it is not unusual. However, the officer does not think so, and in 5:2:29 he cautions the passenger, indicating his assessment that the situation is serious. At the end of this speaking turn the officer checks again if the passenger understands the caution, showing that he is indeed aware of the possible language limitations of an L2 speaker.

At turn 5:2:30 another officer joins in, asking where the passenger's husband is. The passenger says *maybe* he is outside, suggesting either she is uncertain of her husband's whereabouts or doesn't want to tell. L2 speakers, as shown in Table 8.3, use 58% more *maybe* than L1 speakers. In answering the officer's question if her husband also carries jewellery, the passenger in 5:2:39 utters a minimal response *mmm:::*, again appearing to deflect the question. In his next turn officer 2 presses for a more helpful answer, using the booster *very* to emphasise the importance of telling the truth; he also uses the plural form *we/us* in this turn, rather than *I/me/my* as officer 1 did in turns 5:2:14/16/29. Officer 2 may want to emphasise the collective institutional power that he represents when he urges the passenger to cooperate.

In 5:2:41, the passenger says her husband carries *a little bit* of jewellery, and *that's all*, minimising the amount: her *a little bit* turns out to be a huge quantity of undeclared jewellery, so EL is employed here to blur the amount. (In the end the required import duty is paid and the undeclared jewellery is released.)

(8.8)

Data: Episode 11, from turn 11:1:72 to 11:1:83, three speakers, over 12 speaking turns.

Context: Officer Kelly (female in her 30s), officer Kathleen (female in her 30s), and passenger (Australian male of Vietnamese origin in his 50s). The officers are questioning the passenger about positive heroin readings.

8.3 Language competence: L1 vs L2

(8.8) (cont.)

11:1:72 PASSENGER:	But you ask me **so much** questions to waste (arms out) the time.=
11:1:73 KELLY:	=Because we ...=
11:1:74 PASSENGER:	=If you now ... (arms out) =
11:1:75 KELLY:	=Because ...=
11:1:76 PASSENGER:	=... (arms out for 'there') take me down there. (pause) Do it! Your job! (pause) That's it!
11:1:77 KATHLEEN:	Now that's enough.
11:1:78 KELLY:	I explained to you the reason that we're going through everything is because we got heroin readings off your briefcase. So we need to know why ...
11:1:79 PASSENGER:	(holds hands out) I don't know. Honestly I don't know.
11:1:80 KELLY:	Okay, that's fine. But every question we've been asking you, you haven't been telling the truth about things. Do you have **something** inside you?
11:1:81 PASSENGER:	(pause) Don't ask me **so** stupid question.
11:1:82 KELLY:	Okay.
11:1:83 PASSENGER:	See (pause) if you (inaudible) then take me down **somewhere**.

The passenger is an L2 speaker with reasonable English. A swab test shows a residue of heroin on his luggage, but the passenger insists he does not know why. As Kelly presses for explanations, the passenger's temper rises. His language becomes blunt and his body language (e.g. 'arms out') indicates a defiant attitude. In 11:1:72 the booster *so* in *so much* is used by the passenger to strengthen the force of his complaint. In response Kelly explains why so many questions are being asked.

A positive reading on luggage alone does not necessarily indicate illegal activity, as the trace could have been picked up anywhere. The passenger is actually travelling with a drug addict friend; he is a volunteer counsellor helping the friend to recover. However, he does not say this at the start, so the questioning has gone in circles. The passenger refuses to give a straight answer, so Kelly presents a very straight question in 11:1:80: 'Do you have something inside you?' using the general stretcher *something* to tacitly ask if the passenger carries drugs inside his body. In 11:1:81, the passenger again uses the booster *so*: 'Don't ask me so stupid question' to emphasise the unreasonable nature of the question in his view. According to the data in Table 8.3, L2 speakers use 36% more *so* than L1 speakers. In 11:1:83 the passenger makes it clear that if officers suspect him of drugs, they should go ahead with a body search. He uses the general stretcher *somewhere* to indicate his willingness to be searched. (A thorough search confirms that the passenger is not carrying anything illegal and he is allowed to go.)

(8.9)

Data: Episode 17, from turn 17:2:24 to 17:2:45, two speakers, over 22 speaking turns.
Context: Officer Sean (male in his 40s) and passenger (Chinese female in her 20s). Sean is questioning the passenger about bags of undeclared food.

17:2:24 SEAN:	You're looking, for the meat products the foot and mouth disease, BSE ma-er mad cow disease. We're looking at ... (pause) banana products are just er ... are not allowed in the country at all. It's not treatable at all, any banana products. (pause) The mushroom, because there's a variety of mushrooms around the world, and it doesn't **sort of** tell us what mushroom it is.
17:2:25 PASSENGER:	Last time it's okay, so **I think** ...=
17:2:26 SEAN:	=Yeah.=
17:2:27 PASSENGER:	=... this time is also okay.
17:2:28 SEAN:	**Well** I wasn't here last time and I ... I ... I don't believe (pause) that ... this is written in plain English, 'dried beef'. I don't believe any one of our staff here would look at this, see dried beef, and say okay you can go. Dried beef is a prohibited entry into Australia.
17:2:29 PASSENGER:	Okay.
17:2:30 SEAN:	This cannot happen.
17:2:31 PASSENGER:	Okay.
17:2:32 SEAN:	So I ... I'm ... I ... I don't believe that story that you went through last time.
17:2:33 PASSENGER:	What about this one ... isn't this okay? **I trust** that is one is okay and that this one ...=
17:2:34 SEAN:	= Okay. This is a perfect example (pause) okay. We need **things** to come to Australia commercially prepared and packaged, which is great, this is what it is. The problem with this one, it's in Chinese there's no way I can even check or help you on our computer ...=
17:2:35 PASSENGER:	= Oh:::=
17:2:36 SEAN:	=... find out what mushroom these is. Certain mushrooms are not allowed.=
17:2:37 PASSENGER:	=You ... you can't ask er **someone**?=
17:2:38 SEAN:	=I can ask **anyone**, but I'm not going to believe them until I have **some** proof of what I can see that's in front of me. (pause) Okay. I don't know what these mushrooms are.

8.3 Language competence: L1 vs L2

(8.9) (cont.)

17:2:39	PASSENGER:	**I think** this one is okay (pause) because ...=
17:2:40	SEAN:	=Look ...=
17:2:41	PASSENGER:	=... I brought it for **many**, **many** times.
17:2:42	SEAN:	Have you?
17:2:43	PASSENGER:	And for me it's ... it's okay.
17:2:44	SEAN:	Mushrooms ...=
17:2:45	PASSENGER:	=**I think** the mushroom is okay.

A student returning from China attempts to cover her false declaration and also argues about what can be passed through quarantine. In 17:2:24 Sean explains the damage prohibited products may cause. In the end of the turn he says that the existence of a variety of mushrooms 'doesn't sort of tell us what mushroom it is'. The hedge *sort of* indicates that the act of telling here is a non-standard kind. In 17:2:25 the passenger declares that the mushrooms are okay, emphasised by the epistemic stretcher *I think*. The same expression *I think* is repeated in 17:2:39 and 17:2:45; and a similar expression *I trust* is used in 17:2:33. All these *I think/I trust* function to stress the passenger's claim: the mushrooms are fine. The double use of *many* in 17:2:41 serves a similar purpose; the quantifier strengthens the claim that she was okayed many times before when she brought in mushrooms.

In 17:2:28 Sean disagrees with what the passenger says. He starts the turn with the padding expression *well* to lead in to his disagreement. He uses the general stretcher *things* in 17:2:34 to refer to a general category of non-specific items that are commercially prepared and packaged, which suits a situation where he does not know what, exactly, the members of the category are, or where there is no need to provide an exhaustive list of items even if it were feasible. More general stretchers are used in following turns; for example, in 17:2:37 the passenger uses *someone* as a general reference, as she need not, or cannot, identify a person specifically. She is suggesting that the officer should check with another person to verify the kind of mushroom. Sean rejects the suggestion in 17:2:38, saying that 'I can ask anyone, but I'm not going to believe them until I have some proof of what I can see that's in front of me'. *Anyone* seems less specific or more general than *someone*, and *some* (quantifier) refers to either 'at least one' or 'a small amount'. Rowland (2007: 82) points out that in generalising based on evidence, uncertainty is entailed; VL tends to generalisation, leading to 'a case of inductive reasoning that is recognizing what a number of particular cases have in common'. Kirkpatrick (1991) finds that Chinese is more inductive than western languages. In this excerpt, both the L2 Chinese passenger and the L1 speaker Sean use general stretchers in generalising to express uncertainty.

The passenger is refusing to let boxes of undeclared and unidentified mushrooms be seized by quarantine, insists that her mushrooms are all right, and appeals to Sean to trust her. Sean thinks otherwise. (In the end the passenger pays a fine for undeclared food, and the mushrooms are destroyed.)

Not only are there differences between L1 and L2 speakers, as shown in this study, but discrepancies exist among L1 speakers as well. Ruzaitė finds that linguistic patterns of approximators and quantifiers differ between British English (BE) and American English (AE), and that 'negatively loaded lexemes co-occur with quantifiers significantly more frequently in BE than in AE, which may suggest that in BE quantifiers (usually paucal ones) are more frequently used to mitigate negative notions'; consequently there is 'a higher degree of tentativeness in the British than in the American academic discourse' (2007: 214). Ruzaitė demonstrates that while AE and BE used quantifiers and approximators for similar purposes, VL frequency varies significantly between the two English varieties.

Channell (1994: 3) confirms that a language user demonstrates competence by using vagueness at a level suitable to the specific context. She argues that L2 speakers especially have difficulty in the interpretation or inference of implicatures and hidden meanings in English. VL is not covered in their textbooks, usually not taught; so L2 speakers have to rely on accumulated experience from dealing with native speakers. Similarly, Roberts (2003) states that L2 speakers may be disadvantaged by heavily context-dependent language which is associated with the assertion of power, because they lack the background knowledge to construe contextualisation cues and infer hidden cues. Knowing such cues makes a speaker a 'belonger'; not knowing marks a speaker as a minority (2003: 117). Aijmer (2013: 149) states that L2 speakers may find it more difficult to formulate what they want to say than native speakers do because of the constraints on fluency imposed by real-time processing, and they may well use VL such as general extenders more frequently than native speakers of English, and for different reasons.

Cotterill (2007: 113) points out that when someone, especially some of dubious linguistic competence, uses VL, it is not to evade or deceive. This is supported in this study, where L2 speakers often use EL for word search rather than evasiveness or deception. That is, in addition to the usual functions such as emphasising or mitigating, L2 speakers may use EL to avoid making errors of fact, to buy time, to hunt through their vocabulary, to phrase things appropriately, etc. Zhang and Li (1999) find that Chinese L2 speakers frequently produce uncompleted sentences which are meant to be construed (and completed) by the listener. In this study, L2 speakers tend to produce minimal responses, exemplified by frequent yeahs, mhm's, head nods, smiles, and unfinished sentences, all employed to manage discourse fluency and flow of speech, perhaps as a way of getting around the language barriers they face.

Table 8.4 *Statistically verified differences attributed to the three speech factors*

Category	Item	Drug vs non-drug discourse	Monologue vs dialogue	L1 vs L2 speakers
Booster	overall	no	yes (dia more)	no
	individual	yes	yes	yes
Hedge	overall	yes (drug more)	yes (dia more)	no
	individual	yes	N/A	yes
about		no	N/A	no
something		yes (drug more)	no	yes (L1 more)

8.4 Summary

This chapter looks at the impacts of speech event, speech genre and language competence on the use of EL. Speech event refers to drug-case discourse vs non-drug-case discourse, and how the level of severity influences the use of EL. Speech genre refers to the opposing genres of monologue and dialogue. Language competence refers to the competence of L1 and L2 speakers.

As shown in Table 8.4, the most influential factor on the overall frequency of boosters and hedges is the speech genre factor, followed by the speech event; linguistic competence makes no difference at all. All four categories of EL are present more in dialogues than in monologues. These findings indicate that the use of EL works best in interactive and adversarial situations. A common phenomenon is the significant difference of individual types of EL for all three factors, excepting hedges in the speech genre, for which there are no valid data. In terms of individual elastic words, the approximator *about* does not show any difference, so no impact is shown by any of the three speech factors. Variance in the use of the general term *something* occurs in speech events and language competence, but not in the speech genre. This demonstrates that *about* is insensitive to all speech factors, and *something* is more sensitive than *about*.

The two types of speech event, drug case and non-drug case, weigh differently in terms of level of severity. In drug cases accused passengers have more to lose than those in non-drug cases. Table 8.1 shows that hedges are used approximately one-third more in drug cases, indicating it is a favourite tactic, useful for mitigation or evasion in stressful situations. About 10% more boosters are also used, but this difference is not statistically confirmed. The drug-case group tends to hedge more, but both groups strengthen their claims to a relatively similar degree. The speech event does impact in some ways on the use of EL. There is positive correlation between the degree of hedging and the severity of a situation: as severity increases the level of hedging increases, but the level of boosting remains relatively constant.

Speech genre is a style of expression, and there are two speech genres considered in this study: monologue (narrator's voice-over, non-spontaneous) and dialogue (real-world interaction, spontaneous). Table 8.2 shows that every category of EL is used more in dialogue than in monologue except *something*, indicating that the nature of EL is more relational and interactive than it is narrative. Dialogues in particular employ more than twice the number of boosters, and about 30% more hedges, than monologues. The only stretcher not influenced by speech genres is *something*, used equally in monologue and dialogue. These findings align with those of Cheng (2007), who finds that the genre of speech is a greater determining factor than the linguistic ability of the speakers, and of Koester (2007: 58), who states that 'genre is a key factor influencing the frequency of VL (and many other interactive features of discourse)'.

There is no significant overall difference in the frequency of boosters and hedges used by L1 and L2 speakers; both groups emphasise and hedge at similar rates. However, the groups do use different types of EL, which is taken to indicate preference rather than 'appropriate' use. L1 speakers are able to employ all four hedges (*could be*, *probably*, *maybe* and *possibly*) more evenly than the L2 group. L2 speakers use *maybe* much more than the other three, suggesting that a lack of ability to manage language use competently leads to a preference for a term they feel comfortable with. L2 speakers tend to produce minimal responses to manage fluency and flow, which may be attributed to their limited language competence.

9 General discussion

A fundamental finding of this study is that in the Australian Customs corpus, participants speak elastically in various ways and for various purposes. This confirms the existing literature in the field. For example, Popper (1992: 24) points out that 'one should never try to be more precise than the problem situation demands', and Jucker et al. (2003: 1738) state that 'when we speak or write, we are rarely very clear, precise, or explicit about what we mean – and perhaps could not be – but are, on the contrary, vague, indirect, and unclear about just what we are committed to'. This study shows that EL enables language users to achieve communicative tasks that other types of language would not be able to realise.

9.1 Stretchers, pragmatic functions and maxims

The realisation of EL in this study is through four categories of stretcher, and the patterns that emerge confirm the claim made in Evison et al. (2007) that the lexical realisations of vague categories are highly patterned. There are some common tendencies of pragmatic functions, linguistic realisation and the four maxims in relation to EL. The interconnection between the lexical items (stretchers) and their pragmatic functions (elastics) are discussed in Chapter 6 (see Tables 6.1 and 6.2). There seem to be certain correlations between a particular type of EL category and a particular pragmatic function, which conform to certain maxims. For example, hedges tend to serve as mitigating functions and follow the 'go epistemic' maxim. Boosters (e.g. *very*) tend to serve as assertive functions and follow the 'go scalar' maxim. The findings in this study support my previous work (Zhang 2011: 591–2), which finds that VL is stretched in varying directions to serve pragmatic functions and maxims. For example, quality stretchers (e.g. *things*) tend to provide the right amount of information and follow the 'go general' and 'go just-right' maxims. The epistemic stretcher, such as *I think*, follows the 'go subjective' maxim, and *maybe* follows the 'go hypothetical' maxim.

While certain correlations emerge in the data, there is limited one-to-one matching between lexical items and pragmatic functions. A lexical item can perform more than one pragmatic function, and a function can be carried out by more than one lexical item. The relationship is overlapping and fluid, manifesting the elastic nature of language. Participants use stretchers to achieve the purpose of being non-discrete, following the four maxims 'go approximate' (e.g. 'about a month'), 'go general' (e.g. 'something inside the luggage'), 'go scalar' (e.g. 'He is so scared'), and 'go epistemic' (e.g. He probably knows her').

I use 'typically' in my 2011 work to hedge the matches between lexical items and the strategies they perform, because the patterns are observed tendencies situated in specific context, and cannot and should not be taken as rules. Evison et al. (2007) stress that patterns are context-sensitive and must always be explored and decoded in context. In using VL appropriately, interactants need to consider 'the surrounding linguistic context', 'the purpose of the text or conversation', and 'their world knowledge' (Channell 1994: 143). The interpretation of EL is always linked to the situation in which it is uttered. Different contexts specify the role of speakers and specific EL functions associated with the stages of events.

EL in these data serves two general functions: informational (e.g. approximate elastic) and interpersonal (e.g. mitigating elastic, rapport elastic). The informational function is similar to Channell's (1994) 'giving the right amount of information' and Koester's 'transactional' function in 'supplying the appropriate amount of information, obtaining information, or communicating effectively when specific information is lacking' (2007: 44); and the interpersonal function (Carter and McCarthy 2006: 202) is similar to Koester's 'relational' function in being used for politeness and solidarity (2007: 44). Drave (2002: 26) believes that the major function of VL is 'to tailor conversational contributions to the perceived informational needs of the other participant (s) so as to maintain and enhance the ongoing relationship'.

The findings in this study indicate that elasticity is multidimensional. The boosters (e.g. *very, quite, too, so*) tend to stretch a speaker's claim upwards, strengthening the force of speech. Conversely, the hedges (e.g. *could be, probably, maybe, possibly*) tend to stretch a claim downwards, mitigating the force of speech. Other stretchers such as *about* tend to modify utterances horizontally, approximating neighbouring meanings. The manifestation is not monotonic but multifaceted, showing the elastic nature of language use.

9.2 Co-constructed and negotiated elastic language

The elasticity of language is co-constructed and negotiated between speaker and listener. Both parties participate to make EL meaningful in a particular context. For example, in excerpts (6.12) and (6.13) in Section 6.6, there are battles between officer and passengers where EL is used as an effective

9.2 Co-constructed and negotiated elastic language 211

weapon, with officers using it to elicit information from passengers and passengers using it to avoid a direct and compromising response and to play down strategically the seriousness of their allegedly illegal actions. This is in line with Cotterill's finding that, in the courtroom, VL coming from witnesses may call their credibility into question, but from a cross-examiner may incite confrontation (2007: 112): the implication in both cases is that EL is not static, but a facet of dynamic talk-in-interaction.

Negotiation between participants enables an understanding of EL. Kong (2013: 313) states that 'there has been a common consensus that meaning is not necessarily derived from words but through dynamic negotiation in interactions'. For any negotiation to take place, common interests and issues of conflict are two basic elements (Iklé 1968: 13). In these data, a common interest for the participants is to resolve the situation, and conflict occurs when one side tries to expose the truth while the other tries to conceal it. In situations where a speaker wants to hide the truth, EL is used to evade and to thwart the hearer. In situations where a speaker wants the hearer to work out the implicature, shared knowledge and contextual clues are used to co-construct the inference. 'Vague expressions may guide listeners to find the best match between the utterance and the intended meaning' (Jucker et al. 2003: 1742); and this study finds that when a speaker chooses to use EL in a particular negotiation, the hearer normally has no problem in deriving the intended meaning (see Section 9.5 below for discussion on this topic).

Co-construction and negotiation using EL are governed by the communicative purposes of an interaction. This supports my (2011) observation that communicative purpose remains the determining factor in communication. Communication using EL is a social action with a purpose: elasticity is executed according to a moment-to-moment communicative purpose in a specific context. For example, in excerpts (8.1) and (8.3), the communicative goal of the officers in the drug cases is getting an admission from the suspects; the goal of the suspects is to avoid making any damaging statements. These opposing goals dominate EL use in their encounters. While officer and passenger have different goals, sometimes they have similar goals as well. When a suspect is innocent, the goal of both parties is the same: to let truth prevail and to sort out the situation as soon as possible; however, when one party is guilty the situation changes dramatically. In responding to these different situations, EL is co-constructed and negotiated differently because of the different purposes of the speakers.

Drawing on the language of murder cases, Shuy (2014: 17) finds vagueness is ubiquitous in law. Two strategies are employed in the courts to resolve borderline cases: interpretation and construction. Shuy finds that the former only works for ambiguous cases with more than one distinctive meaning, while only construction can deal with vague concepts and texts. He suggests that contextualised linguistic evidence may achieve a clearer understanding of vague legal terms when it is constructed by participants. The findings in this study support Shuy's view, in that the understanding of EL is indeed co-constructed by participants in response to context.

Reciprocity occurs when participants co-construct and negotiate in EL, and is part of the construction and negotiation. Generally speaking, reciprocity indicates a business-like social relationship (Pinker 2011). In this study, reciprocity is defined as a phenomenon whereby speakers behave in the same way other interactants do, as they think their interactants intend to do. Sometimes reciprocity becomes a sort of retaliation or payback using EL. One such case is offered in excerpt (6.5) in Section 6.3, where the officer starts with a soft strategy but the passenger does not cooperate. The officer changes his strategy and becomes more authoritative. A similar example is presented in excerpt (7.6) in Section 7.2 as well, where the passenger's tone softens when the officer uses a mitigating strategy. Excerpt (8.4) in Section 8.2 offers a typical example of reciprocity: the passenger thinks that the officer is trying to convict her of something, so takes the attitude of 'you don't tell me the truth, I won't tell you the truth'. She makes it very clear that she is being deliberately obstructive, evading questions, because she believes that the officer intends to cause her difficulties. Her linguistic behaviour reflects what she thinks is the officer's behaviour.

Participants manipulate EL to their advantage, speaking according to what other participants say to them. Pascale and Athos (1981: 102) argue that 'explicit communication is a cultural assumption; it is not a linguistic imperative. Skilled executives develop the ability to vary their language along the spectrum from explicitness to indirection depending upon their reading of the other person and the situation'. In this way reciprocity mirrors a seller's approach to business communication: telling their own stories to encourage customers to open up and provide the information needed for a sale (Handford 2010). Reciprocity is one of the strategies interlocutors use to 'change trajectory in responding to the other party's attitude' (Zhang 2011: 595). Reciprocal linguistic moves follow a 'repay' kind of behaviour, polite to polite or rude to rude.

9.3 Cooperative and competitive elastic language

Vagueness is a characteristic of natural language (Bolinger 1965; Fodor 1977). VL is a valuable resource that enables us to interact strategically and effectively (Jucker et al. 2003). The general stretcher *thing* can be an interpersonal tool to mitigate negativity, a concluding device, a general superordinate to avoid having to list a wide range of aspects in detail for efficiency, or a filler when a speaker struggles to access more specific lexical resources (Gassner

9.3 Cooperative and competitive elastic language 213

2012: 18–20). Vague expressions are 'deliberately chosen for their contribution on the communicative message' (Channell 1994: 197). Lack of knowledge may lead to vagueness (e.g. Crystal and Davy 1979; Fodor 1977; Lakoff 1973; Ullmann 1962); this study also shows that EL is used strategically even when there is specific information at the speaker's disposal. EL is a shrewd strategic move, and often participants use it not because they don't know precise words, but because they know exactly what to say but choose not to say it. Lyons (1981: 203) states that neither preciseness nor vagueness is always present and desirable, as it depends on what language game we are playing. EL is a pragmatic strategy and its use is closely linked with communicative goals.

Most existing literature on VL focuses on its cooperative strategies (e.g. Channell 1994). For example, a general extender refers to a list of referents, and is an attitude marker showing politeness and conversational cooperation (Overstreet 1999). VL makes an important contribution to the convergent tenor of everyday talk (McCarthy 1998: 108). It is the central feature of daily language in use, both spoken and written, and its convergent nature is used 'mostly with a socially cohesive function as a high-involvement strategy for asserting in-groupness' (Cutting 2007: 15). Adolphs et al. (2007: 75) confirm that 'VL is not merely a symptom of disfluency or communicative uncertainty but strategically motivated by the goal of interactional convergence'. Ruzaitė states that 'people have to communicate cooperatively throughout an interaction and to attend their faces constantly' (2007: 50). However, VL is also employed for competitive purposes. My work is one of the few that observe that VL functions competitively, manifested in various continua of polarities – soft or tough, firm or flexible, cooperative or competitive – and interactants are elastic enough to switch frequently between seemingly opposing strategies to respond to changing discourse needs (Zhang 2011: 594). The tension-prone institutional encounters between officer and passenger discussed in this study reveal that EL is used not only for cooperative but also for competitive purposes. Both officers and passengers employ EL to boost or hedge, depending on the need of the moment. They are soft or flexible one moment, tough and firm the next: EL serves both cooperation and competition.

Words are weapons and bullets, especially in adversative situations. The competitive use of EL tends to occur in conflictual discourse, as has been made clear in this study. In the type of challenging and confrontational situations considered here, it is not surprising to see non-cooperation. The sides have different agendas and motives, and use EL to negotiate moves, cooperative and competitive – whatever works. EL is used for social cohesion as well as confrontation, particularly when it is being deployed for evasive and deceptive purposes.

It is idealised and problematic to claim that only consensual talk is normal. Handford (2010: 178) claims that VL helps to 'address the face needs of the hearers', and failure to use it may be seen as 'highly face-threatening or indicative of conflict' because VL infers a low level of assertion and control in the speaker (McCarthy and Carter 1997; McCarthy and Handford 2004). This study further illustrates that EL is used abundantly to serve both cooperative and competitive functions and in both manifestations is equally effective. EL is not merely face-saving, it is conflict-managing as well.

The use of EL conforms to several maxims of language use, such as Grice's Maxim of Quantity and Maxim of Relevance by providing the right amount of information (Channell 1994; Zhang 1996). However, when it is used for purposes such as withholding information, it intentionally flouts some maxims, such as the Maxim of Quality and Maxim of Manner. Flouting indicates implicature, such as mitigating and evading. Violating a maxim may not be negative if it is justifiable and 'informationally appropriate for the purpose of exchange' (Schiffrin 1994: 225). Perhaps the statement can be expanded to say 'informationally and pragmatically appropriate for the purpose of communication', to reflect the fact that in these data EL is used mostly for pragmatic purposes.

Lakoff (1987: 201) states that in some social situations, being nice is more important than telling the truth. For example, after a dinner at friend's place, we normally say 'it was delicious' even if we didn't like it at all. Examining vague expressions in courtrooms, Cotterill (2007: 100) states that the usual assumptions about cooperation (Grice 1975) and politeness (Brown and Levinson 1987) cannot be taken for granted, particularly during cross-examination, as VL is not necessarily cooperative and polite. In this study, some passengers consider keeping out of jail more important than telling the truth, which affects their judgement when they answer officers' questions. The officers attempt to ascertain precise information, while passengers choose EL to evade trouble. Sometimes the situation and competing priorities force passengers to tell lies.

Cooperative and competitive communication do not have to be exclusive, and speakers may align with or distance themselves from each other depending on the situation. Officers and passengers use EL for cooperative and competitive purposes, choosing whichever suits the moment best. The participants working for the institution tend to work towards achieving institutional goals (Drew and Heritage 1992; Koester 2007), but non-institutional participants may not be happy to do that, as is the case here. The conflict of interests encourages the competitive use of EL. Cooperative and competitive EL play different roles in communication; they are a pair of contradictions, but interact with and complement each other.

Adolphs et al. (2007) find some tension between practical and interpersonal requirements, in that professional health care workers have to provide precise information to their patients to meet their professional responsibilities, but find VL useful in mitigating the negative impact of some things they have to tell a patient. The conflict between these two needs is resolvable by using different levels of vagueness. This study suggests that the tension between an institutional requirement ('tell what it is') and personal maintenance is also managed by using EL: officers use EL to make passengers feel respected (an interpersonal move) in order to find out the truth (an institutional move). Institutional and interpersonal requirements are integrated and complementary, and EL is 'good enough' to achieve both tasks: a phenomenon that is an integral part of the elastic nature of language.

9.4 Universal and specific elastic language

Elasticity consists of universality and specificity. 'Universal' refers to a characteristic that is invariant between opposing groups, and 'specific' refers to a characteristic that differs among groups.

EL serves the communicative needs of all participants in a universal way by stretching in various trajectories, because 'while vagueness is context-governed and culture-dependent, it is universal in terms of its all-round elasticity' (Zhang 2011: 571): that is, universality in its stretchability in various directions and situations.

Table 9.1 shows that universality is primarily manifested at the overall level, in that EL frequency is less variant (six paired groups out of ten, 60%). Particularly, boosters are used at similar rates for four paired groups out of five (80%), but hedges are used at similar rates for only one pair out of five (20%). This suggests that the participants use boosters more consistently than hedges. The speakers of the various groups from various cultures (Australian, Chinese, New Zealand, Greek ...) use EL at similar overall frequencies in the majority of cases, which confirms the previous finding by Koester (2007) that there is no marked difference in the relative frequency of vague terms in American English and British English in workplace settings.

Table 9.1 *Statistically verified differences relating to the influences of five factors*

Category	Item	Officer vs passenger	Men vs women	Drug vs non-drug discourse	Monologue vs dialogue	L1 vs L2 speakers
Booster	overall	no	no	no	yes (dia more)	no
	individual	yes	no	yes	yes	yes
Hedge	overall	no	yes (men more)	yes (drug more)	yes (dia more)	no
	individual	yes	yes	yes	N/A	yes

(Adapted from Tables 7.4 and 8.4 of this study)

Table 9.1 also shows the specificity of EL, in that the frequency of individual types of EL differs in almost every paired group. Different participants prefer different types of stretcher, and the choice of EL is socially (power and gender factors), linguistically (speech event, speech genre, and language competence factors) and culturally (L1 vs L2 factors) specific. This result supports previous work that finds that EL is specific: for example, Cheng (2007) finds that different types of discourse influence the form and frequency of VL use, and Koester (2007) notes that VL is used more often in carrying out institutional tasks than in maintaining interpersonal relationships.

VL is linguistically and culturally specific (Zhang 2011: 596). When talking about gender difference, Sunderland (2004: 14–15) confirms that 'though gender differentiation as expressed in discourse may be a global or near-global phenomenon, *specific* behavioural (including linguistic) differences are likely to be *situated*, or *local*, related to a particular community'. She emphasises the interconnection between gendered talk and the community to which speakers belong. The phenomenon of politeness is universal, but how it is manifested is not the same over cultures (e.g. Blum-Kulka 1990, 1992; Gu 1990; Ide 1989) and is discourse-specific (e.g. Kasper 1999; Lakoff 1990; Myers 1989). Evidence of sociocultural and linguistic influences on elasticity (particularly in terms of the preference for particular types of EL) is also present in this study.

There is a certain degree of universality in the general frequency distribution of EL as well as specificity in the use of individual types of stretcher across five paired sociocultural and linguistic groups, supporting in principle Tárnyiková's (2009: 119) claim that vagueness strategies and manifestations are partly universal (e.g. round number = vague number), but remains language- and culture-specific to a considerable degree. In a broad sense, the elasticity of language is universal in that it is indispensable in communication and plays strategic roles across cultures. At the same time, it is linguistically and culturally specific in that it manifests differently in response to the communicative situation. Interlocutors from different demographics, cultures and societies may stretch EL in similar ways, because globalisation unifies people more closely in how they think and how they realise their thoughts in language; therefore, while this study reveals socioculturally and linguistically specified elasticity, it is not all about discrepancies: similarities are also shown at a general level. Both universality and specificity are important in understanding EL interaction.

9.5 Communicative hero or villain?

VL 'contains referential expressions with undetermined referents, the intended illocutionary force is often not fully specified, and implicatures are not

9.5 Communicative hero or villain? 217

linguistically encoded at all' (Sperber and Wilson 1985/86: 161). The question is: does EL hinder communication?

The data in this study show few occasions where the use of EL causes misunderstanding between interactants. This supports what has been stated in the literature. Vagueness is a 'desirable feature of natural languages. Vague words often suffice for the purpose in hand, and too much precision can lead to time wasting and inflexibility' (Williamson 1994a: 4869). The hearer decides if there is a need to ask for a clarification, or whether a vague expression is acceptable for the context (Jucker et al. 2003: 1751). There are a few cases in this study where clarification is requested, but EL is rarely seen as a communication barrier: it proves itself indispensable, with an important role that precise language is incapable of filling. Cheng and Warren (2001: 81) argue that VL 'facilitates rather than hinders successful communication in intercultural conversations', a point that is also made in Jucker et al.'s work, where 'interlocutors generally do not have problems in understanding vagueness. They are apparently able to find an interpretation, which they consider good enough for the purposes of the conversation' (2003: 1766). Channell (1994: 195) states that 'language users plainly have no particular difficulties with vague language. Human cognition is well set up to process vague concepts.' She states that theoretically VL cannot be assumed to be the exception rather than the rule. Vagueness in language is not a deficiency but an essential ingredient of communicative competence (Rowland 2007: 94) and may be the norm in interactions of many kinds (Koester 2007: 57). This study reveals that EL is treated by the participants as just as normal as other types of language.

EL, then, is a 'hero' in communication rather than a 'villain', because of its effectiveness. 'There is nothing to be ashamed of in vague language; in fact, if people did not have access to it their range of communication would be severely restricted' (Sinclair, in Channell 1994, xviii). Participants use EL to achieve effective interactions that would not be feasible with other types of language. VL conveys far more information effectively than precise language (Moxey and Sanford 1997: 211). Jucker et al. note that vague expressions are 'good-enough substitutes for precise expressions, but are preferable to precise expressions because of their greater efficiency' (2003: 1739); Channell points out that VL is not matter of good or bad, but of appropriate or inappropriate in relation to a particular situation (1994: 197). Everything is about balance; EL is a matter of shoe-fit-foot, when it suits the context.

Why does EL not cause trouble? We take it for granted; most speakers of English are not even aware vagueness exists in their language until it is pointed out to them (Channell 1994: 4). People do not need to have a precise understanding of language; an approximate or prototypical understanding can do the job. Shuy (2014: 22) speculates that 'abstract words such as *intentionality*, *predisposition*, and *voluntariness* convey a prototype meaning in which the semantic categories have blurry edges that permit various degrees of inclusion'. It appears that we somehow absorb and resolve vagueness. Coleman and Kay (1981: 26–7) state that 'a semantic prototype associates a word or phrase with a prelinguistic, cognitive schema or image; and speakers are equipped with an ability to judge the degree to which an object matches this prototype schema or image'. The combination of our pre-linguistic and cognitive schematic ability and shared knowledge of prototypical meaning enables us to communicate in EL with ease.

EL is useful in communication, but this does not mean that it can be used without limitations. In this study there are some cases where EL has to be clarified. Cotterill (2007: 112) points out that whenever VL is used, there is 'an opportunity for confrontation'. Elasticity has limits: overstretch a rubber band and it snaps; overstretch EL and it may hamper rather than help successful communication. In cases where precise information is needed, VL may create miscommunication or incomprehension (Gassner 2012; Hamilton and Mineo 998; Janicki 2002; Janney 2002). This does not mean that VL alone causes miscommunication, because any other type of language (including precise language) can cause miscommunication as well (Ruzaitė 2007: 34).

The term 'vague language' tends to have a negative tone, and is sometimes perceived as 'incomprehensible' (Janicki 2002) or 'obscure communication' (Lakoff 2000). VL usually carries negative associations, such as causing miscommunication (Ruzaitė 2007). For these reasons, this study replaces the term 'VL' with 'EL'. Instead of constantly clarifying the term 'VL', it is wiser to adopt a different term that reflects clearly a positive image of this form of language use.

9.6   Summary

VL permits innate, non-precise interpretation and analysis (Channell 1994: 6–7), not as a marginal form of language use but as a norm (Koester 2006). Five general issues concerning EL are derived in this study. The first is that elasticity is manifested through EL stretchers and their pragmatic functions. There are some interconnections and correlations between lexical items (stretchers), pragmatic functions (elastics), and the four maxims: for example, hedges (e.g. *could be*, *maybe*) tend to serve a mitigating function and follow the 'go epistemic' maxim, but the relationship is overlapping and fluid, which itself is a manifestation of the elastic nature of language. There are two general functions: informational (e.g. approximate elastic) and interpersonal (e.g. mitigating elastic). The two serve different roles and together act as versatile and powerful communicative tools. Elasticity

9.6 Summary

manifestation in this study is multidimensional and non-monotonic, stretching upwards, downwards and horizontally.

The second issue is that elasticity is co-constructed and negotiated among participants. EL is not static; it is dynamic in talk-in-interactions. Co-construction and negotiation are characterised by the following features: (1) common interest, the basis on which to co-construct the understanding of EL; (2) the negotiation of conflict between officer and passenger when one wants the truth and the other does not necessarily wish to reveal it; (3) communicative goals, the determinant factor being that officers and passengers may have different goals at one moment and similar goals the next; and (4) a reciprocal approach in negotiation, as a way of payback or retaliation.

The third issue is that EL performs both cooperative and competitive functions. Most existing literature on EL focuses on cooperative strategies, such as its work in establishing politeness. This study shows officers and passengers employing EL to boost or hedge their utterances. EL is not indicative merely of face-saving, but of conflict management as well. Participants use EL for cooperative and competitive purposes interchangeably, to suit the moment best. Cooperative and competitive EL play different roles in communication and contradiction, but also interact and complement each other.

The fourth issue is that elasticity is both universal and specific. EL is used at largely similar rates at a general level (total instances of boosters and hedges), and serves the communicative needs of all participants by stretching in all trajectories. Specificity exists in that types of individual elastic expression are not the same between most groups, and is socially (power and gender factors), linguistically (speech event, speech genre, L1 and L2) and culturally (L1 vs L2) specific. There is universality in the general frequency distribution of EL, and specificity in the use of individual forms and their frequency of EL.

The fifth issue is that EL is a communicative 'hero', not a 'villain'. The use of EL does not cause misunderstanding between interactants, and there is no indication that EL creates a communication barrier. Participants use EL to achieve effective interactions that would not be feasible using precise language. EL is useful in communication – but this does not mean that it can be used without any boundary, as overstretching may cause problems in communication. EL is not a 'bad' language as long as it is used appropriately.

The lexical patterns and pragmatic functions discussed in this study should be viewed as tendencies rather than rules. Without access to the speakers for personal reflection, we cannot know for certain their real intentions in using EL (O'Keeffe 2003; Powell 1985). While the patterns generated in this study are not meant to be universally applicable, it is hoped that the findings add a new dimension to the study of EL.

10 Conclusions and implications

Why and how do we stretch our words? While there have been some insightful approaches to answer this question, there lacks an overarching theoretical account. This book develops a theoretical framework to explain the theory of elasticity, based on natural language data and a comparative analysis of EL form, function and context. It reveals the significant role EL plays in our communication, particularly in the ways speakers stretch language to negotiate and co-construct meaning in exchanges. Elasticity is an image that allows us to see how EL stretches along and across various continua in a fluid fashion. It works to strengthen and weaken speech tones, firm and soften a speaker's stance, perform institutional roles and resist cooperation, and resolve conflicts between seeking and evading truth. EL adapts to the demands of context, effectively managing the tension between emphasis and mitigation, seeking truth and evading the truth. The maxims of EL use are confirmed in the interactions among interlocutors, as are the interconnections between the elasticisation of language and discursive and social influences. EL is inherently unspecified or underspecified, and strategic: a positive form of language.

The elasticity theory developed in this study consists of three main principles: the fluidity principle (EL is fluid and overlapping); the stretchability principle (EL is stretchable in multiple directions); and the strategy principle (EL strategically meets the demands of a communication). The use of EL observes four maxims: 'go approximate', 'go general', 'go scalar', and 'go epistemic'. There are also three features of EL: elasticity is co-constructed as a result of interactional negotiation between the speaker and the hearer; the manifestation of elasticity is influenced by other factors such as social and speech factors; elasticity of language is universal at macro level and specific at micro level, and they are complementary. In principle, elasticity may be a universal linguistic phenomenon existing across cultures and languages, although its particular manifestation is likely to be specific in response to differences in these factors. These findings confirm that using EL is a positive and deliberate communicative tactic. There is little evidence that using EL causes miscommunication.

EL is non-monotonic and multidimensional (stretching upwards, downwards and horizontally). Elasticity is manifested through stretchers and their pragmatic functions. There are interconnections and correlations between lexical items (stretchers), pragmatic functions (elastics), and the four maxims; these relationships also overlap.

Elasticity is co-constructed and negotiated among participants. The process features both a common interest in resolving a situation and conflicts between interlocutors. The stretch work features local and global elasticity and reciprocity, and is determined by communicative goals. Both cooperative and competitive EL functions appear to be frequent and powerful, challenging the present idealised focus on cooperative functions. EL tends to be used for cooperation in win–win discourses and for competitive purposes in win–lose discourses. While these functions appear oppositional, participants readily switch between them as best suits their immediate discursive need.

This book promotes the term 'elastic language', which does justice to the desirability of a form of language that has not been given the attention it rightly deserves. The concept of elasticity interconnects with other concepts such as vagueness, generality, and unspecificness. The findings of this study demonstrate the fruitfulness of stretching words to suit communicative needs, and the analysis carried out within the proffered elasticity-theoretical framework provides plausible explanations of stretching at work. Specifically, the findings provide answers to the three research questions raised in Section 1.3 and reprised below.

10.1 How is elastic language distributed?

Determining how EL is distributed requires a quantitative approach. EL is realised through four linguistic categories: (1) approximate stretcher (e.g. *about 20, many*); (2) general stretcher (e.g. *things, and things like that*); (3) scalar stretcher (e.g. *very, a bit*); (4) epistemic stretcher (e.g. *maybe, I think*). The top 20 stretchers, ranking from the most frequent, are *very, some, anything, something, lot (a lot, a lot of, lot of, lots of), quite, things, a bit, much, probably, sort of, could be, about, possible/possibly, maybe, stuff, a little bit, too, so, or something*. The ranking provides an overall picture of EL distribution. Further analysis of the four categories of stretcher and their versatile clusters reveals the non-discrete nature of the category boundaries, suggesting the fluidity of EL. It finds that participants are less variable in overall frequency level, but more variable in using individual items. They use boosters more consistently than they use hedges.

10.2 What are the pragmatic functions of elastic language?

The pragmatic functions of EL are revealed through a qualitative approach. The naturally occurring data used in this study were undoubtedly advantageous in their wealth of empirical evidence of the different functions of EL, showing how it stretches and adjusts its 'rubber band' qualities to achieve communicative goals.

Six pragmatic functions – just-right, rapport, mitigating, intensifying, self-protection, and evasive – are selected for scrutiny. The just-right elastic expresses tentativeness when precise information is unavailable or unimportant. Approximate stretchers are typically used with the just-right elastic, when an estimate is good enough for the context. Rapport elastic is a strategy for establishing solidarity, informality, and friendliness, and general extenders such as *things like that* typically realise this function by establishing sameness and group identity. Mitigating elastic wards off face threats, toning down or lowering the force of a claim, and is typically accomplished by using downtoners and softeners in discourses of a negative or sensitive nature. Intensifying elastic increases the strength of a claim, typically by using scalar words such as *very* and *a lot*, also called boosters or intensifiers. Intensifying elastic is an emphatic, authoritative and institutional marker, as well as a device used to hide information.

Self-protection elastic hedges a statement to safeguard the speaker's interests, typically realised by shields (e.g. *I think, probably, seem to*) which convey the speaker's lack of full commitment and their reluctance to let others know their true intention. Evasive elastic is used to withhold information and deflect questions – signs of non-cooperation. When evasiveness occurs, the hearer tends either to accept it if it does not interfere with the communication, or challenge it if it becomes obstructive. There are some correlations between the four categories of stretcher and the six EL strategies, but no systematic correlation can be established because of the non-linear behaviour of EL. For example, *some* can be both an approximate stretcher and a general stretcher, and *many* can be both an approximate stretcher and a scalar stretcher. Some disfluencies occur around EL expressions, exemplified by padding expressions (e.g. *well, you know*) and non-verbal activities (pause). These indicate that the speaker has stopped to think about how to make the best use of EL for the immediate need.

10.3 How does elastic language interact with social and speech factors?

EL is socially situated, and a speaker's stance may be shaped and influenced by certain social factors. This study found a limited impact of power and gender on the use of EL at overall distribution level. The lack of significant difference in the total number of hedges and boosters used by officers and passengers indicates that each group is as assertive or unassertive as the other – a rather surprising result, given the assumed authoritative

10.3 How does elastic language interact with social and speech factors? 223

position of the officers, and suggesting that EL is not necessarily indexical of power status at a general level. More impact is revealed at the individual level, however.

The power asymmetry between officer and passenger, in the sense that officers tend to initiate conversations and ask questions, does not stop both groups using similar rates of boosters and hedges. There is no evidence that passengers are less emphatic or tentative than officers. The groups take turns in claiming, reclaiming or adjusting power, in a manner that indicates how changeable power relations may be. EL is a powerful device in handling tension: caught between trusting what a passenger says and carrying out their duties, officers often resort to elasticity. EL also enables them to show empathy with passengers who are distressed and confused, without abandoning their institutional duties.

Men (male officers and passengers) and women (female officers and passengers) use similar frequencies of boosters in total number and of individual types as well. Gender difference is evident in the use of hedges: men use more hedges, and differ from women in their choice of hedge. This finding goes against the common assumption that women use more hedges, and does not support the claim that EL is women's language. In this study, men are the more tentative and women the more assertive. Power and gender factors have certain impacts on the use of EL, but not necessarily in the same way. For example, men use more hedges than women, but there is no difference between officers and passengers. Men prefer the same types of booster as women, but officers and passengers prefer different types.

Speech event (drug vs non-drug case), speech genre (monologue vs dialogue) and language competence (L1 vs L2) impact on the use of EL in one way or another. Participants use more EL in severe situations such as drug cases. In particular, they use fewer hedges in non-drug cases, suggesting that EL is beneficial in dangerous encounters. The most influential factor is speech genre (dialogues use much more EL than monologues), while language competence (L1 vs L2) makes no difference at all to the overall frequencies of booster and hedge but does affect their individual frequencies. This finding indicates that EL is more frequently employed in interactive than in non-interactive situations. This indicates that EL is interactive and simultaneous in nature, and it is relational rather than narrative. Drug and non-drug cases are different in terms of severity of outcome, and hedges appear more in drug cases, indicating that mitigating or evading tactics are employed more in stressful situations. The severity of a situation and hedging are positively related. L1 and L2 speakers emphasise and hedge at similar overall rates, but prefer different types of EL; and L1 speakers employ all four hedges more adeptly than L2, suggesting a lack of linguistic ability to manage many different forms of EL by L2 speakers. There is one cross-board phenomenon: a significant difference in the use of individual forms of EL for all three speech factors. *About* is insensitive to speech factors, but *something* is more sensitive.

As this study is carried out on an institutional corpus, the conclusions should not be over-claimed. While it may be too soon to claim that the patterns derived from this study are universal and apply across languages, these findings have value as they put EL in the spotlight.

10.4 Implications

Language without elasticity is a dead reef and going nowhere. EL is a live ocean and reaches everywhere. This study investigates how EL games are played in tension-prone situations and explicates the pragma-linguistic use of stretch work. The elasticity theory developed in this book adds an important theoretical dimension to the study of EL.

The notion of elasticity promoted in this study implies there are degrees and relativity of certainty in language. The concept of elasticity reconceptualises how EL is perceived in linguistics and positions it as a legitimate and valuable interactional construct. EL is dynamic, not fixed. In proposing an elasticity theory, this work calls for a paradigm shift in the way we think about language, something that may be profoundly challenging for many because the theory challenges the deeply ingrained ideology that precise language is always better than EL. EL should not be a taboo topic: it is a natural part of the fabric of our language, and the sooner we acknowledge it the better we can maximise its power in communication.

The new knowledge of this overlooked phenomenon raises a fundamental question for linguistics research: Does language have to be clear-cut? The answer is no, as linguistic communication is naturally elastic. The findings in this study offer an early map of the linguistic landscape of adversarial discourse, where operations of a cooperative and competitive nature are as integral to each other as mountains and valleys. Rescher (2008) states that vagueness does not stop a statement from being true and useful, and VL is just as true and useful as any other type of language, if not more. This study may help people to take a less idealised view of the necessity for precision.

This study highlights features of institutional interaction, including discursive negotiations and multimodal exchanges, where elasticity is a ubiquitous feature. Elasticity is expected to be applicable to other parts of linguistics and to cross cultures, particularly with its principles of fluidity, stretchability and strategy.

This study has some practical implications. It may provide guidance in training customs officers by strengthening their interactional skills, and by extension may be useful in training other groups engaged in adversarial discourses, such as police, attorneys and politicians; the findings of this study may also be useful to witnesses or people standing accused of crime. It may educate businessmen in how EL is used cross-culturally. Adding EL to training curricula will enable professionals to use EL effectively and avoid misunderstanding people who use EL. There are institutional requirements for officers, and everyone else in various situations, to be more skilful when they convey less specific information through EL.

This study may also be beneficial for language education, if language courses incorporate EL. Vagueness is part of communication skills teaching (Channell 1994: 205). Cotterill (2007: 113) points out that people may use VL for purposes other than evasiveness or deception, especially L2 speakers whose linguistic knowledge is limited. It is important for language educators to be aware that VL is not a sign of linguistic inadequacy: vague expressions in fact are 'part of the linguistic repertoire of the competent language user, who uses them to accomplish particular communicative goals' (Channell 1994: 197), and it is misleading to exclude it. A language learner who does not know how to use VL in the target language 'may sound rather bookish and pedantic to a native speaker' (1994: 21). It is important, particularly at the advanced level, to master EL to become a competent speaker. Students need to know things like how to mitigate, how to express politeness, and how to speak imprecisely.

While there is currently a preference for non-existent 'precise language', EL represents the real-life patterns of language use, which have important implications for ways in which language is analysed, for the study of real-world human communication, and for the field of linguistics as a whole.

10.5 Future research

Wardhaugh (1993: 181) predicts that 'vagueness rather than precision will prevail'. This study contributes to the theory and knowledge of the complexity of EL by developing the elasticity theory and offering fresh insight into the use of EL in institutional settings. Although the elasticity theory is proposed here primarily to explain the pragmatic behaviour of EL, it may also be applicable to other linguistic phenomena such as syntax and prosody.

Further research includes the application of elasticity theory to inter-cultural or cross-cultural communication. This will demonstrate if the theory is universal or specific, and if there is a need for more than one theory to deal with EL in various cultures and languages: Will one theory fit all, or do we need to have a separate theory for each language? For example, English and Chinese are typologically far apart, so if evidence shows that the realisation of EL is similar in both languages, and that speakers use EL similarly in ways that can be explained adequately by elasticity theory, then EL and elasticity theory are universal as far as these two languages are concerned. Such findings will not only make a contribution to EL itself, but also to inter- and cross-cultural communication in general.

Further theoretical explorations can be pursued as well. For example, the data show that men use more hedges than women. Are men socially conditioned to be more accommodating and so use these techniques, or is there another reason for this gender difference? Is the difference social or innate? Is EL inherent or developmental?

EL is a 'broad and fruitful area of language study' (Channell 1994: 198). Further EL research could be cross-discourse (e.g. classroom, police interviews, political speech), cross-disciplinary (e.g. engineering texts, arts texts), cross-genre (e.g. written language, non-verbal), cross-time (e.g. longitude, diachronic), or cross-approach (e.g. psychological, cognitive): all of these will enhance the richness of EL study.

References

Adolphs, S. (2006), Advances in corpus linguistics. *Journal of Pragmatics* 38(2): 292–6.
Adolphs, S., S. Atkins and K. Harvey (2007), Caught between professional requirements and interpersonal needs: vague language in healthcare contexts. In J. Cutting (ed.), *Vague Language Explored*, pp. 62–78. Basingstoke (UK): Palgrave Macmillan.
Adolphs, S., B. Brown, R. Carter, C. Crawford and O. Sahota (2004), Applying corpus linguistics in a health care context. *Journal of Applied Linguistics* 1(1): 9–28.
Aijmer, K. (1984), 'Sort of' and 'kind of' in English conversation. *Studia Linguistica* 38: 118–28.
   (1985), What happens at the end of our utterances? The use of utterance-final tags introduced by *and* and *or*. In O. Togeby (ed.), *Papers from the Eighth Scandinavian Conference of Linguistics*, pp. 366–89. Institut for Nordisk Filologi, Københavns Universitet.
   (1997), *I think*: an English modal particle. In T. Swan and O. J. Westvik (eds), *Modality in Germanic Languages: Historical and Comparative Perspectives*, pp. 1–47. Berlin: Mouton de Gruyter.
   (2002), *English Discourse Particles: Evidence from a Corpus*. Amsterdam: John Benjamins.
   (2013), *Understanding Pragmatic Markers: A Variational Pragmatic Approach*. Edinburgh: Edinburgh University Press.
Andersen, G. (2010), A contrastive approach to vague nouns. In G. Kaltenböck, W. Mihatsch and S. Schneider (eds), *New Approaches to Hedging*, pp. 35–48. Bingley (UK): Emerald.
Anderson, J. (1973), Universal quantifiers. *Lingua* 31: 125–76.
Ariel, M. (2000), *Defining Pragmatics*. Cambridge: Cambridge University Press.
Atkinson, J. M. and J. Heritage, eds (1984), *Structures of Social Action. Studies in Conversation Analysis*. Cambridge: Cambridge University Press.
Austin, J. L. (1962), *Sense and Sensibilia*. Oxford: Clarendon Press.
Banfield, A. (1973), Narrative style and the grammar of direct and indirect speech. *Foundations of Language* 10: 1–39.
Bavelas, J. B., A. Black, N. Chovil and J. Mullett (1990), *Equivocal Communication*. Newbury Park (CA): Sage.
Biber, D., S. Johansson, G. Leech, S. Conrad and E. Finegan (1999), *Longman Grammar of Spoken and Written English*. London: Longman.

(2010), *Longman Grammar of Spoken and Written English*, 8th edition. London: Longman.

Birner, B. J. (2013), *Introduction to Pragmatics*. West Sussex: Wiley-Blackwell.

Blakemore, D. (1992), *Understanding Utterances: An Introduction to Pragmatics*. Oxford: Blackwell.

Blum-Kulka, S. (1990), 'You don't touch lettuce with your fingers': parental politeness in family discourse. *Journal of Pragmatics* 14: 259–88.

(1992), The metapragmatics of politeness in Israeli society. In R. J. Watts, S. Ide and K. Ehlich (eds), *Politeness in Language: Studies in its History, Theory and Practice*, pp. 255–80. Berlin: Mouton de Gruyter.

Blum-Kulka, S., J. House and G. Kasper (1989), *Cross-Cultural Pragmatics: Requests and Apologies*. Norwood (NJ): Ablex.

Bolinger, D. (1961), *Generality, Gradience, and the All-or-None*. The Hague: Mouton.

(1965), The atomization of meaning. *Language* 41(4): 555–73.

(1972), *Degree Words*. The Hague: Mouton.

(1975), *Aspects of Language*. New York: Harcourt Brace Jovanovich.

Bradac, J. J. and R. L. Street, Jr (1989/90), Powerful and powerless styles of talk: a theoretical analysis of language and impression formation. *Research on Language and Social Interaction* 23: 195–241.

Bradac, J. J., A. Mulac and S. A. Thompson (1995), Men's and women's use of intensifiers and hedges in problem-solving interaction: molar and molecular analyses. *Research on Language and Social Interaction* 28(2): 93–116.

Briggs, C. L. (1997), Introduction: from the ideal, the ordinary, and the orderly to conflict and violence in pragmatic research. *Pragmatics* 7(4): 451–59.

Brockway, D. (1981), Semantic constraints on relevance. In H. Parret, M. Sbisà and J. Verschueren (eds), *Possibilities and Limitations of Pragmatics*, pp. 57–78. Amsterdam: John Benjamins.

Brown, P. (1980), How and why are women more polite: some evidence from a Mayan community. In S. McConnell-Ginet, R. Borker and N. Furman (eds), *Women and Language in Literature and Society*, pp. 111–36. New York: Praeger.

Brown, P. and S. C. Levinson (1978), Universals in language usage: politeness phenomena. In E. N. Goody (ed.), *Questions and Politeness: Strategies in Social Interaction*, pp. 56–311. Cambridge: Cambridge University Press.

(1987), *Politeness: Some Universals in Language Usage*. Cambridge: Cambridge University Press.

Bucholtz, M. and K. Hall (2005), Identity and interaction: a sociocultural linguistic approach. *Discourse Studies* 7(4–5): 585–614.

Burnett, H. (2012), The puzzle(s) of absolute adjectives on vagueness, comparison, and the origin of scale structure. *UCLA Working Papers in Linguistics: Papers in Semantics* 16: 1–50.

Bybee, J. (2004), Mechanisms of chance in grammaticization: the role of frequency. In B. D. Joseph and R. D. Janda (eds), *The Handbook of Historical Linguistics*, pp. 602–23. Malden (MA): Blackwell.

Caffi, C. (1999), On mitigation. *Journal of Pragmatics* 31: 881–909.

Carter, R. (1980), The language of sisterhood. In L. Michaels and C. Ricks (eds), *The State of the Language*, pp. 226–34. Berkeley (CA): University of California Press.

(1998), Orders of reality: CANCODE, communication, and culture. *ELT Journal* 52(1): 43–56.
(2003), The grammar of talk: spoken English, grammar and the classroom. *New Perspectives on English in the Classroom*, pp. 5–13. London: Qualifications and Curriculum Authority.
Carter, E. (2013), *Analysing Police Interviews: Laughter, Confessions and the Tape*. London: Continuum.
Carter, R. and M. McCarthy (1997), *Exploring Spoken English*. Cambridge: Cambridge University Press.
(2004), This, that and the other: multi-word clusters in spoken English as visible patterns of interaction. *TEANGA* 21: 30–52.
(2006), *Cambridge Grammar of English: A Comprehensive Guide*. Cambridge: Cambridge University Press.
Channell, J. (1990), Precise and vague quantities in writing on economics. In W. Nash (ed.), *The Writing Scholar: Studies in the Language and Conventions of Academic Discourse*, pp. 95–117. Beverly Hills: Sage.
(1994), *Vague Language*. Oxford: Oxford University Press.
Chapman, S. (2011), *Pragmatics*. Basingstoke (UK): Palgrave Macmillan.
Chase, S. (1950), *The Tyranny of Words*, 7th edition. London: Methuen.
Chefneux, G. (2012), Mitigation at work: functions and lexical realisations. In S. Măda and R. Săftoiu (eds), *Professional Communication across Languages and Cultures*, pp. 169–92. Amsterdam: John Benjamins.
Chen, W. Z. and S. X. Wu (2002), *Fanchou yu Mohu Yuyi Yanjiu (in Chinese) [A Study on Category and Semantic Fuzziness]*. Fujian (China): Fujian Renmin Press.
Cheng, W. (2007), The use of vague language across spoken genres in an intercultural Hong Kong corpus. In J. Cutting (ed.), *Vague Language Explored*, pp. 161–81. Basingstoke (UK): Palgrave Macmillan.
Cheng, W. and A. O'Keeffe (2014), Vagueness. In C. Rühlemann and K. Aijmer (eds), *Corpus Pragmatics: A Handbook*, pp. 360–78. Cambridge: Cambridge University Press.
Cheng, W. and A. B. M. Tsui (2009), 'Ahh ((laugh)) well there is no comparison between the two I think': how do Hong Kong Chinese and native speakers of English disagree with each other? *Journal of Pragmatics* 41(11): 2365–80.
Cheng, W. and M. Warren (2001), The use of vague language in intercultural conversations in Hong Kong. *English World-Wide* 22(1): 81–104.
(2003), Indirectness, inexplicitness and vagueness made clearer. *Pragmatics* 13(3): 381–400.
Chierchia, G. (2004), Scalar implicatures, polarity phenomena, and the syntax/pragmatics interface. In A. Belletti (ed.), *Structures and Beyond: The Cartography of Syntactic Structures* 3, pp. 39–103. Oxford: Oxford University Press.
Clark, B. (2013), *Relevance Theory*. Cambridge: Cambridge University Press.
Clark, H. H. and D. Wilkes-Gibbs (1986), Referring as a collaborative process. In H. H. Clark (ed.), *Arenas of Language Use*, pp. 107–43. Chicago: University of Chicago Press.
Coleman, L. and P. Kay (1981), Prototype semantics: the English word *lie*. *Language* 57(1): 26–44.

Conrad, S. and D. Biber (2000), Adverbial marking of stance in speech and writing. In S. Hunston and G. Thompson (eds), *Evaluation in Text: Authorial Stance and the Construction of Discourse*, pp. 56–73. Oxford: Oxford University Press.

Cook, G. (2007), 'This we have done': the vagueness of poetry and public relations. In J. Cutting (ed.), *Vague Language Explored*, pp. 21–39. Basingstoke (UK): Palgrave Macmillan.

Cotterill, J. (2007), 'I think he was kind of shouting or something': uses and abuses of vagueness in the British courtroom. In J. Cutting (ed.), *Vague Language Explored*, pp. 97–114. Basingstoke (UK): Palgrave Macmillan.

Creswell, J. W. (1994), *Research Design: Qualitative and Quantitative Approaches*. Thousand Oaks: Sage.

(2008), *Educational Research: Planning, Conducting, and Evaluating Quantitative and Qualitative Research*, 3rd edition. New Jersey: Prentice Hall.

(2009), *Research Design: Qualitative, Quantitative, and Mixed Methods Approaches*, 3rd edition. Los Angeles: Sage.

Creswell, J. W. and V. L. Plano Clark (2007), *Designing and Conducting Mixed Methods Research*. Thousand Oaks: Sage.

Cruse, A. (1986), *Lexical Semantics*. Cambridge: Cambridge University Press.

(2006), *A Glossary of Semantics and Pragmatics*. Edinburgh: Edinburgh University Press.

Crystal, D. (2008), *A Dictionary of Linguistics and Phonetics*, 6th edition. Malden (MA): Blackwell.

Crystal, D. and D. Davy (1969), *Investigating English Style*. New York: Longman.

(1975), *Advanced Conversational English*, 5th edition. London: Longman.

(1979), *Advanced Conversational English*, 8th edition. London: Longman.

Cutting, J. (1998), The function of inexplicit language in 'CANCODE' casual conversations. Conference paper presented at *Sociolinguistics Symposium* 12, University of London.

(2000), Vague language and international students. In J. Cutting (ed.), *The Grammar of Spoken English and EAP Teaching*, pp. 39–54. Sunderland: University of Sunderland Press.

(2001), Speech acts of the in-group. *Journal of Pragmatics* 33(8): 1207–33.

(2002), The in-group code lexis. *Hermes Journal of Linguistics* 28: 59–80.

(2007), *Vague Language Explored*. Basingstoke (UK): Palgrave Macmillan.

(2008), *Pragmatics and Discourse*, 2nd edition. London: Routledge.

Daitz, E. (1956), The picture theory of meaning. In A. Flew (ed.), *Essays in Conceptual Analysis*, pp. 53–74. London: Macmillan.

Deese, J. (1974), Towards a psychological theory of the meaning of sentences. In A. Silverstein (ed.), *Human Communication: Theoretical Explorations*, pp. 67–80. Hillsdale (NJ): Lawrence Erlbaum Associates.

Dines, E. R. (1980), Variation in discourse: 'and stuff like that'. *Language in Society* 9: 13–31.

Dobson, I. (2010), Mind your language! *Advocate: Journal of the National Tertiary Education Union (Australia)* 17(4): 28.

Dörnyei, Z. (2007), *Research Methods in Applied Linguistics*. Oxford: Oxford University Press.

References

Drave, N. (2002), Vaguely speaking: a corpus approach to vague language in intercultural conversations. In P. Peters, P. Collins and A. Smith (eds), *Language and Computers: New Frontiers of Corpus Research 16 (Papers from the Twenty-First International Conference of English Language Research and Computerized Corpora)*, pp. 25–40. Amsterdam: Rodopi.

Drew, P. (1992), Contested evidence in courtroom cross-examination: the case of a trial for rape. In P. Drew and J. Heritage (eds), *Talk at Work*, pp. 470–520. Cambridge: Cambridge University Press.

Drew, P. and J. Heritage (1992), Analyzing talk at work: an introduction. In P. Drew and J. Heritage (eds), *Talk at Work*, pp. 3–65. Cambridge: Cambridge University Press.

Du Bois, B. L. (1987), 'Something on the order of around forty to forty-four': imprecise numerical expressions in biomedical slide talks. *Language in Society* 16(4): 527–41.

Du Bois, J. W. (2007), The stance triangle. In R. Englebretson (ed.), *Stancetaking in Discourse: Subjectivity, Evaluation, Interaction*, pp. 139–82. Amsterdam: John Benjamins.

Duffley, P. J. and P. Larrivée (2012), Exploring the relation between the qualitative and quantitative uses of the determiner *some*. *English Language and Linguistics* 16(1):131–49.

Ediger, A. (1995a), *An analysis of set-marking tags in the English language*. PhD thesis, University of California.

(1995b), Vague language. *Applied Linguistics* 16(1): 127–31.

Eisenberg, E. M. (1998), Flirting with meaning. *Journal of Language and Social Psychology* 17(1): 97–108.

Englebretson, R. (2007), Stancetaking in discourse: an introduction. In R. Englebretson (ed.), *Stancetaking in Discourse: Subjectivity, Evaluation, Interaction*, pp. 1–25. Amsterdam: John Benjamins.

Evison, J., M. McCarthy and A. O'Keeffe (2007), 'Looking out for love and all the rest of it': vague category markers as shared social space. In J. Cutting (ed.), *Vague Language Explored*, pp. 138–57. Basingstoke (UK): Palgrave Macmillan.

Fairclough, N. (1989), *Language and Power*. London: Longman.

(1992), *Discourse and Social Change*. Cambridge: Polity Press.

Fillmore, C. J. (1982), Frame semantics. In Linguistic Society of Korea (ed.), *Linguistics in the Morning Calm*, pp. 111–37. Seoul: Hanshin Publishing Company.

Fodor, J. D. (1977), *Semantics: Theories of Meaning in Generative Grammar*. New York: Crowell.

Fowler, R. (1985), Power. In T. van Dijk (ed.), *Handbook of Discourse Analysis* vol. 4: *Discourse Analysis in Society*, pp. 61–82. Orlando (FL): Academic Press.

Fraser, B. (1980), Conversational mitigation. *Journal of Pragmatics* 4(4): 341–50.

(2010), Pragmatic competence: the case of hedging. In G. Kaltenböck, W. Mihatsch and S. Schneider (eds), *New Approaches to Hedging*, pp. 15–34. Bingley (UK): Emerald.

Fronek, J. (1982), *Thing* as a function word. *Linguistics* 20: 633–54.

Gassner, D. (2012), Vague language that is rarely vagueP: a case study of 'thing' in L1 and L2 discourse. *International Review of Pragmatics* 4(1): 3–28.

Gazdar, G. (1979), *Pragmatics: Implicature, Presupposition, and Logical Form.* New York: Academic Press.
Geeraerts, D. (1989), Introduction: prospects and problems of prototype theory. *Linguistics* 27(4): 587–612.
 (2006a), Introduction: a rough guide to cognitive linguistics. In D. Geeraerts (ed.), *Cognitive Linguistics: Basic Readings*, pp. 1–28. Berlin: Mouton de Gruyter.
 ed. (2006b), *Words and Other Wonders: Papers on Lexical and Semantic Topics.* Berlin: Mouton de Gruyter.
Glinert, L. (2010), Apologizing to China: elastic apologies and the meta-discourse of American diplomats. *Intercultural Pragmatics* 7(1): 47–74.
Goffman, E. (1974), *Frame Analysis: An Essay on the Organization of Experience.* Boston: Northeastern University Press.
 (1981), *Forms of Talk.* Philadelphia: University of Philadelphia Press.
Grice, P. H. (1975), Logic and conversation. In P. Cole and J. L. Morgan (eds), *Syntax and Semantics* vol. 3: *Speech Acts*, pp. 41–58. New York: Academic Press.
Gu, Y. G. (1990), Politeness phenomena in modern Chinese. *Journal of Pragmatics* 14: 237–57.
Guilbaud, G. (1977), Mathematics and approximation. In H. Asher and H. Kunle (eds), *Proceedings of the Third International Conference on Mathematics Education*, pp. 125–34. Norwood (NJ): Ablex.
Gumperz, J. (1982), *Discourse Strategies.* Cambridge: Cambridge University Press.
Halliday, M. A. K. and R. Hasan (1985), *Language, Context and Text: Aspects of Language in a Social-Semiotic Perspective.* Burwood: Deakin University Press.
Hamilton, M. and P. J. Mineo (1998), A framework for understanding equivocation. *Journal of Language and Social Psychology* 17: 3–35.
Handford, M. (2010), *The Language of Business Meetings.* Cambridge: Cambridge University Press.
Hatch, E. and C. Brown (1995), *Vocabulary, Semantics and Language Education.* Cambridge: Cambridge University Press.
Hinkel, E. (2003), Adverbial markers and tone in L1 and L2 students' writing. *Journal of Pragmatics* 35: 1049–1068.
Holdcroft, D. (1979), Speech acts and conversation I. *Philosophical Quarterly* 29: 125–41.
Holmes, J. (1982), Expressing doubt and certainty in English. *RELC Journal* 13(2): 9–28.
 (1985), Sex differences and miscommunication: some data from New Zealand. In J. B. Pride (ed.), *Cross-Cultural Encounters: Communication and Miscommunication*, pp. 24–43. Melbourne: River Seine.
 (1990), Hedges and boosters in women's and men's speech. *Language and Communication* 10(3): 185–205.
 (1995), *Women, Men and Politeness.* London: Longman.
 (2000), Women at work: analysing women's talk in New Zealand workplaces. *Australian Review of Applied Linguistics* 22(2): 1–17.
 (2006), *Gendered Talk at Work.* Oxford: Blackwell.
Horn, L. R. (1972), On the semantic properties of logical operators in English. PhD thesis, University of California.

References

Huang, Y. (2012), *The Oxford Dictionary of Pragmatics*. Oxford: Oxford University Press.
Hübler, A. (1983), *Understatements and Hedges in English*. Amsterdam: John Benjamins.
Hurford, J. R. (1987), *Language and Number*. Oxford: Blackwell.
Hutchby, I. and R. Wooffitt (1998), *Conversation Analysis: Principles, Practices and Applications*. Cambridge: Polity Press.
Hyland, K. (1998a) Boosting, hedging and the negotiation of academic knowledge. *Text* 18(3): 349–82.
 (1998b), *Hedging in Scientific Research Articles*. Amsterdam: John Benjamins.
 (1998c), Persuasion and context: the pragmatics of academic metadiscourse. *Journal of Pragmatics* 30: 437–55.
 (2000), Hedges, boosters and lexical invisibility: noticing modifiers in academic texts. *Language Awareness* 9(4): 179–97.
Ide, S. (1989), Formal forms and discernment: two neglected aspects of universals of linguistic politeness. *Multilingua* 8(2/3): 223–48.
Iklé, F. C. (1968), *How Nations Negotiate*. New York: Praeger.
Jaffe, A. (2012), *Stance: Sociolinguistic Perspectives*. Oxford: Oxford University Press.
Janicki, K. (2002), A hindrance to communication: the use of difficult and incomprehensible language. *International Journal of Applied Linguistics* 12(2): 194–217.
Janney, R. W. (2002), Cotext as context: vague answers in court. *Language and Communication* 22: 457–75.
Jefferson, G. (1990), List construction as a task and resource. In G. Psathas (ed.), *Interaction Competence*, pp. 63–92. Lanham (MD): University Press of America.
Jick, T. D. (1979), Mixing qualitative and quantitative methods: triangulation in action. *Administrative Science Quarterly* 24: 602–11.
Jucker, A. H. (1993), The discourse marker *well*: a relevance theoretical account. *Journal of Pragmatics* 19(5): 435–52.
Jucker, A. H., S. W. Smith and T. Lüdge (2003), Interactive aspects of vagueness in conversation. *Journal of Pragmatics* 35(12): 1737–69.
Kaltenböck, G. (2013), Development of comment clauses. In B. Aarts, J. Close, G. Leech and S. Wallis (eds), *The Verb Phrase in English: Investigating Recent Change with Corpora*, pp. 286–317. Cambridge: Cambridge University Press.
Kaltenböck, G., W. Mihatsch and S. Schneider, eds (2010), *New Approaches to Hedging*. Bingley (UK): Emerald.
Kasper, G. (1999), Data collection in pragmatics research. *University of Hawaii Working Papers in ESL* 18 (1): 71–107.
Kay, P. (1984), The *kind of/sort of* construction. In C. Brugman (ed.), *Proceedings of the Tenth Annual Meeting of the Berkeley Linguistics Society*, pp. 157–71. Berkeley (CA): BLS, University of California.
 (2004), Pragmatic aspects of grammatical constructions. In L. R. Horn and G. Ward (eds), *The Handbook of Pragmatics*, pp. 675–700. Malden (MA): Blackwell.
Kärkkäinen, E. (2003), *Epistemic Stance in English Conversation: A Description of its Interactional Functions, with a Focus on I think*. Amsterdam: John Benjamins.
 (2007), The role of *I guess* in conversational stancetaking. In R. Englebretson (ed.), *Stancetaking in Discourse: Subjectivity, Evaluation, Interaction*, pp. 183–219. Amsterdam: John Benjamins.

(2010), Position and scope of epistemic phrases in planned and unplanned American English. In G. Kaltenböck, W. Mihatsch and S. Schneider (eds), *New Approaches to Hedging*, pp. 203–36. Bingley (UK): Emerald.

(2012), *I thought it was very interesting*: conversational formats for taking a stance. *Journal of Pragmatics* 44(15): 2194–210.

Kecskes, I. (2014), *Intercultural Pragmatics*. New York: Oxford University Press

Kendon, A. (2004), *Gesture: Visible Action as Utterance*. Cambridge: Cambridge University Press.

Kiesling, S. F. (2009), Style as stance: stance as the explanation for patterns of sociolinguistic variation. In A. Jaffe (ed.), *Stance: Sociolinguistic Perspectives*, pp. 171–94. Oxford: Oxford University Press.

Kirkpatrick, A. (1991), Information sequencing in Mandarin in letters of request. *Anthropological Linguistics* 33(2): 183–203.

Koester, A. (2006), *Investigating Workplace Discourse*. London: Routledge.

(2007), 'About twelve thousand or so': vagueness in North American and UK offices. In J. Cutting (ed.), *Vague Language Explored*, pp. 40–61. Basingstoke (UK): Palgrave Macmillan.

(2010), *Workplace Discourse*. London: Continuum.

Kong, K. (2013), Epilogue: what makes Chinese unique in discourse and interaction? In Y. L. Pan and D. Z. Kádár (eds), *Chinese Discourse and Interaction: Theory and Practice*, pp. 310–20. London: Equinox.

Labov, W. (1972), *Sociolinguistic Patterns*. Pennsylvania: University of Pennsylvania Press.

Lakoff, G. (1973), Hedges: a study in meaning criteria and the logic of fuzzy concepts. *Journal of Philosophical Logic* 2(4): 458–508.

(1987), *Women, Fire, and Dangerous Things: What Categories Reveal about the Mind*. Chicago: The University of Chicago Press.

Lakoff, G. and M. Johnson (1999), *Philosophy in the Flesh*. New York: Basic Books.

Lakoff, R. T. (1990), *Talking Power: The Politics of Language*. New York: Basic Books.

(2000), *The Language War*. Berkeley(CA): University of California Press.

Langacker, R. W. (1986), An introduction to cognitive grammar. *Cognitive Science* 10(1): 1–40.

Larrivée, P. and P. Duffley (2014), The emergence of implicit meaning: scalar implicatures with *some*. *International Journal of Corpus Linguistics* 19(4): 530–47.

Leech, G. (1983), *Principles of Pragmatics*. London: Longman.

Lehrer, A. (1975), Talking about wine. *Language* 51(4): 901–23.

Levinson, S. C. (1983), *Pragmatics*. Cambridge: Cambridge University Press.

(2000), *Presumptive Meanings: The Theory of Generalized Conversational Implicature*. Cambridge (MA): MIT Press.

Lewis, D. (1979), Scorekeeping in a language game. *Journal of Philosophical Logic* 8: 339–59.

Linell, P. and M. Bredmar (1996), Reconstructing topical sensitivity: aspects of face-work in talks between midwives and expectant mothers. *Research on Language and Social Interaction* 29(4): 347–79.

Lyons, J. (1981), *Language, Meaning and Context*. London: Fontana.

References

Macaulay, R. K. S. (1991), *Locating Dialect in Discourse: The Language of Honest Men and Bonnie Lasses in Ayr.* New York: Oxford University Press.

Martinich, A. P. (1980), Conversational maxims and some philosophical problems. *The Philosophical Quarterly* 30: 215–28.

Martinovski, B. (2006), Framework for analysis of mitigation in courts. *Journal of Pragmatics* 38(12): 2065–86.

Matthews, P. H. (1997), *The Concise Dictionary of Linguistics.* Oxford: Oxford University Press.

Mauranen, A. (2004), 'They're a little bit different ...': observations on hedges in academic talk. In K. Aijmer and A. B. Stenström (eds), *Discourse Patterns in Spoken and Written Corpora,* pp. 173–97. Amsterdam: John Benjamins.

Maynard, S. K. (1993), *Discourse Modality: Subjectivity, Emotion and Voice in the Japanese Language.* Amsterdam: John Benjamins.

McCarthy, M. J. (1998), *Spoken Language and Applied Linguistics.* Cambridge: Cambridge University Press.

McCarthy, M. J. and R. A. Carter (1997), Grammar, tails and affect: constructing expressive choices in discourse. *Text* 17(3): 231–52.

McCarthy, M. J. and M. Handford (2004), 'Invisible to us': a preliminary corpus-based study of spoken business English. In U. Connor and T. Upton (eds), *Discourse in the Professions: Perspectives from Corpus Linguistics.* Amsterdam: John Benjamins.

McCarthy, M. J., A. O'Keeffe and S. Walsh (2005), 'Post-colonialism, multi-culturalism, structuralism, feminism, post-modernism and so on and so forth': vague language in academic discourse, a comparative analysis of form, function and context. Conference paper presented at AAACL/ICAME Conference, University of Michigan.

McCawley, J. D. (1981), *Everything that Linguists Have Always Wanted to Know about Logic, but Were Ashamed to Ask.* Chicago: University of Chicago Press.

Mehl, M. R., S. Vazire, N. Ramírez-Esparza, R. B. Slatcher and J. W. Pennebaker (2007), Are women really more talkative than men? *Science* 317(5834): 82.

Metsä-Ketelä, M. (2006), 'Words are more or less superfluous': the case of *more or less* in academic lingua franca English. *Nordic Journal of English Studies* 5(2): 117–43.

Mey, J. L. (1993), *Pragmatics: An Introduction.* Oxford: Blackwell.

— (2001), *Pragmatics: An Introduction,* 2nd edition. Malden (MA): Blackwell.

Morris, W. C. (1938), *Foundations of the Theory of Signs,* special issue of *International Encyclopaedia of Unified Science* 1(2). Chicago: The University of Chicago Press.

Morse, J. M. (1991), Approaches to qualitative–quantitative methodological triangulation. *Nursing Research* 40: 120–23.

Mortensen C. D. (1997), *Miscommunication.* Thousand Oaks: Sage.

Moxey, L. and A. Sanford (1993), *Communicating Quantities: A Psychological Perspective.* Hove (UK): Lawrence Erlbaum.

— (1997), Choosing the right quantifier: usage in the context of communication. In T. Givón (ed.), *Conversation: Cognitive, Communicative and Social Perspectives,* pp. 207–31. Amsterdam: John Benjamins.

Murphy, B. (2010), *Corpus and Sociolinguistics: Investigating Age and Gender in Female Talk.* Amsterdam: John Benjamins.

Myers, G. (1989), The pragmatics of politeness in scientific articles. *Applied Linguistics* 10: 1–35.

Newman, M. L., C. J. Groom, L. D. Handelman and J. W. Pennebaker (2008), Gender differences in language use: an analysis of 14,000 text samples. *Discourse Processes* 45: 211–36.

Ochs, E. (1996), Linguistic resources for socializing humanity. In J. Gumperz and S. Levinson (eds), *Rethinking Linguistic Relativity*, pp. 407–37. Cambridge: Cambridge University Press.

Okamoto, S. (2002), Ideology and social meanings: rethinking the relationship between language, politeness, and gender. In S. Benor, M. Rose, D. Sharma, J. Sweetland and Q. Zhang (eds), *Gendered Practices in Language*, pp. 91–113. Stanford (CA): Center for the Study of Language and Information Publications.

O'Keeffe. A. (2002), Exploring indices of national identity in a corpus of radio phone-in data from Irish radio. In A. Sanchez-Macarro (ed.), *Windows on the World: Media Discourse in English*. Valencia (Spain): University of Valencia Press.

(2003), 'Like the wise virgins and all that jazz': using a corpus to examine vague language and shared knowledge. In U. Connor and T. Upton (eds), *Applied Corpus Linguistics: A Multidimensional Perspective*, pp. 1–20. Amsterdam: Rodopi.

(2004), 'How to be vague and that kind of thing'. Presented at the *38th International Association of Teachers of English as a Foreign Language Conference*, Liverpool.

(2006), *Investigating Media Discourse*. London: Routledge.

O'Keeffe, A., M. McCarthy and R. Carter (2007), *From Corpus to Classroom: Language Use and Language Teaching*. Cambridge: Cambridge University Press.

Overstreet, M. (1995), *The form and function of general extenders in English interactive discourse*. PhD thesis, The University of Hawaii.

(1999), *Whales, Candlelight, and Stuff Like That: General Extenders in English Discourse*. New York: Oxford University Press

Overstreet, M. and G. Yule (1997a), On being explicit and stuff in contemporary American English. *Journal of English Linguistics* 25(3): 250–58.

(1997b), Locally contingent categorization in discourse. *Discourse Processes* 23: 83–97.

Parvaresh, V. and T. Tayebi (2014), Vaguely speaking in Persian. *Discourse Processes* 51(7): 565–600.

Parvaresh, V., M. Tavangar, A. E. Rasekh and D. Izadi (2012), About his friend, how good she is, *and this and that*: general extenders in native Persian and non-native English discourse. *Journal of Pragmatics* 44: 261–79.

Pascale, R. T. and A. G. Athos (1981), *The Art of Japanese Management*. New York: Simon and Schuster.

Peirce, C. S. (1902), Vagueness. In M. J. Baldwin (ed.), *Dictionary of Philosophy and Psychology* II, p. 748. London: Macmillan.

Pennebaker, J. (2011), *The Secret Life of Pronouns: What Our Words Say about Us*. New York: Bloomsbury Press.

Peräkylä, A. (1993), Invoking a hostile world: discussing the patient's future in AIDS counselling. *Text* 13(2): 291–316.

Pinker, S. (2011), Language is a window into social relations. *Cognitive Media.* www.cognitivemedia.co.uk, retrieved 5 December 2011.

Pocheptsov, O. G. (1992), Mind your mind: or some ways of distorting facts while telling the truth. *Et Cetera: A Review of General Semantics* 49(4): 398–404.

Pomerantz, A. (2005), Using participants' video stimulated comments to complement analyses of interactional practices. In H. T. Molder and J. Potter (eds), *Conversation and Cognition*, pp. 93–113. Cambridge: Cambridge University Press.

Popper, K. (1966), *The High Tide of Prophecy: Hegel, Marx, and the Aftermath*, special issue of *The Open Society and its Enemies II.* London: Routledge and Kegan Paul. (1992), *Unended Quest: An Intellectual Autobiography.* London: Routledge.

Powell, M. J. (1985), Purposive vagueness: an evaluative dimension of vague quantifying expressions. *Journal of Linguistics* 21(1): 31–50.

Pratt, M. L. (1981), The ideology of speech act theory. *Centrum* 1: 5–18.

Preacher, K. J. (2010–2015), Calculation for the chi-square test: an interactive calculation tool for chi-square tests of goodness of fit and independence (computer software). Available at http://quantpsy.org.

Preisler, B. (1986), *Linguistic Sex Roles in Conversation: Social Variation in the Expression of Tentativeness in English.* Berlin: Mouton de Gruyter.

Prince, E. F., J. Frader and C. Bosk (1982), On hedging in physician–physician discourse. In R. J. Di Pietro (ed.), *Linguistics and the Professions*, pp. 83–97. Norwood (NJ): Ablex.

Quaglio, P. (2009), *Television Dialogue: The Sitcom Friends vs. Natural Conversion.* Amsterdam: John Benjamins.

Quirk, R. and S. Greenbaum (1973), *A Concise Grammar of Contemporary English.* New York: Academic.

Quirk, R., S. Greenbaum, G. Leech and J. Svartvik (1985), *A Comprehensive Grammar of the English Language.* London: Longman.

Raffman, D. (2014), *Unruly Words: A Study of Vague Language.* Oxford: Oxford University Press.

Rescher, N. (2008), Vagueness: a variant approach. *Informal Logic* 28(4): 282–94.

Roberts, C. (2003), Language acquisition or language socialization in and through discourse? Towards a redefinition of the domain of SLA. In C. Candlin and N. Mercer (eds), *English Language Teaching in its Social Context: A Reader*, pp. 108–21. London: Routledge.

Romero Trillo, J. (2002), The pragmatic fossilization of discourse markers in non-native speakers of English. *Journal of Pragmatics* 34(6): 769–84.

Rosch, E. (1975), Cognitive reference points. *Cognitive Psychology* 7: 532–47.

Rowland, T. (2007), 'Well maybe not exactly, but it's around fifty basically?': vague language in mathematics classrooms. In J. Cutting (ed.), *Vague Language Explored*, pp. 79–96. Basingstoke (UK): Palgrave Macmillan.

Rue, Y. J. and G. Q. Zhang (2008), *Request Strategies: A Comparative Study in Mandarin Chinese and Korean.* Amsterdam: John Benjamins.

Russell, B. (1923), Vagueness. *Australian Journal of Philosophy and Psychology* 1: 84–92.

Ruzaitė, J. (2007), *Vague Language in Educational Settings: Quantifiers and Approximators in British and American English.* Frankfurt am Main: Peter Lang.

Sabet, P. and G. Q. Zhang (in press), *Communicating through Vague Language: A Comparative Study of L1 and L2 Speakers*. London: Palgrave Macmillan.

Sadock, J. M. (1977), Truth and approximations. *Berkeley Linguistic Society Papers* 3: 430–9.

Sassoon, G. W. (2013), *Vagueness, Gradability and Typicality: The Interpretation of Adjectives and Nouns*. Leiden: Brill.

Schick, L. (2014), *Some people*: from referential vagueness to social-moral socialization in middle school dance classes. *Pragmatics and Society* 5(2): 243–70.

Schiffrin, D. (1994), *Approaches to Discourse*. Oxford: Basil Blackwell.

Schönefeld, D., ed. (2011), *Converging Evidence: Methodological and Theoretical Issues for Linguistic Research*. Amsterdam: John Benjamins.

Scollon, R. and S. Scollon (1995), *Intercultural Communication: A Discourse Approach*. Oxford: Blackwell.

Scott, M. (2010), *WordSmith Tools, version 6.0*. Liverpool: Lexical Analysis Software.

Shirato J. and P. Stapleton (2007), Comparing English vocabulary in a spoken learner corpus with a native speaker corpus: pedagogical implications arising from an empirical study in Japan. *Language Teaching Research* 11(4): 393–412.

Shuy, R. W. (2014), *The Language of Murder Cases*. Oxford: Oxford University Press

Simpson R. C. (2004), Formulaic expressions in academic speech. In U. Connor and T. A. Upton (eds), *Discourse in the Professions*, pp. 37–64. Amsterdam: John Benjamins.

Sinclair, J. M. (1991), *Corpus Concordance Collocation*. Oxford: Oxford University Press.

Smith, P. M. (1985), *Language, the Sexes and Society*. Oxford: Blackwell.

Smith, S. W. and A. H. Jucker (2014), 'Maybe, but probably not': negotiating likelihood and perspective. *Language and Dialogue* 4(2): 284–98.

Speer, S.A. (2002), 'Natural' and 'contrived' data: a sustainable distinction? *Discourse Studies* 4: 511–25.

Spencer-Oatey, H. (2000), Rapport management: a framework for analysis. In H. Spencer-Oatey (ed.), *Culturally Speaking: Managing Rapport through Talk across Cultures*, pp. 11–46. London: Continuum.

Sperber, D. and D. Wilson (1985/86), Loose talk. *Proceedings of the Aristotelian Society New Series* 86: 153–71.

(1995 [1986]), *Relevance: Communication and Cognition*. Oxford: Blackwell.

(1991), Loose talk. In S. Davis (ed.), *Pragmatics: A Reader*, pp. 540–9. New York: Oxford University Press.

Stenström, A. B. (1994), *An Introduction to Spoken Interaction*. London: Longman.

Stubbe, M. and J. Holmes (1995), *You know, eh* and other 'exasperating expressions': an analysis of social and stylistic variation in the use of pragmatic devices in a sample of New Zealand English. *Language and Communication* 15(1): 63–88.

Stubbs, M. (1986a), A matter of prolonged fieldwork: notes towards a modal grammar of English. *Applied Linguistics* 7(1): 1–25.

(1986b), *Educational Linguistics*. Oxford: Basil Blackwell.

(1996), *Text and Corpus Analysis*. Oxford: Blackwell.

Sunderland, J. (2004), *Gendered Discourses*. New York: Palgrave Macmillan.

References

Swales, M. J. (1990), *Genre Analysis: English in Academic and Research Settings*. Cambridge: Cambridge University Press.
Tannen, D. (1989), *Talking Voices*. Cambridge: Cambridge University Press.
— (1990), *You Just Don't Understand: Women and Men in Conversation*. New York: William Morrow.
— (1996), *That's Not What I Meant*. London: Virago Press.
Tárnyiková, J. (2009), Vague reference to notional categories (English–Czech interface). *Philologica: Anglica III Linguistica* 99: 115–32.
Tausczik, Y. R. and J. W. Pennebaker (2010), The psychological meaning of words: LIWC and computerized text analysis methods. *Journal of Language and Social Psychology* 29(1): 24 –54.
Terraschke, A. and J. Holmes (2007), 'Und tralala': vagueness and general extenders in German and New Zealand English. In J. Cutting (ed.), *Vague Language Explored*, pp. 198–220. Basingstoke (UK): Palgrave Macmillan.
Thomas, J. (1995), *Meaning in Interaction: An Introduction to Pragmatics*. London: Longman.
Tong, R. M., H. T. Nguyen, R. R. Yager and S. Ovchinnikov, eds (1987), *Fuzzy Sets and Applications: Selected Papers by Lotfi A. Zadeh*. New York: Wiley.
Trappes-Lomax, H. (2007), Vague language as a means of self-protective avoidance: tension management in conference talks. In J. Cutting (ed.), *Vague Language Explored*, pp. 117–37. Basingstoke (UK): Palgrave Macmillan.
Trickett, L. (2012), 'I get to fly home business class', retrieved from http://media.smh.com.au/sport (29 July 2012).
Ullmann, S. (1962), *Semantics*. Oxford: Blackwell.
Van Deemter, K. (2010), *Not Exactly: In Praise of Vagueness*. Oxford: Oxford University Press.
Vygotsky, L. S. (1978), *Mind in Society*. Cambridge (MA): Harvard University Press.
Wachtel, T. (1980), Pragmatic approximations. *Journal of Pragmatics* 4(3): 201–11.
— (1981), Distinguishing between approximations. *Journal of Pragmatics* 5(4): 311–22.
Ward, G. and B. Birner (1992), The semantics and pragmatics of 'and everything'. *Journal of Pragmatics* 19(3): 205–14.
Wardhaugh, R. (1985), *How Conversation Works*. Oxford: Basil Blackwell.
— (1993), *Investigating Language: Central Problems in Linguistics*. Oxford: Blackwell.
Warren, M. (2007), {/[Oh]Not a < ^ Lot >}: discourse intonation and vague language. In J. Cutting (ed.), *Vague Language Explored*, pp. 182–97. Basingstoke (UK): Palgrave Macmillan.
Widdowson, H. G. (1984), Reference and representation as modes of meaning. In H. G. Widdowson (ed.), *Explorations in Applied Linguistics* 2 (Chapter 11). Oxford: Oxford University Press.
Wierzbicka, A. (1986), Precision in vagueness: the semantics of English 'approximatives'. *Journal of Pragmatics* 10(5): 597–613.
Williamson, T. (1994a), Vagueness. In R. Asher and S. Simpson (eds), *The Encyclopedia of Language and Linguistics*, pp. 4869–71. Oxford: Pergamon Press.
— (1994b), *Vagueness*. London: Routledge.

Wilson, J. (1990), *Politically Speaking: The Pragmatic Analysis of Political Language*. Oxford: Blackwell.
Wilson, D. and D. Sperber (2012), *Meaning and Relevance*. Cambridge: Cambridge University Press.
Wittgenstein, L. (1953), *Philosophical Investigations*. Oxford: Blackwell.
Wodak, R. (1996), *Disorders of Discourse*. London: Longman.
Wright, J. W. and L. A. Hosman (1983), Language style and sex bias in the courtroom: the effects of male and female use of hedges and intensifiers on impression formation. *Southern Speech Communication Journal* 48:137–52.
Wu, T. P. (1999), *Mohu Yuyanxue (in Chinese) [Fuzzy Linguistics]*. Shanghai: Shanghai Foreign Language Education Press.
Yule, G. (1996), *Pragmatics*. Oxford: Oxford University Press.
Zadeh, L. A. (1965), Fuzzy sets. *Information and Control* 8(3): 338–53.
Zhang, G. Q. (1996), The semantics of fuzzy quantifiers. PhD thesis, The University of Edinburgh.
 (1998), Fuzziness-vagueness-generality-ambiguity. *Journal of Pragmatics* 29(1): 13–31.
 (2004), *Mohu Yuyixue (in Chinese) [Fuzzy Semantics]*, 2nd edition. Beijing: China Social Sciences Press.
 (2005), Fuzziness and relevance theory. *Waiguo Yuyan Wenxue [Foreign Language and Literature Studies]* 22(2): 73–84.
 (2011), Elasticity of vague language. *Intercultural Pragmatics* 8(4): 571–99.
 (2013), The impact of touchy topics on vague language use. *Journal of Asian Pacific Communication* 23(1): 87–118.
 (2014), The elasticity of *I think*: stretching its pragmatic functions. *Intercultural Pragmatics* 11(2): 225–57.
Zhang, G. Q. and H. B. Feng (2013), Hanyu zhong de mohu yuyan he huati de minganxing (in Chinese) [The sensitivity of conversational topics and vague language in Mandarin Chinese]. *Dangdai Yuyanxue [Contemporary Linguistics]* 15(1): 45–61.
Zhang, G. Q. and P. Sabet (in press), Elastic 'I think': stretching over L1 and L2. *Applied Linguistics*, advance access published 1 July 2014, doi:10.1093/applin/amu020
Zhang, Y. P. and J. L. Li (1999), *Culture and Communication*. Beijing: China Renmin University Publishing House.
Zhao, X. H. and G. Q. Zhang (2012), *Negotiating with Vague Language: A Chinese Perspective*. Beijing: China Social Sciences Press.

Index

Adolphs, 45, 159, 197
Aijmer, 33, 59, 114, 116, 163, 167
ambiguity, 22, 25
approximate stretcher, 36, 80, 128
approximator, 27
attitude stance marker, 34
attribution shield, 43

Biber, 33, 106
Bradac, 177
Burnett, 14

Carter and McCarthy, 39
Channell, 1, 26–7, 30, 38, 44, 49, 51, 143, 190, 206, 217
Cheng, 15, 32, 78, 99, 190
chi-square test, 73
co-construction, 211
competitive function, 55
competitive strategy, 214
Cooperative Principle, 49
cooperative strategy, 213
Cotterill, 46, 128, 147, 159, 194, 206
Creswell, 66
Cruse, 59, 92
Crystal, 12, 14
Crystal and Davy, 27
Cutting, 23, 50, 54

dialogue, 191–2
discourse filler, 119
Dörnyei, 72
Drave, 10, 38

elastic language, 4
elasticisation, 62
elasticity, 5, 57–8, 60–1
  boundaries of elasticity, 59
  mechanisms of elasticity, 62
  principles of elasticity, 57
  processes of elasticity, 62

properties of elasticity, 60
structures of elasticity, 61
epistemic stance marker, 13, 34, 106
epistemic stretcher, 36, 105
epistemic vagueness, 33
evasive elastic, 44, 146, 152
Evison, 133

face-threatening act, 40
fluidity principle, 54
four maxims, 63
fuzziness, 11, 15

gender, 172, 182
general stretcher, 36, 88
general term, 31
generality, 24
Glinert, 5
global elasticity, 61, 123, 155
go approximate maxim, 83
go epistemic maxim, 63, 112–13
go general maxim, 63, 95
go scalar maxim, 63, 104
Grice, 24, 49–50

Handford, 97, 134, 193
hedge, 20–1, 42
hedging, 20, 22
hidden meaning, 123
Holmes, 33, 172
Hyland, 21

implicature, 24, 50, 99, 123
implicitness, 23
indirect language, 23–4
indirectness, 25
inexplicitness, 23
informality, 40
informational function, 210
institutional data, 72
intensifier, 32, 42

241

Index

intensifying elastic, 44, 140, 152
interpersonal function, 210

Jucker, 27, 53, 87, 127
just-right elastic, 44, 127, 152

Kay, 20
Kecskes, 3
Koester, 18, 198

L1, 198
L2, 198
Lakoff, 169
Larrivée and Duffley, 84
literal meaning, 59, 123
local elasticity, 61, 155

Maxim of Manner, 50, 214
Maxim of Quality, 50
Maxim of Quantity, 39
Maxim of Relevance, 51
mitigating elastic, 44, 135, 152
mitigation, 40
mixed research design, 66
monologue, 191–2
Morris, 3

naturally occurring data, 71
negative goal, 146
negotiation, 211
non-literal meaning, 59
non-verbal activities, 120

O'Keeffe, 31
on-screen documentary data, 71

padding expression, 113, 125
Peirce, 14
placeholder, 32
plausibility shield, 43
politeness, 40
Popper, 16
power asymmetry, 159, 223
power imbalance, 158, 182
pragmatics, 2
Prince, 27, 35, 43, 45

Quaglio, 197

rapport elastic, 44, 130, 152
reciprocity, 212
referential vagueness, 33
relational meaning, 124

Relevance Theory, 13, 54
Rowland, 21, 38, 46, 184
Russell, 11, 14
Ruzaitė, 2, 27, 35, 38, 43–4, 88, 127, 206

scalar stretcher, 36, 97
Schick, 85
self-distancing, 42
self-protection, 42
self-protection elastic, 44, 143, 152
semantic vagueness, 16
semantics, 2
Shuy, 158
slingshot, 6
softener, 33
specificity, 215
speech competence, 184
speech event, 184, 207
speech factors, 184
speech genre, 184, 191, 208
Sperber and Wilson, 13, 50–1, 61
stance marker, 13, 34
strategy principle, 54
stretch work, 6
stretchability principle, 54
stretcher, 36, 123
Stubbs, 1, 136
style stance marker, 34
Sunderland, 172

tension management device, 138
tentativeness, 45
Terraschke and Holmes, 133
Trappes-Lomax, 17, 26, 40, 46, 138

uncertainty, 17, 43, 45
universality, 215

vague category indicator, 13, 30–1
vague language, 1, 10, 13–14, 18–19, 23
vague quantifier, 13, 27, 29
vagueness, 10–11, 13–14, 19
Vygotsky, 194

Wierzbicka, 28
Wilson and Sperber, 15, 51–2
withhold information, 43
Wodak, 23
WordSmith Tools, 73

Zadeh, 10, 15, 59
Zhang, 12–13, 22, 34, 43–4, 47, 54–6, 58, 60, 100, 209

Lightning Source UK Ltd.
Milton Keynes UK
UKHW022234160519
342838UK00018B/411/P